ECONOMICS
AND SOCIAL CHOICE

JACK W. NICKSON, JR.
CHAIRMAN AND PROFESSOR OF ECONOMICS
OLD DOMINION UNIVERSITY

McGRAW-HILL BOOK COMPANY

NEW YORK ST. LOUIS SAN FRANCISCO DÜSSELDORF JOHANNESBURG
KUALA LUMPUR LONDON MEXICO MONTREAL NEW DELHI
PANAMA RIO DE JANEIRO SINGAPORE SYDNEY TORONTO

TO PAMELA

ECONOMICS
AND SOCIAL CHOICE

Library of Congress Catalog Card Number 75–134601

ISBN 07-046516-9
567890 HDMM 75432

This book was set in Baskerville by Brown Bros. Linotypers, Inc.,
printed on permanent paper by Halliday Lithograph Corporation,
and bound by The Maple Press Company.
The designer was J. Paul Kirouac;
the drawings were done by BMA Associates, Inc.
The editors were Jack Crutchfield, Hiag Akmakjian, and Cynthia Newby.
Peter D. Guilmette supervised production.

PREFACE

Almost everyone recognizes the importance of having some knowledge of the elementary principles by which our body and mind operate. Even a fraction of the knowledge a person requires to be licensed as a medical doctor helps to safeguard the majority of us against ignorant, irrational actions which might damage our mental and physical wellbeing. And so some knowledge in these areas has become everybody's concern.

But are we taking the same precautions for our *economic* health? It is impossible to find a person in our society who is immune from attack on his economic wellbeing. Furthermore, everyone is a functional part of our economic framework and as such is directly or indirectly affected by changes and disturbances in the operation of our economy. Whatever we may do to secure the material necessities of life (whether we are bankers or farmers), the majority of us are vitally interested in continually improving the economic health of both ourselves and our nation. These considerations more than warrant a widespread knowledge of the functioning of our economy. The fact is, however, that the majority of us are trying to care for our economic health without the benefit of a basic knowledge of the economy.

Because we are confronted with economic problems, we all have some notion —correct or incorrect—about the functioning of the complex economic activities of our society. When significant economic developments occur, we try to interpret the possible effects on our personal position. How will spending huge amounts for defense affect me? Do the extensive problems of poverty, pollution, and poor housing conditions for millions have individual economic relevance for my family? In short, we all to a degree explain economic and social phenomena in the light of our own personal standing in the economy. It is much easier for a poor man to be a "liberal" than for a rich man. It is easier for a black man to be sympathetic with the poverty problem than for a white man. And the conservationist and sportsman will likely be more concerned with pollution and preservation than will the small-town apartment dweller. As a consequence, individual economic explanations and predictions usually vary greatly.

Our economic framework is highly complex. An analysis of the effects and consequences of certain changes involves the consideration of many important factors and the ways in which they influence each other. In the solution of economic problems, many opportunities exist for honest differences of opinion about which factors are the most important ones and what the actual relationship is among all the important factors. Only by further research into the complexities of our economic framework will we be able to reduce these differences of economic opinion. It is the task of the economist to analyze the guiding principles underlying the economic life of our society. The more secrets he can uncover, the fewer arguments we will have about effective remedies for the illnesses and malfunctions afflicting our economic system.

A much more serious reason for differing economic opinions is that the knowledge of the functioning of our economy runs from complete ignorance, for many of us, to the high degree of competence possessed by a small group of trained specialists. Many opinions on economic problems are formed without benefit of the slightest amount of knowledge of the way in which our economy operates. The correctness of decisions based on such opinions is a matter of pure chance. It is more likely that such decisions will have disastrous effects on our economic health. The words of a German philosopher that "nothing is more frightful than ignorance in action" apply well to much of our economic decision making.

While each of us is an individual, we nevertheless must make our decisions within the framework of our society. Moreover, the basic principles and characteristics of our economic system determine to a large extent whether individual decisions and activities will be economically successful.

But it is not enough to concern ourselves with individual economic decisions only. Of equal importance are the many economic problems which must be solved by the society as a whole. In a democracy such as ours the members of the society make an important contribution toward deciding these issues by electing a representative government. To meet our responsibilities as members of this democracy, we must know what makes our economic system work. As voters, we will be constantly forced to form an opinion on many economic issues affecting our individual circumstances and affecting the economic strength of our nation. Knowledge, not ignorance, must guide us in the responsible exercise of our political rights and duties.

The purpose of this text is to familiarize the student with the functioning of the total economic framework of our democratic society. Or, to use different words, to explain how the parts of the economic machine are related to one another in the total performance of the economy. To achieve this goal, extensive attention must be paid to the characteristics, functions, and influences of specific economic factors. These more detailed discussions, however, are presented in such a way that the student will be able to see clearly what role these topics play in the total economic framework.

It is common practice to explain complicated technical processes with simplified diagrams, charts, and descriptive narrative. The advantages of such a broad simplification are obvious. Before turning to detailed explanations, the student becomes aware of the most important relationships existing in the technical mechanism. A similar approach has been employed in this book to help the student understand the more complex parts of our economic system.

In Part 1, the economy is sketched in very broad terms and the basic tools of analysis are introduced. This section can be compared to a road map on which only the interstate highways and the most influential metropolitan and rural areas are shown. Using this road map, we can study the functioning of our economy without the confusion of too many details at one time.

Some tools are required to draw a simplified picture of our economy's operation. We have first to explore the driving forces behind our economic activities. And we must be introduced to some concepts and terms which we need to sketch the broad picture of our economy.

The function of subsequent parts of this book is to refine the simplified broad explanation of Part 1. In these chapters, the student learns how to measure the nation's economic performance and how to correct economic disturbances. Specific national "problems" are introduced, together with some possible solutions.

I have tried to follow four major guidelines. (1) The purpose of this text should be to explain how and why the economy performs as it does. Description of the economy should be restricted to the extent necessary for a clear and readily understandable explanation of the operation of the economy. (2) Without sacrificing scientific truth, the material should be presented with a minimum of technical terminology and theoretical detail. (3) The presentation should be interesting, so that the student will be encouraged to study further the many fascinating aspects of our economic system. (4) The treatment of each separate topic should never leave any doubt about the role played by that topic in the total economic picture.

It is my sincere wish that this book succeed in achieving these goals and that students gain an objective understanding of our economy. The rewards for the student will be worthwhile—for his individual economic well-being, as well as the strength and growth of our nation, depends upon such an understanding.

My special thanks go to Sean Schmitz, who was so patient while typing (and retyping) the manuscript and who corrected many of my clumsy mistakes. The errors that remain are my own.

JACK W. NICKSON, JR.

CONTENTS

PART 1

WHAT IS
AN ECONOMIC SYSTEM?

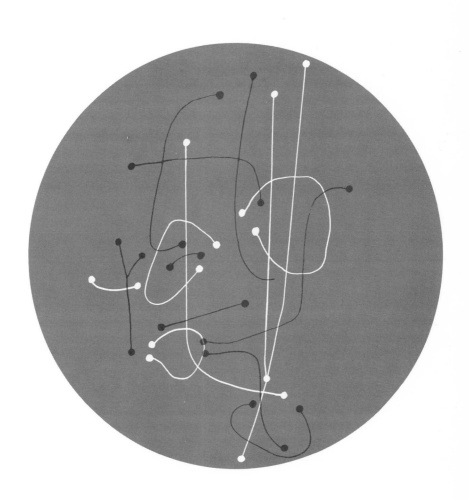

CHAPTER 1

THE ECONOMIC PROBLEMS

THE NOTION OF RELATIVE SCARCITY

There are many reasons why everyone in our society cannot have as much of some particular economic good as he or she may want. But the most important reason is that our human mind has an unlimited capacity to create, without a noticeable effort, a host of desires and wants. Unfortunately, however, our ability to produce everything necessary to satisfy all our wants is very limited. We continually have to decide which of our wants we consider the most important. These wants we try to satisfy, and the rest remain dream-castles, with little chance of becoming reality. To put this in more technical terms: *the resources which determine our capacity to produce material goods and services are scarce in relation to the multitude of our needs, wants, and desires.*

Thus any economic good can be scarce—whether it be peanuts or diamonds. Its degree of scarcity depends upon how much we want it, reflected by its capacity to command a price.

OUR PRODUCTIVE RESOURCES

In the creation or production of any worthwhile product or service, three basic ingredients are necessary. These ingredients of the production process are called the *factors of production,* or *productive resources.* The three basic groups of our productive resources are *labor, capital,* and *natural resources.* Imagine that you want to build (produce) your own radio receiver rather than buy one ready-made in the store.   What do you need?

FACTORS OF PRODUCTION

Labor
+
Capital   } Productive resources
+
Natural resources

Labor

First of all, you need your human effort to do the most important work involved in the project.   In economics we call that *labor*.   All people who are willing and able to contribute their efforts to the production of goods and services make up the *labor force* in our society.   The president of General Motors, the school janitor, the army private, the construction worker, and your instructor are all part of the labor force. They continually busy themselves with providing some kind of desirable product or service.   They all go together to make up one of our productive resources—labor.

Capital

Coming back to our radio project, would you not have a hard time completing the job with just your labor?   You need tools, don't you? At least a soldering iron and a pair of pliers.   Tools have an important function in the production process.   They make the job of producing something much easier and thus save us time; that is, they save labor! And furthermore, they make possible the production of many products and services which we could not produce with labor alone.   All the tools, machines, and equipment which are necessary if we are to produce things are known as *capital,* another of our productive resources.

The word "capital" has several meanings.   You may think of it in terms of money.   But to understand our economic system we need a clear distinction between the real thing and its equivalent in money. To the economist, therefore, capital means *those real products which are used to make the production of other products and services possible.*   The factory building and the machines in it, the delivery truck of the milkman, the accountant's fountain pen, and the instruments of the doctor are all products not intended to satisfy our needs directly but to help produce the goods and services we are ultimately interested in.

Natural Resources

To complete your radio set, you also need supplies which are provided by nature. Your completed project could justly be described as pieces of nature converted into a different form by your labor and tools (capital). For all the tangible pieces of your receiver can be traced back to a natural production process in which they were created without human efforts. Natural forces supplied us with the different metals. Fertile land was necessary to grow the lumber for your radio's cabinet and to raise the agricultural products which make up the major part of the plastic insulating the wires. We could go on like this almost indefinitely. In short, *natural resources are all those useful things nature provides for us.* Our coal, oil, and other mineral deposits, the timber, the arable land, the fish in the sea, and the sea itself, which makes cheap transportation possible, are all useful to us in the process of creating products and services to satisfy our needs. The more abundantly nature has blessed a society with these resources, the more productive such a society can be.

PUTTING OUR RESOURCES TO WORK

We can now understand that the production of anything means combining some labor, some capital, and some natural resources. But it is not enough for an economy to have resources; those resources must be *put to use*—they must be converted into goods and services, for it is in this way that we satisfy human wants. It is not raw resources but the things made from those resources that we are really after. An individual and the total society both want to do a good job in com-

UTILIZING THE RESOURCES

Technical know-how + Entrepreneurship	Applied to factors of production	=	Productive capacity

bining the productive resources so that we will obtain a satisfactory quantity of well-constructed products and needed services.

Technical Know-how

Through the years we have collected a whole stock of technical know-how which determines what we are able to do with our available resources. Technical know-how, or technology, leads to many benefits. Through improvements in technical know-how we have developed machines which have taken the toil out of the major part of human labor. The more our technology enables us to build machines to do the work which once took human labor, the more we can use this saved labor for the production of other desirable things which before had to be left unproduced due to a scarcity of labor.

But improvement in our technical know-how not only saves us labor through the development of better machines and production processes; it also literally creates new natural resources! Remember how we defined natural resources? They are all those *useful* things nature provides for us. Do you think the oil deposits in the Western Plains were very useful to the Indian tribes? They simply did not know what to do with them. But our technology has developed the gasoline engine, the oil furnace, and a multitude of other technical processes which require oil for fuel and lubrication. Through our technology, therefore, the oil deposits are now a very valuable and useful natural resource. In the same way, the recent development of atomic science has created an almost unlimited supply of energy for the future—energy which has always existed but which had to await the development of our technical know-how before it became a *useful* resource. Our human intellect is often called our most valuable resource. It is encouraging that this intellect seems to have an unlimited potential to come up with new solutions for a better life.

Entrepreneurship

To actually apply improvements of our technical know-how in the production process we need a group of people who are willing to experiment with new ideas—we need *entrepreneurship*. This high-sounding word means nothing more than "enterprising ability." Entrepreneurs are people who like to experiment with new production processes, who like to try out new machinery and tools, and who dare to produce new, unproved goods and services.   They are risk takers and are considered as vital assets in our society.   They help provide for the continual improvement of our economic performance.

We have now seen that labor, capital, and natural resources are our basic factors of production.   What we do with our labor, how we use our capital, and how useful our resources are depend upon our technical know-how.   And a highly developed entrepreneurship assures us that these factors of production will be put to new uses for the benefit of our economy.

WHAT, HOW, AND FOR WHOM?

We know now what the productive resources are that determine our capacity to produce desirable goods and services.   We have also discussed the idea that we will never have sufficient resources to produce everything we desire.   This brings us to three very significant economic problems: (1) *What* will we produce with our relatively scarce productive resources?   (2) *How* will we combine the resources in the production process?   (3) *For whom* will the products and services be produced?

What

We must make up our minds about what will be produced with the productive resources and what will remain unproduced.   For what are we to use our limited amount of human effort, our capital, and our natural resources?   The scarcity of our productive resources forces us to make choices.   These choices are further complicated by the fact that our resources can be used for a vast variety of purposes.   Every economic system must in one way or another decide what will be produced—how the available resources will be allocated to the production of the many desirable goods and services.

For example, what portion of the limited quantity of bauxite (aluminum ore) provided by nature should we allocate to the production of planes and missiles to satisfy our need for security from the threats of our enemies?   The same material and human effort could produce many other desirable things.   We could use it to produce more pleasure boats, to satisfy our wants for recreation; or we could use it to produce more modern siding for our houses, to make them more attractive and easier to maintain.

How

At the same time that we decide for what we will use our productive resources, we must determine how we will combine the resources in the production process.   You can easily visualize this problem, for example, in the production of wheat.   We could simply combine only land and labor to grow this desired product.   But a better approach would be to use our labor and other natural resources to first produce farm equipment (capital), after which we could work the land more efficiently with both labor and capital.   Capital increases our productive capacity, as we will see in the next chapter, but it requires resources which we otherwise could have used for present-day consumption.

The problem of how to combine the productive resources is a problem of finding the most advantageous proportions of labor, capital, and natural resources in the production of each product and service.

For Whom

Finally, the society faces one more major problem.   We must decide for whom we shall produce.   We must find out how the economy distributes the finished products and services of the factory workers, the doctors, the lawyers, and all other consumers.

THE BASIC ECONOMIC PROBLEMS

Factors of production
+
Technical know-how   Productive capacity →   What?
+   How?
Entrepreneurship   For whom?

COST OF PRODUCTION

Because there is a scarcity of productive resources, we find ourselves with the need to "economize."   Or we might say that we must learn to allocate or distribute our available productive resources in such a way as best to satisfy the wants of the people in our society.

For this purpose we need a basis of comparison. We must determine what it will cost us to create each product or service we have decided to produce. Each product or service will require a certain amount of our scarce resources. What did we actually sacrifice to obtain the product? Our sacrifice is the next best product that we could have produced with the resources. We can say, therefore, that the *alternative cost* of any product or service is the value of the next best product or service we have to do without.

Such alternative costs, or opportunity costs, include the cost of raw material to the firm (say, the cost of using money to buy steel instead of using the money for additional research and development). Alternative costs are also involved when the business firm decides to invest. If the firm uses its own money to build a plant, the opportunity cost will be the interest return the firm could have obtained by loaning the money to someone else at, say, 6 percent. Thus the firm's profit rate on this particular investment must exceed 6 percent before a real profit is realized.

The society must solve the problems of "what," "how," and "for whom" in such a way that the most desirable products will be produced and the value of the alternatives we have to sacrifice will be kept at a minimum.

OUR PRIVATE-ENTERPRISE ECONOMY

The basic problems of "what," "how," and "for whom" do not exist only in our economy. But the way in which the economy's resources are put to use varies greatly among nations. In the United States we allow a higher degree of freedom of choice in determining the way we use our resources than do most other countries.

In an economic system such as ours, businessmen are relatively free to decide what they will produce. Nobody dictates to them or requires them to obtain permission to use and own resources except as is necessary to safeguard the public welfare. The businessmen are guided in their decisions by their desire to make a profit. They try to produce only those goods and services which the consumer wants, for otherwise they will not be able to sell their products at profitable prices.   The consumers, in turn, try to maximize the satisfaction derived from the products they buy.   That is, they spend their money income in such a way that the goods and services they choose will satisfy a maximum amount of their needs and wants.   And those who own resources attempt to maximize their return on those resources.

Such a reliance upon economic freedom to pursue profits and to consume on the basis of personal satisfaction does, of course, create problems.   Sometimes, in the desire to produce larger quantities of goods, we ignore the *quality* of the goods produced.   Or, in our wish to outshine our neighbors, we may become overly committed to personal credit and debt.   Moreover, some assert that our desire to maintain a private market system leads to a deprived public sector—so that we have tremendous automobiles, but poor highways; the largest industrial output in the world, but air and water pollution.

Nevertheless, we say that we prefer the private-enterprise economy, with businesses and individuals working hard to better their economic wellbeing.   Individual freedom is an essential part of our economy.   Of course, we must sometimes limit an individual's freedom for the benefit of the whole society, but all in all, we want to provide to the members of our society as much freedom to make economic decisions for themselves as possible.

It is well to emphasize that even if we were able to find the best solutions to the many aspects of the problem of allocating our scarce resources at this very moment, our job would not be finished. The world we live in is continually changing, and there will always be room for improvements because of these changes.   The *right* answer today may not be the best solution in the world of tomorrow.

CHAPTER SUMMARY

In this chapter we examined the notion of relative scarcity and the requisites to production.   Even in a society as productive as ours, we found that our resources are scarce in relation to our virtually unlimited needs and desires.   Turning these scarce resources into goods and services was seen to depend upon the factors of production (labor, capital, and natural resources) and upon our technical know-how and entrepreneurship.

Because we will never be able to fully satisfy our economic needs and desires, we face three significant economic problems: (1) What will we produce with our relatively scarce resources?   (2) How will we combine those resources in the production process?   (3) For whom will the goods and services be produced?

These three fundamental economic problems are faced by *all* economic systems.   However, we in the United States prefer to attempt solutions in the relatively free atmosphere of a private-enterprise economy.

STUDY QUESTIONS
1.   In a society as highly productive as ours, how can we say that economics is concerned with the allocation of *scarce* resources? What determines our ability to produce these scarce resources?
2.   What, exactly, do we mean when we refer to the basic economic problems of *what, how,* and *for whom?*

IMPORTANT CONCEPTS IN CHAPTER 1
Relative scarcity
Factors of production
Labor force
Capital
Technical know-how
Entrepreneurship
The economic problems: what, how, for whom
Alternative cost
Private-enterprise economy

CHAPTER 2

SOLVING THE ECONOMIC PROBLEMS: DEMAND AND SUPPLY

In Chapter 1 we saw that the three basic questions in economics are (1) what to produce, (2) how to produce, and (3) for whom to produce. Now we will see how these questions are answered in our economic system. The solution to these "economic problems" depends upon the price system and the notions of demand and supply.

THE ROLE OF THE MARKET PRICE SYSTEM

Let us suppose, for the sake of discussion, that you have chosen for your life's vocation to be a fisherman (or doctor, lawyer, or Indian chief!). You have decided to spend your working hours catching fish, which you will then sell to others. What induces you to use all your productive labor to produce fish? You know by experience that the other members of the society want fish so badly that they are willing to pay you a good price per pound. You could have used your labor to produce something else, but you know that you would end up with less money for a day's labor spent on the production of another product than for a day spent producing fish. This assures you that the society considers your labor resource best applied in the production of fish. How would the society tell you, otherwise?

Assume that some people have taken up cattle raising and that the society now demands considerably less fish because people have taken a fancy for beef. You will find that you can no longer sell the same quantity of fish for the same prices as before. The demand for fish has decreased, and you have only one course of action—to rid yourself of the fish by offering it at lower prices, which will induce your customers to buy more. But all together you end up with much lower receipts for a day's work than before. Assume that this process of decline continues. Each day you receive less for your fish than before because people no longer want as much fish. This means that you get less money to buy other products and services for yourself; in other words, your income from fishing continues to decline.

You learn now that the increase in the demand for beef is causing the prices that cattle growers get per pound of beef to increase. People offer higher and higher prices for the much-desired beef. The higher prices mean that the cattle growers receive more money for their labor, and they now are willing to buy anybody's labor at good prices per hour (wages) to help them in the production of beef.

You, faced with a declining demand and consequently lower prices for your fish, make some quick calculations. You find that if you take the total amount you get for your daily catch and divide this by the number of hours you fish, you get less income per hour fishing than the cattle growers are offering per hour to able cowhands. You can improve yourself by changing jobs. Or, what is more important to our problem, you will be better off if you reallocate your productive labor from fishing to the production of beef. And is that not what the society wanted to achieve by offering less for your fish and more for beef on the market?

The Price System and the Problem of WHAT to Produce

What will be produced with our scarce resources? Those products that yield the highest prices on the market in relation to the amount of resources necessary to produce them will be supplied first. The producers of these products will certainly continue to apply their resources in this direction. But it is also these producers who will receive the most purchasing power and thereby induce other productive resources to help them produce what the consumers want so badly that they are willing to pay high prices for it.

But the more resources that are applied in the production of beef, for instance, the more beef will be brought on the market. When the supply of beef increases, the consumers do not necessarily want to buy this greater quantity at the same high prices per pound as before.   To induce them to consume this greater supply, the prices will have to be lowered.   This game of supply and demand reacting on each other goes on until the price reaches a level at which the consumers want to buy the total supply of beef of those producers who still believe that they get the highest reward per hour of labor by producing beef, even at this lower price.   Then there is no reason to attract more productive resources to produce beef, nor is there any reason for the still-employed resources to find another application.

The Price System and the Problem of HOW to Produce

Demand and supply also largely determine *how* we are going to use our productive resources in the production process.   Are we going to raise cattle by letting them run loose on the prairie and using our labor to keep track of them?   Or will we apply a more roundabout production method, by first producing capital in the form of strong fences, buildings for winter shelter, drinking wells, and other facilities?   To create all this capital, which will increase the productivity of labor in raising cattle, somebody has to release the necessary resources by real saving.   The cattle industry believes that the production of cattle can be so greatly improved by the use of labor-saving capital that they are willing to borrow money at a high interest rate.   You and others hear about this, and you find that $1 invested now would be repaid to you later plus a good return in interest.   This reward might induce you to save some of your money rather than spend it for present consumption.   You find out that you get paid to save.   You get paid for postponing your consumption to some time in the future.   The resources you thus save will be invested by the cattle industry to produce the desired capital.

But the cattle industry might not be the only economic activity which likes to borrow money to invest in capital.   Who will get your money, which will enable them to command the saved resources to produce capital for them?   Again, we have to look at the consumer.   The higher the consumers value a product, the higher will be the price the producer of that product receives and the better able that producer will be to promise you a high interest rate on your money if you lend your money to him rather than to somebody else.   Once again, the saved money, which can command saved resources to produce capital, will go to the highest bidder. It is in the *capital market* that the saved funds will find the demand for funds to be invested. Those producers who can offer the highest price (in the form of a higher rate of interest) will gain command over the resources which were not used for the production of consumer goods and which are thus available to produce capital.

It is logical that if our income is so low we can barely buy the most necessary things for the present, we will not easily be induced to postpone some consumption and save money and resources to produce capital. The more wealthy we become, the more easily we can save and the more capital we can produce to become even wealthier.

The Price System and the Problem of FOR WHOM to Produce

Our last big problem is determining *for whom* we will produce. To all of us, it is a well-known fact that the finished products our society produces are not equally distributed among the members of our society. What determines the actual share of each? Here again, it is the market price mechanism which plays a major role. Remember when we used you in our example as a fisherman expending labor on fish? When the fish were in high demand, you received a good price for your catch. The higher the price of fish, the more money you received per hour of labor spent catching fish. And the more money you received per hour, the more money you had to buy other products for your own satisfaction. But what happened when the demand for fish declined? To sell your fish you had to accept lower and lower prices for it, leaving you with a much lower income than before; consequently, you could not buy as many consumption goods for yourself as before. The society did not value the product of your labor as much as before and was not willing to give you the same quantity of other products in exchange.

Now, as of your hours of labor is not necessarily the same as an hour of your neighbor's labor. He might use his hours to conduct a very intricate production process for which he needed years of training. Just as your labor is specialized on fishing, he might have specialized as a highly skilled engineer. If the society values the products of his labor highly, this will be expressed in a high market price. Apparently many want to have his products, and the highest bidders will be most successful in obtaining them.   This causes the engineer to receive a high wage for his labor and enables him to buy a great quantity of other products and services for his own enjoyment.

In the price system, therefore, the *money income* (the dollars you receive) and the *real income* (what you can buy with your money income) are determined by the value the consumers attach to your labor, as expressed by the market price of the products of your labor.

Another reason why our economy distributes more to one than to another lies in the fact that we have different amounts of savings.   Those people who did not consume in the past all they could have consumed on the basis of their incomes but instead loaned their money out for investment will receive income not only for their present labor services but also for the use of their money (in the form of interest).   The more savings you lend out, the higher your interest income will be and the more able you will be to command products and services for your own consumption.   Some members of our society are so lucky that their ancestors did the saving for them.   They inherited accumulated assets.   The continual interest returns assure these owners an income with which they can demand a varying amount of consumption goods, depending upon the size of the monetary assets and the height of the interest rates.

Thus we find that the market price system in large part determines what will be produced, how it will be produced, and for whom it will be produced.   The market price system was seen to solve these problems through an equating of the *demand* and *supply* of various products.   *What* will be produced?   Those products that yield the highest prices on the market in relation to the amount of resources necessary to produce them.   *How* will the products be produced?   The amount of capital that will be combined with labor and natural resources in the production process is determined by the willingness and ability of the consumers to save in money and the willingness of the businessman to borrow these funds to command the real savings for capital creation. *For whom* will the products be produced?   The higher one's labor products are valued or the larger one's accumulated wealth is, the larger will be the share one receives of the finished goods and services for consumption.

Now let us turn to a more formal presentation of the all-important notions of demand and supply—to see how these important "market forces" set the level of prices, which, in turn, answer the questions of what, how, and for whom.

CONSUMER DEMAND

Consumer demand (or, simply, demand) can be defined as "the willingness and ability of consumers to purchase goods and services at particular prices in a set of given prices at a point in time." Keep this definition in mind as we examine its various components.

Diminishing Marginal Utility

The willingness of consumers to purchase goods and services is based upon something called the "law of diminishing marginal utility." This sophisticated-sounding phrase is really quite simple in concept, especially if we take it word by word. "Diminishing" means declining; "marginal" means extra; and "utility" means satisfaction. Thus, the law of diminishing marginal utility suggests that the satisfaction derived from an extra unit of a product or service declines as we get more of that product or service.

Take, for example, the hot dog. If you are very hungry, you will derive a lot of satisfaction from one hot dog. But after you have eaten that one, you will derive less satisfaction from the second one, still less from the third, and so on. And because you derive less utility from each succeeding unit, you are willing to pay less and less for each one offered to you. A very hungry man might pay $5 for his first hot dog, but by the time he has eaten six, he will be willing to pay very little (or nothing) for the seventh.

In broader terms, this relation between diminishing marginal utility and price allows us to establish what is called a *demand schedule*. (See Table 2-1.) Note that there is an inverse relationship between price and quantity demanded; the higher the price, the fewer will be the units demanded. We might be willing to buy one item for $5, but we will buy fifteen items only if the price drops to $1.

The data in Table 2-1 can be plotted on a graph to yield what is called a *demand curve*. A demand curve graphically relates the price of a product to the quantity demanded of that product. This graph is

TABLE 2-1   Demand Schedule for Product A

PRICE OF A	QUANTITY DEMANDED OF A
$5	1
4	3
3	5
2	9
1	15

drawn in Figure 2-1.   The plotted points are the pairs of figures (price and quantity demanded) in Table 2-1.   These points are simply connected with a smooth line to obtain the demand curve.   (Can you tell from the graph about how many items would be demanded at a price of $2.50?)

The demand curve slopes downward and to the right.   This is the *law of demand*—that there will be an inverse relationship between the price of any commodity and the quantity demanded of that commodity.

Elasticity of Demand

We have said nothing yet about the degree to which demand responds to a change in price.   We know that it must rise as price falls (and

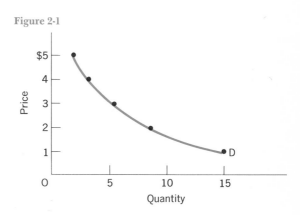

Figure 2-1

vice versa)—the law of demand tells us that; however, is it steeply sloped or almost flat?   When we refer to the degree of response of quantity changes to price changes, we are talking about an economics notion called *elasticity of demand*.

"Elasticity" simply refers to the degree of consumer responsiveness to price changes.   There are three possible degrees of elasticity of demand: demand may be relatively *elastic,* relatively *inelastic,* or of *unitary elasticity.*

If demand is *elastic,* we know that a change in price leads to a more than proportionate change in quantity demanded; that is, that a 1 percent change in price will lead to a more than 1 percent change in quantity demanded.   The demand curve in Figure 2-2 is elastic over the range shown.   Note that a small price change (from O*P* to O*P'*) will lead to a much larger change in the quantity demanded (from O*X* to O*X'*).   Demand is generally elastic for luxury goods—where consumers are quite responsive to price changes.

At the other extreme is *inelastic demand.*   In this case, a price change leads to a less than proportionate change in quantity demanded; that is, a 1 percent change in price (in either direction) will lead to a less than 1 percent change in the quantity demanded.   The demand curve shown in Figure 2-3 is inelastic over the range shown.   A relatively large price change (from O*P* to O*P'*) leads to a much smaller change in the amount demanded (from O*X* to O*X'*).   Such a demand curve usually applies to commodities which are considered necessities by the

Figure 2-2   Elastic Demand

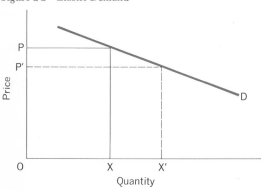

Figure 2-3 Inelastic Demand

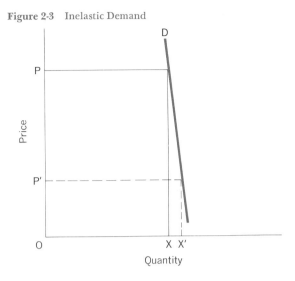

consumer—so that the consumer will continue to buy about the same amount regardless of price fluctuations.

When a percentage price change is exactly offset by a percentage change in the opposite direction in the quantity demanded, we have *unitary elasticity*.

Why do we care about the degree of elasticity of demand? One reason is its effect upon a firm's total revenue. The total revenue (TR) earned by any firm is equal to the price (P) of its product multiplied by the quantity (Q) of that product sold: $TR = P \times Q$. A knowledge of the degree of elasticity of demand aids the firm in making pricing decisions. Let us take two cases.

Suppose first that the demand is relatively elastic. Should the firm raise the price of its product, lower it, or leave it unchanged? If the firm raises its price when demand is elastic, we know that the quantity sold will *decrease* more than proportionately. Hence, total revenue would fall. If the firm were to lower its price, the quantity sold would *increase* more than proportionately and total revenue would rise. Hence, price changes and changes in total revenue move in opposite directions when demand is relatively elastic. The signal to the firm

A second determinant of the level of demand is consumer *tastes*.   The demand for midiskirts, for example, is much greater today than, say, ten years ago.

A final determinant of the level of demand is *the price of substitutes*. If a good substitute for an existing product is introduced in the economy, the demand for the old product normally falls.   One of the best examples of this occurred with the introduction of margarine.   When margarine came onto the market, the demand for butter fell considerably.

Our discussion has covered most of the significant elements of consumer demand.   We will now turn to the other important market force—*supply*.   Once we are familiar with the idea of supply, we will combine the notions of demand and supply to show how these two forces determine the prices of virtually all the goods and services produced in our economy.

MEETING CONSUMER DEMAND

As we mentioned above, when we speak of consumer demand we may say it refers to consumers' willingness and ability to *buy* goods and services.   The counterpart to this notion is supply.   Thus we may say that supply is the willingness and ability of producers to produce for sale goods and services at particular prices in a set of given prices at a point in time.

The Law of Supply

It stands to reason that the higher the price of a good, the more willing will be a producer to supply that good.   He is induced to supply more because, all other things being equal, he will make more per unit profit from each item at the higher price.   On this basis, the law of supply tells us that there is a *direct* relationship between the price and the quantity supplied of a commodity or service; as the price of the commodity rises, more units of the commodity will appear on the market.

Just as we constructed a demand schedule, we can construct a supply schedule, relating various prices of a product to the amount of that

TABLE 2-3   Supply Schedule for Product A

PRICE OF A	QUANTITY SUPPLIED OF A
$5	12
4	10
3	5
2	3
1	1

product which will be supplied.   Table 2-3 shows such a supply schedule.

From Table 2-3, it is apparent that the producer is willing to offer for sale twelve units, providing the market price per unit is $5.   However, only one unit will be offered for sale if the price drops to $1.

The data in Table 2-3 can be plotted on a graph to yield a *supply curve*.   A supply curve graphically relates the price of a product to the quantity supplied of that product.   Such a graph is shown in Figure 2-5.   The pairs of data from the supply schedule provide us with the points to plot.   These points are then connected with a smooth line to form the supply curve.

Note that the supply curve slopes upward and to the right, showing a

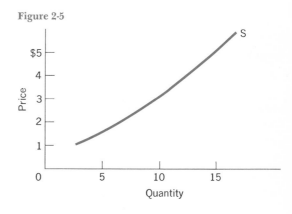

Figure 2-5

direct relationship between the price of a commodity and the quantity supplied of that commodity.

Supply versus Quantity Supplied

As with demand, we have again been very careful thus far to talk about changes in the *quantity* supplied, not changes in *supply*. A change in the quantity supplied refers to a movement along a given supply curve, that is, to a change in the amount supplied due *solely* to a price change. A change in *supply*, on the other hand, refers to a *shift* in the supply curve, that is, a willingness on the part of businesses to produce more of a product at the same prices.

Table 2-4 shows a shift in the supply schedule. In this case, assume that the original supply schedule is represented by the price column and the quantity supplied in period 1. Assume further that the costs of production for this business are suddenly halved. Now the business can supply twice as many units as before without affecting the level of profits. This is a change in supply. Figure 2-6 shows this change graphically. An increase in supply is depicted by a shift of the supply curve to the right. A decrease in supply would be shown by a shift to the left.

The Determinants of Supply

We have indicated that supply can be changed by a change in the *costs of production*. This is one determinant of supply. If costs rise, other things being equal, supply should fall. And vice versa.

TABLE 2-4   Supply Curves for Product A

PRICE OF A	QUANTITY SUPPLIED OF A IN PERIOD 1	QUANTITY SUPPLIED OF A IN PERIOD 2
$5	12	17
4	10	15
3	5	10
2	3	6
1	1	2

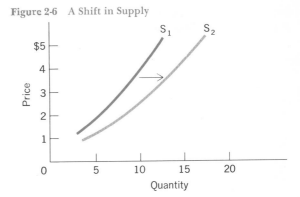

Figure 2-6   A Shift in Supply

Another determinant of the level of supply is *technological develop-ment*. If technology advances to the point, say, that cost-saving ma-chinery can be introduced into the production process, supply should increase. And, of course, it is impossible to produce a commodity at all if the level of technology is not far enough advanced. Color tele-vision, for example, could not have been produced in the 1800s.

A third determinant of supply is the *number of sellers*. Obviously, the more producers we have, the larger will be the supply; and the fewer the producers, the lower the number of goods supplied.

We have now covered most of the important aspects of supply. Next we will turn to a discussion of how demand and supply act together to determine prices.

HOW PRICES ARE DETERMINED

As we indicated earlier, the very important market forces of supply and demand act together to determine the price of virtually every good or service sold in the United States. Now we will see how.

The Interaction of Supply and Demand

To fully understand how supply and demand act together, it will be helpful to look at Figure 2-7. In this figure, the supply curve has been superimposed on the demand curve. The demand curve is denoted by *D,* and the supply curve by *S.* The intersection of these two curves determines the price which will be charged for the commodity under consideration and the amount of that commodity which will be bought and sold.

To determine the *market price* (or *equilibrium price,* as it is sometimes called), locate the point of intersection of the two curves (point *E*). Now look across from that point of intersection to the price axis. The market price is O*P.* To determine the quantity demanded and sold, look down from the point of intersection to the quantity axis. The amount both demanded and supplied is O*X.*

Why must this be the only price and quantity which can persist? Let us see. Suppose that momentarily the price of this particular commodity were to rise to a higher level, say to O*A.* We know, from looking at the demand curve, that at a price of O*A* only O*Y* units will be demanded. But we also know, from looking at the supply curve, that at the same price of O*A,* producers would be willing to supply O*Z* units.

Figure 2-7   Supply and Demand

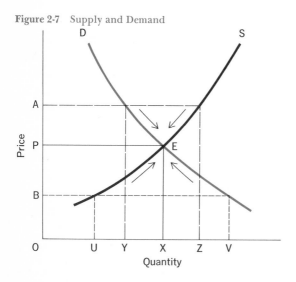

Thus, at this higher price, the quantity supplied of this good will exceed the quantity demanded (by the amount YZ).

Now, if there are more goods coming onto the market than people are willing to buy, something must happen to the price.   If you were a businessman facing this situation, you would probably lower your prices to prevent an inventory buildup and to sell the excess of goods which resulted from the higher price.   As you lower your price, the market price of course moves downward—back toward its original position.   The general rule is that anytime the quantity supplied is greater than the quantity demanded, the price will fall.

But what if the reverse were true?   Suppose the price had momentarily fallen below the equilibrium level to OB.   At this lower price the demand curve shows us that consumers are willing to buy a larger number of units, OV.   However, because the price is momentarily reduced, businesses are willing to produce only OU number of goods.   Thus, at this lower price, the amount demanded exceeds the amount supplied (by the amount UV).   This is a situation commonly referred to as "too much money chasing too few goods."   The result will be that consumers, who are competing now for relatively scarce goods, will bid up the price in an attempt to secure those goods.   The rule is that anytime the quantity demanded exceeds the quantity supplied, the price will rise.

For these reasons, the only price which will persist is the market price OP, where the amount demanded and the amount supplied are exactly equal (point E).

TABLE 2-5

PRICE OF A	QUANTITY DEMANDED OF A	QUANTITY SUPPLIED OF A	PRICE MOVEMENT
$5	1	12	Downward
4	3	10	Downward
3	5	5	None
2	9	3	Upward
1	15	1	Upward

To get a numerical look at these forces, let us return to our original supply and demand data (contained in Tables 2-1 and 2-3). In Table 2-5, we put them together into a supply *and* demand schedule.

At a high price of $5, consumers are demanding only one unit of commodity A but businesses are willing to supply twelve units. The quantity supplied exceeds the quantity demanded, so the price must fall. But at a price of $4, the same situation exists, exerting further downward pressure on the price of commodity A.

If the price were to fall to $1, consumers would demand fifteen units but producers would be willing to supply only one unit at this low price. The quantity demanded would exceed the quantity supplied, and the price would rise. The same situation would exist if the price rose to $2, exerting further upward pressure on the price.

Thus, the only price at which there is no pressure for further change is $3. At this price level, consumers are demanding five units and businesses are willing to supply five units. The equilibrium price is therefore $3, and the equilibrium quantity demanded and supplied is five units.

Shifts in Supply and Demand

Now that we know what is meant by the "market" price and quantity, or the "equilibrium" price and quantity, we will examine the different ways in which this price and quantity can be changed. For ease of comprehension, we will first take the case in which *either* demand *or* supply changes, but not both. Figure 2-8 shows all the possible alternatives.

In Figure 2-8a, we are assuming that the demand for a particular commodity increases (perhaps due to a change in consumers' tastes) but that the supply of that commodity remains unchanged. What will be the effects of this increase in demand? The demand curve shifts to the right from D to D' (indicating an increase in demand). The original equilibrium price was OP, and the original equilibrium quantity was OX, both of these being determined by the intersection of the demand and supply curves at point E. But with the increase in demand to D', a new point of equilibrium is established at E'. The new equilibrium price then rises to OP', and the new equilibrium quantity demanded and supplied rises to OX'. Anytime there is an *increase* in

Figure 2-8

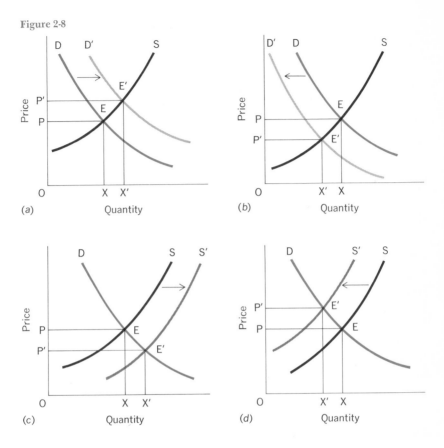

demand for a product, with the *supply* of that product remaining *constant*, there will be an *increase* in the *price* and an *increase* in the number of *units* of that product bought and sold.[1]

Turning next to Figure 2-8b, we will assume that the demand for this commodity decreases (perhaps due to a declining level of income) but that the supply of the commodity again remains constant. The original equilibrium price was OP, and the original equilibrium quantity

[1] Technically, this movement represents an increase in *demand* and an increase in the *quantity supplied.*

was OX (again determined by the point of intersection of demand and supply, point E). With the decrease in demand to D' (a shift to the left of the demand curve), a new point of intersection is established at E'. Hence, the new price will be OP' and the new amount bought and sold will be OX'. When there is a *decrease* in *demand* for a product, with the *supply* of that product remaining *constant,* the *price* of the product will *fall* and the *quantity* bought and sold will *fall.*[2]

So far, we have talked about changes in demand only. In Figure 2-8c and d, the supply changes but the demand holds constant. In Figure 2-8c, the supply increases while the demand remains steady. This shift in the supply curve will move the point of intersection of demand and supply from E to E'; the price will drop to OP', and the quantity bought and sold will increase to OX'. When the *supply* increases and *demand* remains *constant,* the *price* will *fall* and the *quantity* bought and sold will *rise.*[3]

Finally, in Figure 2-8d, the supply decreases and the demand remains constant. Here the point of intersection moves from point E to point E', causing a price rise from OP to OP' and causing the quantity bought and sold to fall from OX to OX'. When the *supply* of a product *decreases* and the *demand* remains *constant,* the *price* will *rise* and the *quantity* bought and sold will *fall.*[4]

Now we can move to a slightly more complicated case—where demand and supply *both* change, but in the *same direction.* Figure 2-9 shows these possibilities.

Figure 2-9a shows an equal increase in both demand and supply (both curves shifting to the right). The point of intersection of these two curves moves from point E to point E'. Clearly, in this case the amount bought and sold will increase (from OX to OX'). But what happens to the equilibrium price? Because we have let demand and supply increase by *equal* amounts, the price will remain unchanged. If, however, as in the case shown in Figure 2-9c, demand had increased *more* than supply had increased, the price level would have risen. In either case, the equilibrium quantity will increase, but the effect upon the price is said to be indeterminate—that is, the price can rise, fall,

---

[2] This is technically a decrease in *demand* and a decrease in the *quantity supplied.*
[3] This is an increase in *supply* and an increase in the *quantity demanded.*
[4] This represents a decrease in *supply* and a decrease in the *quantity demanded.*

Figure 2-9

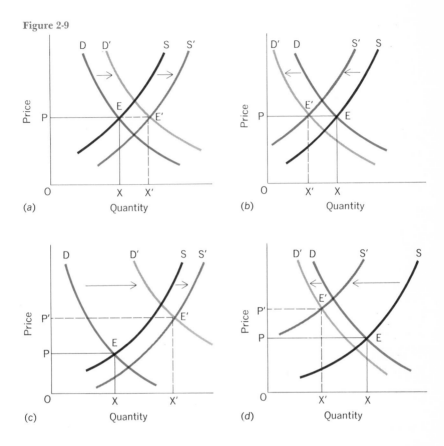

or remain constant, depending upon the *relative magnitudes* of the changes in demand and supply. To summarize, if *demand and supply* both *increase,* the *amount* of any commodity bought and sold will *increase* but the *effect* upon the *price* will be *indeterminate* (dependent upon the relative magnitudes of the increases in supply and demand). If demand increases more than does supply, the price will rise. If supply increases more than does demand, the price will fall. And if demand and supply both increase by equal amounts, the price will remain constant.

A like case is shown in Figure 2-9*b* and *d,* except that now we are letting both demand and supply decrease. In Figure 2-9*b,* both decrease by equal amounts, so that the quantity bought and sold declines and the price remains constant.   Figure 2-9*d* shows what would happen if supply decreased by a greater amount than the decrease in demand. The quantity bought and sold would decline, but the price would rise (to OP').   Thus, if *demand* and *supply both decrease,* the amount bought and sold will *decrease* but the effect upon *price* will again be *indeterminate* (dependent upon the relative magnitudes of the changes in demand and supply).   If supply decreases more than does demand, the price will rise.   If supply decreases less than does demand, the price will fall.   And if demand and supply decrease by equal amounts, the price will remain unchanged.

We have only one final case to examine.   Let us now see what would happen to the price of a commodity and the amount of that commodity bought and sold if demand and supply both change, but in *opposite* directions.   Figure 2-10 shows this possibility.

In Figure 2-10*a,* we see that *demand increases* and *supply decreases,* and by equal amounts.   The point of intersection moves from point *E* to point *E'*.   What happens to the price of this commodity?   It rises, from OP to OP'.   But the quantity bought and sold remains constant.   In this case, the change in quantity is said to be *indeterminate*.   Figure 2-10*c* shows a situation where, again, demand increases and supply decreases.   However, this time the increase in demand is greater than the decrease in supply.   The price, of course, still rises, but now the quantity bought and sold rises also.   The rule is that when *demand increases* and *supply decreases,* the *price* will *rise* but the effect on the *quantity* bought and sold will be *indeterminate*.   If demand rises more than supply falls, the quantity will increase.   If demand rises less than supply falls, the quantity will decrease.   If demand rises and supply falls by equal amounts, the quantity will remain unchanged.

Figure 2-10*b* shows the reverse situation.   Now *demand* is *decreasing* while *supply* is *increasing* (again by equal amounts).   The point of intersection moves from point *E* to point *E'*.   Clearly, the price must fall.   But, again, the effect on quantity is indeterminate.   A glance at Figure 2-10*d* will show that if the supply increases more than the demand decreases, the quantity bought and sold will increase.   If supply increases less than demand decreases, the quantity will decrease. The rule: if *demand decreases* while *supply increases,* the equilibrium

Figure 2-10

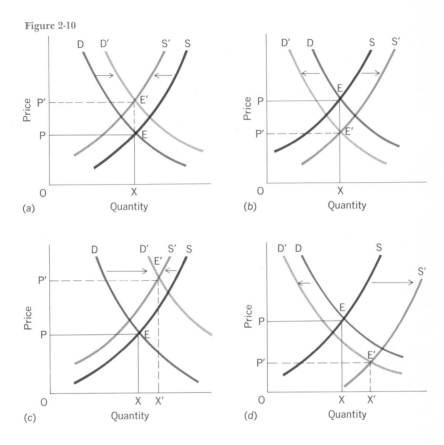

price will decline but the effect on the *quantity* bought and sold will be *indeterminate*. If supply rises more than demand falls, the quantity will increase. If the increase in supply is exactly offset by a decrease in demand, the quantity will remain constant.

CHAPTER SUMMARY

Chapter 1 introduced the economic problems of *what*, *how*, and *for whom*. In this chapter we saw how these problems are answered in a market price system such as ours. Specifically, the very important notions of demand and supply were seen to provide the answers.

Demand was defined as the willingness and ability of consumers to purchase goods and services at particular prices in a set of given prices and was seen to be based upon the idea of diminishing marginal utility. The elasticity of demand was also examined, and we found that demand could be elastic, inelastic, or of unitary elasticity—depending upon the degree of consumer responsiveness to price changes. The important difference between a change in demand and a change in quantity demanded was also pointed out. Price was seen to be the sole cause of a change in quantity demanded; a change in demand was shown to be the result of a change in income, tastes, or the price of substitute products.

We defined supply as the willingness and ability of producers to produce for sale goods and services at particular prices in a set of given prices. Just as with demand, a change in the *quantity* supplied was seen to be dependent upon price changes (though in a direct, rather than an indirect, relationship). A change in the supply function itself was seen to be dependent upon costs of production, technological development, and the number of sellers.

It is the interaction of supply and demand which determines the equilibrium (market) price of any good or service and the quantity of that good or service both bought and sold. This interaction between supply and demand was discussed in some detail, and the effect of changes in each upon price and quantity was presented. At this point it may be helpful to summarize the rules regarding changes in demand and supply:

1. If demand increases and supply remains constant, the price will rise and the quantity bought and sold will rise.
2. If demand decreases and supply remains constant, the price will fall and the quantity bought and sold will fall.
3. If supply increases and demand remains constant, the price will fall and the quantity bought and sold will rise.
4. If supply decreases and demand remains constant, the price will rise and the quantity bought and sold will fall.
5. If demand and supply both increase, the quantity bought and sold will increase but the effect upon price will be indeterminate.
6. If demand and supply both decrease, the quantity bought and sold will decrease but the effect upon price will be indeterminate.
7. If demand increases and supply decreases, the price will rise but

the effect upon the quantity bought and sold will be indeterminate.

8. If demand decreases and supply increases, the price will fall but the effect upon the quantity bought and sold will be indeterminate.

A knowledge of the market forces of supply and demand provides us with a very important tool for determining price and output levels in the economy. A mastery of these concepts is vital to an understanding of the nation's economy.

In Part 2, which follows, we will take a close look at the economic performance of our economy. We will learn how to measure that performance and how to affect the level of output, income, and employment in the economy. We will also apply some of our tools of analysis to suggest possible solutions to current economic problems.

STUDY QUESTIONS

1. How does the price system solve the problem of *what* to produce? *How* to produce? *For whom* to produce? In this framework, can you explain why the Beatles may receive more income from a single performance than a schoolteacher may receive for a lifetime of work?
2. Name several products or services for which you would expect the demand to be relatively elastic. Relatively inelastic. Justify your conclusions.
3. Explain very carefully how supply and demand together determine the equilibrium price and quantity for any good or service.
4. Tell what would happen to the equilibrium price and quantity of a good under all the following conditions: demand rises, supply remains constant; demand falls, supply remains constant; supply rises, demand remains constant; supply falls, demand remains constant; demand rises, supply falls; demand falls, supply rises; demand and supply both rise; demand and supply both fall.

IMPORTANT CONCEPTS IN CHAPTER 2

The economic problems: what, how, for whom
Capital market

Money income
Real income
Demand
Supply
Diminishing marginal utility
Demand schedule
Demand curve
Law of demand
Elasticity of demand: elastic, inelastic, unitary elasticity
Demand versus quantity demanded
Determinants of demand
Law of supply
Supply schedule
Supply curve
Supply versus quantity supplied
Determinants of supply
Interaction of supply and demand
Equilibrium price; equilibrium quantity

PART 2

AGGREGATE ECONOMIC PERFORMANCE

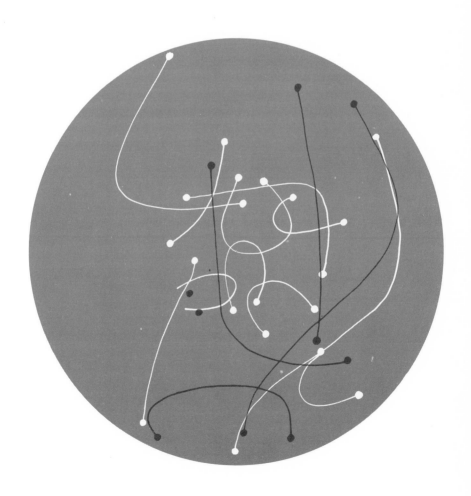

CHAPTER 3

MEASURING ECONOMIC PERFORMANCE

We must now turn our attention to measuring the economic performance of our society. We will first examine the accounting techniques
used to measure our economic output and income. Then we will take
a brief look at some of the predominant theories of the business cycle.

NATIONAL–INCOME ACCOUNTING

In a complex society such as ours, we need some way in which to state
our output and growth in quantitative terms. Are we more productive this year than last? What has been our growth trend? Are we
more or less productive than other societies? Exactly how wealthy are
we? These are questions which can be at least partially answered by
an understanding of national-income accounting.

The Department of Commerce periodically gathers data dealing with
the economic performance of the society. These data are manipulated
in such a way that we derive six basic measures: gross national product,
net national product, national income, personal income, disposable
personal income, and saving. Each of these items measures a different,
but important, aspect of output and income. We will have a look at
these figures to see exactly what each measures and how each is
computed.

Gross National Product (GNP)

The National Income Division of the U.S. Department of Commerce
officially defines gross national product as *the market value of the out-*

put of goods and services produced by the nation's economy before deduction of depreciation charges and other allowances for business and institutional consumption of durable goods.

At first glance this definition may appear a bit cumbersome. But if we break it down, we will see that it is quite descriptive. The definition tells us that we are measuring the *market value* of goods and services. Immediately we know that we are measuring the nation's output in terms of its value in dollars. (GNP is measured in current dollars—that is, the 1970 GNP is measured in terms of 1970 dollars.) Further, we know that we are considering only those goods and services which are bought and sold in the legitimate marketplace. (We exclude income from crime, for example.)

Thus we are obtaining the dollar value of the nation's output. But the second part of the definition tells us something important, too. Specifically, it tells us that we are valuing the nation's output *before* deducting the capital cost of producing those goods. That is, we have not accounted for the capital equipment used up in the production of the new goods. It is for this reason that this measure is called *gross* national product.

The production of the nation (GNP) is measured by adding up the level of total spending necessary to buy that output. There are four types of spending (or categories of spending) which make up the level of total spending in the economy and hence the level of the GNP:

1. PERSONAL-CONSUMPTION EXPENDITURES This element of spending measures the total purchases of final output by the consumer sector of the economy. This is by far the largest part of the gross national product, accounting for about two-thirds of it, except in wartime. And about half of this spending is for food, housing, and household operation. Personal-consumption expenditures in 1967 amounted to $491.7 billion.

2. GROSS PRIVATE DOMESTIC INVESTMENT Just as consumers buy part of the GNP, so do businesses—in the form of investment expenditures for new plant and equipment (capital) and in the form of increased inventory. Such spending by private business in 1967 was $112.1 billion.

3. GOVERNMENT PURCHASES OF GOODS AND SERVICES Federal, state, and

local governments also purchase part of the nation's output. Such expenditures are for goods (tanks, guns, etc.) and for services (salaries for Congressmen, firemen, teachers, etc.). In peacetime, the government normally buys about 20 to 25 percent of the GNP. In 1967, this figure amounted to $176.3 billion.

4.   NET EXPORTS OF GOODS AND SERVICES   Other countries also buy part of our nation's production. But we also buy some of theirs. So we deduct what we spend on foreign goods from the revenues coming to us from foreign nations. The result is the *net* exports of goods and services. In 1967, net exports accounted for $4.8 billion of the GNP.

In terms of symbols, let:

GNP = gross national product
    C = personal-consumption expenditures
     I = gross private domestic investment
    G = government purchases of goods and services
    E = net exports of goods and services

Then: GNP = C + I + G + E

Table 3-1 shows the dollar amounts of the components of GNP.

Net National Product (NNP)

As we mentioned above, gross national product is one measure of the nation's output—but it is a *gross* measure; that is, it does not take into

TABLE 3-1   Gross National Product in the United States, 1967

	DOLLARS, BILLIONS
Personal-consumption expenditures	491.7
Gross private domestic investment	112.1
Government purchases of goods and services	176.3
Net exports of goods and services	4.8
Gross national product	785.0*

* Total does not equal the sum of the parts due to rounding.
SOURCE: U.S. Department of Commerce, *Survey of Current Business.* February, 1968, Table 1, p. 3.

account the capital consumed in the production of that output.   If we desire a *net* measure of output, we seek the net national product.

To obtain this figure, an item called "capital-consumption allowances" is subtracted from the GNP.   Capital-consumption allowances take account of the capital used up by depreciation, accidental damage to fixed capital, and capital outlay charged to current expense.   (The important element is depreciation, which normally accounts for about 90 percent of the total capital consumption.)

In 1967, the GNP was $785.0 billion, as we have seen.   Capital-consumption allowances in the same year were $67.1 billion; thus the net national product stood at $717.9 billion ($785.0 − $67.1 = $717.9). Net national product is perhaps a better estimate of output because it takes into account the cost of producing that output.

National Income (NI)

Both of the above measures are indicators of *output*.   Now we turn to a measure of *income* for the nation as a whole.   National income is defined as *the sum of the payments to the factors of production for engaging in current economic activities.*   Thus we are measuring basically business and personal income in the economy—payments for producing the nation's output.

To obtain this measure, the National Income Division subtracts indirect business taxes (e.g., sales and excise taxes) and business transfer payments (e.g., donations and bad debts) from the net national product.   (These subtractions are made because indirect business taxes and transfer payments are not part of business or personal income.)   Then government subsidies are added, on the assumption that subsidies are a payment for current production and are thus part of the nation's income.   After these two subtractions and one addition, the resultant figure is national income.   In 1967, national income amounted to $649.6 billion.

Personal Income (PI)

Another measure of income in which we are interested is personal income.   National income, we noted, measured business and personal income.   Thus, if we desire a measure of personal income only, we

must subtract out undistributed business income.   We must also add
in certain types of government spending (interest payments and transfer payments).   If we make these adjustments, we will have a measure
of personal income.   Personal income in 1967 was $626.4 billion.

Disposable Personal Income (DPI)

Not all the income received by persons in the private sector of the
economy is available for spending.   Part of it is taxed away.   Hence,
if personal taxes are subtracted from personal income, disposable personal income is derived.   This is income which individuals are free
to use as they choose.   In 1967, it amounted to $544.7 billion.

Saving (S)

A final figure in which we are interested is saving.   Out of a given
disposable income, what is not spent is saved.   Therefore, if we deduct
personal-consumption expenditures from disposable personal income,
we will derive a residual figure reflecting the level of personal saving
in the economy.

These, then, are the basic measures we use to evaluate the level of the
nation's output and income.   A brief summary of the steps followed in
obtaining these measures is given below:

GNP − (Capital consumption allowances) = NNP
NNP − (Indirect business taxes) − (Business transfer payments) +
(Government subsidies) = NI
NI − (Undistributed corporate profits) + (Net interest paid by govern-
ment) + (Government transfer payments) + (Business transfer pay-
ments) = PI
PI − (Personal taxes) = DPI
DPI − (Personal-consumption expenditures) = S

The Need for Constant Dollars

We have stated that the various output and income measures are given
in *current* dollars.   But inflations and depressions, of course, cause
prices to rise and fall.   What is needed for comparison of GNP from
year to year is a statement of GNP in terms of *constant* dollars, using

any given year as the "base." For example, we could state the 1967 GNP in terms of 1966 dollars. Then the 1967 GNP would be directly comparable with the 1966 GNP. If we wished to talk about long-run trends in the GNP, we could state each year's GNP in terms of, say, 1933 dollars. Then we could see the growth of the GNP, inflation aside. Adjusted GNP is called *real* GNP.

Converting current dollars to constant dollars is easily done by using a *price index* (which can be obtained from the U.S. Department of Commerce, *Survey of Current Business*, and elsewhere). Table 3-2 shows such a conversion. In column 1, the GNPs for both 1966 and 1967 are given in current dollars, as originally reported. If we want the 1967 GNP in terms of 1966 dollars, we let 1966 be the "base" year and set the price index equal to 100 for that year. Now, supposing that the price level rose 3 percent in 1967, we know that the price index for 1967 is 103.0.

To compute the real GNP (constant 1966 dollars), the money GNP (current dollars) is divided by the price index for the appropriate year. The result is multiplied by 100 to convert the decimal figure to a percentage figure. These computations are shown in column 3 of Table 3-2. As we would expect, the 1966 GNP remains unchanged because 1966 was taken as the base year. But the 1967 GNP is deflated and becomes $762.1 billion when stated in 1966 dollars. It can readily be seen, then, that part of the increase in money GNP between 1966 and 1967 was due simply to price-level increases.

Figure 3-1 traces the changes in real and money GNP from 1950 to 1967 (1958 = 100).

TABLE 3-2   Sample Calculation of Real Gross National Product

YEAR	(1) BILLIONS OF CURRENT DOLLARS	(2) PRICE INDEX	(3) REAL GNP IN BILLIONS OF 1966 DOLLARS
1966	743.3	100.0	$\dfrac{743.3}{100.0} \times 100 = 743.3$
1967	785.0	103.0	$\dfrac{785.0}{103.0} \times 100 = 762.1$

Figure 3-1 Real and Money GNP, 1950–1967

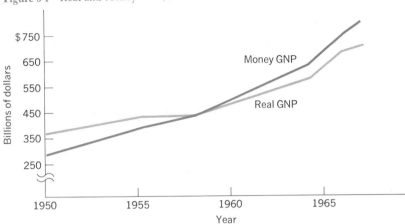

The national-income accounts provide us with one type of measure of economic activity over the years. We will now turn to a more detailed discussion of economic fluctuations—the "business cycle."

BUSINESS CYCLES

It has been said that "the statistical records of business activity . . . indicate that the course of business, like true love, is not smooth. Fluctuation rather than stability is the rule. . . ." [1] Our economy has, in fact, been characterized by various kinds of business fluctuations, of varying lengths and of varying degrees of severity.

Some of these changes in business activity have been of a nonrecurring nature, caused by accidental factors or by structural changes in the economy. But others have been of a recurring, rhythmic character—and it is this type of fluctuation which is normally referred to as a "business cycle."

[1] James A. Estey, *Business Cycles*, 3d ed., Prentice-Hall, Inc., Englewood Cliffs, N.J., 1956, p. 3.

Phases of the Business Cycle

Although economists may use various terms to identify the phases of cyclical fluctuations, we may adequately describe such phases as periods of (1) prosperity, (2) recession, (3) depression, and (4) recovery. These phases are shown in Figure 3-2.

The most severe period of depression and unemployment in our nation's history was the Great Depression, encompassing almost the entire decade of the 1930s. This was followed by a period of tremendous recovery during the war years of 1940 to 1945. Since 1945, we have experienced a series of recessions and recoveries. Recessions were in evidence in 1946 (as we reconverted from wartime to peacetime activity), in 1949, in 1954, and in 1957–1958. Since 1959, we have, in general, had a rather prolonged period of prosperity.

Major Business-cycle Theories

What has caused these swings in business activity, employment, and income? Unfortunately, this is not a question for which we can provide an easy answer. Over the years several theories have been advanced to explain these cyclical fluctuations. We will examine some of the more important types of theories.

As early as 1875, W. Stanley Jevons, an English economist, maintained that variations in the sun's atmosphere, as shown by the frequency and magnitude of sunspots, caused cyclical fluctuations. His conclusion was based upon the coincidence of the cycle of sunspots and the early English business cycles. Jevons reasoned that sunspots

Figure 3-2

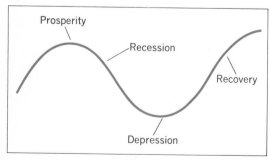

affected the weather, the weather caused changes in agricultural production, and changes in agricultural output caused equivalent changes in commercial activities.   This so-called *sunspot theory* of the cycle has, of course, since been discounted.

Other popular explanations of cyclical variation come under the general heading of *psychological theories.*   Psychological causes of cycles arise from mistaken judgment and changing public attitudes.   For example, in a period of recovery, businessmen may tend to exaggerate their profit expectations.   If this is the case, these businessmen may expect an even larger growth in business activity than is warranted by the facts.   Hence, they may tend to increase their investment and output beyond the level justified by the current growth period.   Such an unwarranted expansion would, of course, eventually lead to a downturn in the cycle.

Another example of psychological causes of the cycle is related to the attitudes of consumers.   If, for some reason, consumers become overly pessimistic about the future, they may curtail their spending activities.   If they do, demand will fall and sales will therefore decline.   A pessimistic attitude (an expectation of a downturn) can, in fact, cause such a downturn.

Still another group of theories purporting to explain cycles falls under the heading of *innovation theories.*   The idea of the effect of innovations on cyclical behavior was most notably advanced by Joseph Schumpeter.

An "innovation" can be defined as "a new or old idea put to work." Very briefly, Schumpeter maintained that if, for example, a businessman found a new cost-saving method of production and put this method to work, a "thundering herd" of businessmen would follow this innovative technique.   Consequently, as more and more businessmen invested in the new technique, the level of spending and output would rise.   Eventually this expansion would come to an end as the consumer-goods market became saturated.

There are many other theories suggesting causes of the business cycle. We have made no attempt to be complete in our coverage of cycle theory.   Other theories which the interested student should examine are the monetary theories, overinvestment theories, and underconsumption theories.

CHAPTER SUMMARY

Chapter 3 had two objectives: one was to examine the techniques used to measure this nation's economic performance, and the other was to look at a few of the theories of the business cycle.

Several measures of output and income were presented. These were gross national product, net national product, national income, personal income, disposable personal income, and saving.

We found that GNP is a measure of the nation's output prior to the deduction of the capital consumed in the process of producing those goods and services. GNP is composed of (1) personal-consumption expenditures, (2) gross private domestic investment, (3) government purchases of goods and services, and (4) net exports of goods and services ($GNP = C + I + G + E$).

Net national product was seen to be a similar measure of the nation's output, except that it is a "net" measure in that capital consumption has been accounted for.

National income was described as the prime measure of the nation's total income. Specifically, it was defined as the sum of the payments to the factors of production for engaging in current economic activities.

Another measure of income of interest to us in this chapter was personal income—which measures the income of persons and excludes that part of national income not distributed to persons (e.g., retained business income).

The remaining two accounts discussed in Chapter 3 were disposable personal income and saving. We found that disposable personal income is simply personal income with taxes removed. That portion of disposable personal income which is not spent becomes saving.

As a final point regarding the national-income accounts, we discussed the need to convert the various measures from current dollars to constant dollars if meaningful comparisons are to be made over time.

Next, Chapter 3 discussed some aspects of the business cycle. The four phases of the business cycle were described as (1) prosperity, (2) recession, (3) depression, and (4) recovery.

Attempts have been made to develop cycle theories at least since the late 1800s, beginning with W. Stanley Jevon's "sunspots" theory. Other theories are the psychological theories (in which it is suggested

that attitudes of consumers and businessmen actually cause or ac-
celerate cyclical fluctuations) and the innovation theory of Joseph
Schumpeter.

The most widely accepted notion of business cycles is based upon the
theory of John Maynard Keynes. This is the so-called "modern"
theory of employment, income, and demand. It will be necessary for
us to examine modern theory in some depth, and it is to this end that
Chapters 4 to 7 are dedicated. In Chapter 4, we examine the basic
Keynesian theory. In Chapters 5 to 7, we will see how business
cycles can be controlled.

STUDY QUESTIONS
1. Define GNP, NNP, NI, PI, DPI, and S. How are each of these
   computed? What is the difference between real and money GNP?
   Why do we care about this difference?
2. Discuss the various theories of the business cycle. Which appears
   most relevant to you? Why?

IMPORTANT CONCEPTS IN CHAPTER 3
Gross national product
Personal-consumption expenditures
Gross private domestic investment
Government purchases of goods and services
Net exports of goods and services
Net national product
National income
Personal income
Disposable personal income
Saving
Money GNP versus real GNP
Phases of the business cycle
Sunspot theory of the cycle
Psychological theories of the cycle
Innovation theories of the cycle

CHAPTER 4

EMPLOYMENT, INCOME, AND OUTPUT

We are now going to turn to one of the most important areas in the study of economics—the theory of the determination of the levels of employment, income, and output. In other words, we are going to find out what forces determine the amount of productive output in our economy, what causes the nation's income to rise and fall, and finally, what causes high or low levels of employment in our economic system.

It is a common error among students of economics that they fail to relate together three notions—employment, income, and output. These three notions are interdependent; that is, they both cause and are caused by each of the others.

Broadly speaking, the level of output determines how many people will be employed to produce that output. Further, the higher the number of people employed, the larger will be the nation's income. And the larger the nation's income, the greater will be the demand for increased output. Thus it is clear that output, employment, and income are dependent upon each other.

Fortunately, we have recently developed a body of theory which enables us to deal rather specifically with these questions of the nation's performance in these economic areas.[1] This body of theory is gen-

---

[1] This theory was first presented by John Maynard Keynes, a British economist, in his book *The General Theory of Employment, Interest and Money*, published in 1936. Later refinements on this theory have been made by many economists, but most notably by Alvin Hansen in *A Guide to Keynes*.

erally known as *modern economic theory,* and it is to an understanding of this modern theory that we will now turn.

THE DETERMINANTS OF THE LEVEL OF EMPLOYMENT, INCOME, AND OUTPUT

We have already alluded to the two most important forces operative in a private economy such as ours.   These forces are demand and supply (see Chapter 2).   We know that the business community will *supply* only what consumers *demand*—no more and no less.   Thus we could say that consumer demand determines the nation's output.   But the problem is a bit more complicated than this.

In reality it is not just consumer demand which determines output; rather, it is *total demand,* or as we will call it, *total spending.*   We are looking, then, for a figure representing the total amount of spending in our economy.   Such a figure is not as elusive as it might seem.

As we indicated in Chapter 3, total spending is composed of four categories of spending: (1) personal-consumption expenditures, C; (2) gross private domestic investment, I; (3) government purchases of goods and services, G; and (4) net exports of goods and services, E.   If we add together these four types of spending, we have a measure of total spending.

Symbolically, we can say then that

$$TS = C + I + G + E$$

where: TS = total spending

C = personal-consumption expenditures

I = gross private domestic investment

G = government purchases of goods and services

E = net exports of goods and services

Because net exports are a relatively minor portion of total spending and because the level of net exports is difficult to manipulate by policy decisions, we may ignore them as an element of total spending.   Thus we abstract somewhat from reality and say that $TS = C + I + G$.   This, then, is our measure of total spending.

On the other hand, total output will be measured by *net national product* (NNP), that is, the market value of the goods and services produced by the nation's economy (after allowing for capital-consumption allowances).   Further, the nation's income is reflected by national income (NI), that is, payments to the factors of production for engaging in current economic activity.

Therefore, when we said earlier that total spending determines total output (or that demand determines supply), what we were really implying is that $C + I + G = NNP$ or NI.   The higher the level of total spending, the higher will be the nation's output, income, and employment.

A CLOSER LOOK AT CONSUMPTION

If we are fully to understand how consumption spending affects total demand, we must take a more comprehensive look at the nature of consumption spending.   Specifically, we must understand what is meant by the *propensity-to-consume* and the *marginal propensity-to-consume.*

The Propensity-to-Consume

By "propensity-to-consume," we mean simply the tendency of persons to consume out of a current level of income.   Stated another way, the propensity-to-consume measures the percentage of current income which is spent.   If, for example, disposable personal income stood at $550 billion and personal-consumption expenditures were $500 billion, then the propensity-to-consume would be $500/$550, which is equal to .909, or 90.9 percent.   What this means, then, is that we are spending 90.9 percent of our income.

The Propensity-to-Save

Whatever portion of our income we do not spend, we must save—since our only choice with disposable income is to spend it or to save it. The propensity-to-save, then, is the complement of the propensity-to-consume.   It is the tendency to *save* out of current level of income; that is, it measures the percentage of current income which is saved. Using the figures above, if disposable personal income is $550 billion and if we are spending $500 billion, then we must be saving $50 billion ($550 − $500). The propensity-to-save, therefore, must be $50/$550, which is equal to .091, or 9.1 percent. (*Note:* The propensity-to-consume plus the propensity-to-save must always be equal to 100 percent. In our case, 90.9 + 9.1 = 100.0. Or, stated in decimal form, .909 + .091 = 1.00.)

Table 4-1 shows some hypothetical levels of disposable income, with corresponding levels of consumer expenditures. In each case, saving, the propensity-to-consume, and the propensity-to-save have been computed.

Note that as income rises, the propensity-to-consume declines and, of course, the propensity-to-save rises. What this means is that at higher income levels we tend to *spend less as a percentage of our income and to save more as a percentage of our income.* Of course, in *absolute amounts,* as our income rises our spending also rises.

It will be helpful to us to graph the relationship we have been discussing. This is done in Figure 4-1.

So that we can better envision saving and dissaving, a 45-degree "helping line" has been introduced in the graph. The helping line is equidistant from both axes, so that at any point on the line spending is just equal to income.

Next, the data from Table 4-1 were plotted. At point *A,* disposable income is $200 billion and consumption spending is $210 billion. Note that this point falls *above* the 45-degree helping line, indicating the existence of "dissaving" (in the amount of $10 billion). At point

TABLE 4-1 Hypothetical Income and Saving Data ($ Billions)

	DISPOSABLE INCOME	CONSUMPTION EXPENDITURES	SAVING (+) OR DISSAVING (−)	PROPENSITY-TO-CONSUME	PROPENSITY-TO-SAVE
A	$200	$210	−$10	1.05	−.05
B	250	250	0	1.00	0.00
C	300	285	15	.95	.05
D	350	315	35	.90	.10
E	400	340	60	.85	.15
F	450	360	90	.80	.20

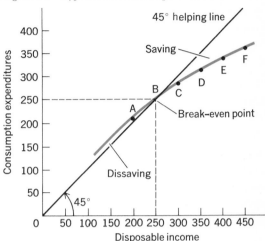

Figure 4-1   Hypothetical Consumption Function

B, disposable income stands at $250 billion and consumption spending at $250 billion. The remaining pairs of data from Table 4-1 were plotted in similar fashion. These points were then connected with a smooth line to form the *consumption function. The consumption function graphically relates spending to income.*

Where the consumption function crosses the 45-degree line, we have a "break-even point"—spending is just equal to income. To the left of the break-even point is *dissaving.* Graphically, dissaving is shown by the distance the consumption function lies *above* the 45-degree line. (Actually, of course, it is the amount by which spending exceeds income.) To the right of the break-even point is *net positive saving.* Graphically, net positive saving is measured by the distance the consumption function lies *below* the 45-degree line. (Actually, it is the amount by which income exceeds spending.)

We will shortly expand the consumption function to include private investment and government spending—the other two elements of total spending. Before turning to these other spending components, however, we have two final notions to examine in the area of consumption spending—the marginal propensity-to-consume and the marginal propensity-to-save.

The Marginal Propensity-to-Consume

It is important that the marginal propensity-to-consume not be confused with the propensity-to-consume. These are two distinctly different notions. You will recall that the propensity-to-consume measures the percentage of current income which is spent. Symbolically, we can say that

$PC = C/Y$ where: PC = propensity-to-consume

C = consumption spending

Y = disposable income

When we speak of the *marginal* propensity-to-consume, however, we are concerned with *changes* in spending associated with *changes* in income. In other words, if income increases, what percentage *of that increase* will be spent? Symbolically, then, the marginal propensity-to-consume is shown as

$MPC = \dfrac{\Delta C}{\Delta Y}$ where: MPC = marginal propensity-to-consume

ΔC = a change in spending

ΔY = a change in the level of disposable income

Table 4-2 again presents the income and consumption data which first appeared in Table 4-1. Here we assume a change from a $200 billion level of disposable income at point *A* to a $250 billion level at point *B*. This represents, of course, an increase in disposable income of $50 billion. At the same time, consumption expenditures rise from $210 billion at point *A* to $250 billion at point *B*, an increase of $40 billion. The marginal propensity-to-consume, then, is found by relating the change in spending ($40) to the change in income ($50). This computation is made in column 3 of the table, and the result is plotted between point *A* and point *B* to show that we are dealing with changing levels of spending and income. A marginal propensity-to-consume of .80 means that we will spend 80 percent of the *increase* in income between point *A* and point *B*.

As income again rises from $250 (point *B*) to $300 (point *C*), consumption spending rises from $250 (point *B*) to $285 (point *C*). Thus the MPC would be equal to $35/$50 = .70. This process is continued throughout the possible ranges of income, and the results are plotted in column 3. Note that as income levels rise, the MPC declines. This

TABLE 4-2 Hypothetical Income and Expenditure Data ($ Billions)

	(1) DISPOS-ABLE INCOME	(2) CONSUMP-TION EX-PENDITURES	(3) MARGINAL PROPENSITY-TO-CONSUME	(4) SAVING	(5) MARGINAL PROPENSITY-TO-SAVE
A	$200	$210	$\frac{\Delta C}{\Delta Y} = \frac{40}{50} = .80$	$-\$10$	$\frac{\Delta S}{\Delta Y} = \frac{10}{50} = .20$
B	250	250	$\frac{\Delta C}{\Delta Y} = \frac{35}{50} = .70$	0	$\frac{\Delta S}{\Delta Y} = \frac{15}{50} = .30$
C	300	285	$\frac{\Delta C}{\Delta Y} = \frac{30}{50} = .60$	15	$\frac{\Delta S}{\Delta Y} = \frac{20}{50} = .40$
D	350	315	$\frac{\Delta C}{\Delta Y} = \frac{25}{50} = .50$	35	$\frac{\Delta S}{\Delta Y} = \frac{25}{50} = .50$
E	400	340	$\frac{\Delta C}{\Delta Y} = \frac{20}{50} = .40$	60	$\frac{\Delta S}{\Delta Y} = \frac{30}{50} = .60$
F	450	360		90	

tells us that the higher the level of income, the lower will be the proportion spent out of *additions* to income.

The Marginal Propensity-to-Save

The complement of the MPC is the marginal propensity-to-save (MPS). The MPS measures the change in saving associated with a change in the level of income.

$$MPS = \frac{\Delta S}{\Delta Y}$$ where: MPS = marginal propensity-to-save

ΔS = a change in saving

ΔY = a change in the level of income

In Table 4-2, as income rises from $200 billion (point *A*) to $250 billion (point *B*), saving increases from $-\$10$ billion to zero. Thus the increase in saving is $10 billion, while the increase in income is $50 billion. Therefore, the MPS must be $10/$50 = .20. An MPS of .20 tells us that we will save 20 percent of an increase in income from $200 to $250 billion.

As we would expect, when income levels rise, the marginal propensity-to-save also rises.   The higher the level of income, the greater will be the proportion saved of any added increments to that income.

Note, too, that the marginal propensity-to-consume plus the marginal propensity-to-save must be equal to 1.00, or 100 percent, in all cases. This concludes, for the moment, our discussion of consumption spending.   The major conclusion at this point is a recognition that the single most important determinant of the level of consumption spending is the level of disposable income.   As income rises, spending rises, but by a decreasing amount.

We will now turn our attention to a second element of total spending—private investment.

A CLOSER LOOK AT INVESTMENT

We found above that level of income determines the level of consumption spending.   Now we must find out what determines the level of investment spending.   The discussion which follows regarding the determinants of investment is an oversimplification but should serve to provide us with an idea of the basic determinants of investment levels.

Remember that investment is an addition to plant, equipment, and the like and that it occurs in the business community.   Whether or not a businessman will invest in, say, a new plant depends upon two very important notions—the marginal efficiency of capital and the cost of capital.

The marginal efficiency of capital can be defined as the *anticipated rate of return on investment.*   Thus, if a businessman expects a return of, say, 10 percent on a new piece of equipment, then we say that the marginal efficiency of capital is 10 percent.

But in order to buy this new piece of equipment, the businessman must raise funds. He does this by issuing new stocks and bonds, by borrowing from financial institutions, or by retaining part of the business profits.   Regardless of where he obtains his funds, the businessman must pay for the use of this money.   And it is this cost which we refer to as the *cost of capital.*

Now, if the marginal efficiency of capital (the anticipated return on investment) is greater than the cost of capital (the cost of obtaining investment funds), the businessman will invest.   Suppose, for example, that he believes a new machine will bring the business a 15 percent return.   Suppose further that it will cost him 10 percent to obtain the funds to buy the new machine.   Obviously, then, it would pay the businessman to go ahead and make the investment.

Let us return now to our consumption function, considering investment as well as consumption spending.   Previously we were relating consumption spending to disposable income.   Now, however, we are going to expand our notion to relate *total* spending to the *nation's* income (or output).   This is shown in Figure 4-2.

The level of consumption spending associated with national income is shown (as it was previously) by the consumption function (labeled "C").   But since investment spending is also a part of total spending, we must add investment to consumption spending.   Assuming a constant level of investment, we can graphically show this addition simply by shifting the consumption function to a higher level, at C + I.   The distance between C and C + I represents the level of investment.   This new consumption function then represents both consumption spending and investment spending.

Finally, we can add the last element of total spending—government

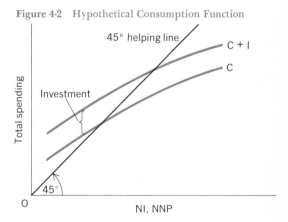

Figure 4-2   Hypothetical Consumption Function

Figure 4-3   Hypothetical Consumption Function

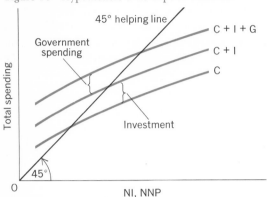

purchases of goods and services. This addition is shown in Figure 4-3. To consumption spending and investment spending, we have now added government spending (shown by the distance between C + I and C + I + G). Thus the *aggregate* consumption function (aggregate demand) is one containing all three major elements of total spending (C + I + G). Henceforth, when we talk about the "consumption function," we will be referring to this aggregate consumption function, or aggregate spending.

THE EQUILIBRIUM LEVEL OF INCOME AND OUTPUT

Let us now see to what use we can put our analysis of the consumption function. Figure 4-4 shows the aggregate consumption function, including all elements of total spending.

Economic theory tells us that the economy is in "equilibrium" when total spending is equal to total output, that is, when everything that is produced is also purchased (in other words, when aggregate demand is equal to aggregate supply). This point of equilibrium is shown graphically by point *E* in Figure 4-4. This is, of course, the point where the consumption function crosses the 45-degree helping line. Because point *E* lies on the 45-degree line, we know that the point is equidistant from the spending axis and the output axis.

Figure 4-4   Hypothetical Consumption Function

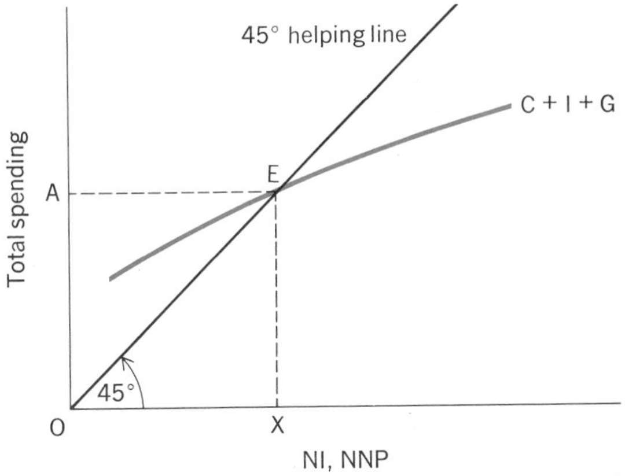

Thus total spending (*OA*) is just equal to total output (*OX*), or demand (*OA*) is just equal to supply (*OX*).

The point of intersection of the consumption function and the 45-degree line is called an *equilibrium* point because there is no tendency to change from this level of spending and output.   Figure 4-5 shows the economy in disequilibrium.

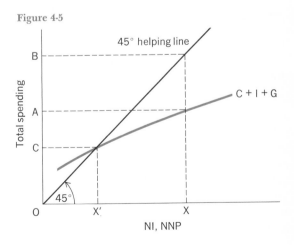

Figure 4-5

Suppose that the economy is producing OX level of output (net national product). We can see from the consumption function that at this level of output and income we would be willing to spend only OA amount in total spending. Yet the 45-degree line tells us that if we are to "clear the market" at this higher level of output, it would be necessary for the level of total spending to be at OB. Clearly, then, total spending is *not* sufficient to buy all the goods and services produced at OX level of net national product. (Put another way, the supply of goods and services is greater than the demand for those goods and services.)

What will be the result? If the economy is producing more than is being demanded, there will be a cutback in the level of output until supply readjusts to demand. Graphically, output must fall from OX to OX' and spending must fall from OA to OC. At this point, and at this point only, will total spending be sufficient to clear the market of all the goods and services produced. Hence, we have moved back to the equilibrium level of spending and output.

Just as the economy will not produce *more* goods and services than are demanded, neither will the economy produce *fewer* goods and services than are demanded. Figure 4-6 shows why this situation is not possible.

Assume, as in Figure 4-6, that the economy is producing at the OX level

Figure 4-6

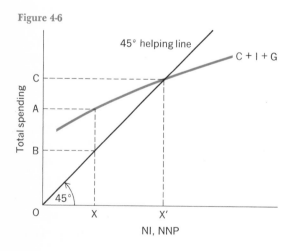

of net national product. The consumption function shows that total spending at this level of output will be O*A*. Yet the 45-degree line tells us that only O*B* amount of spending is necessary to clear the market. Hence, we are faced with overspending (in the amount *AB*). If total spending (demand) exceeds total output, there will, of course, be an increase in the dollar volume of output of goods and services. This is so because of rising prices and because the business community will expand production to meet the high demand.

For the reasons stated above, the economy must be in equilibrium where the aggregate consumption function intersects the 45-degree helping line. But note that we have said nothing yet about the level of employment associated with the equilibrium level of output. Our economy may be producing at a level of NNP which is insufficient to fully employ the factors of production. Or we may be producing at an inflationary level of output. It is to these possibilities that we now turn our attention.

THE DEFLATIONARY GAP

A deflationary gap can be defined as *the amount by which total spending falls short of what would be necessary to clear the market at a full-employment level of net national product.* Let us see exactly what this means.

Figure 4-7 depicts the economy in equilibrium. Based on our previous discussion, we know that the level of output and income is O*X*. We know, too, that the level of total spending is O*A*. And finally, we know that total spending (O*A*) is just equal to total output and income (O*X*). Therefore, we are demanding all the goods and services being produced by the economy.

But let us suppose that a net national product in the amount of O*X* is *not* sufficiently high to provide for full employment. (That is, we are not producing at a high enough level to provide jobs for all who are willing and able to work.) The economy finds itself in what is referred to as an *under-full-employment equilibrium.*

Now suppose further that if we were somehow able to increase our net national product to O*F*, we *could* provide full employment. But we face a problem. Point *E'* (on the 45-degree line) tells us that we

Figure 4-7

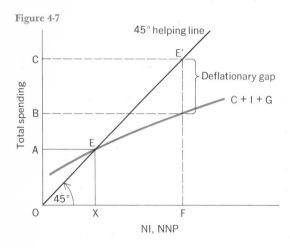

must spend O*C* amount if we are to clear the market at a full-employment level of output. Yet the consumption function at O*F* level of output shows that we *would* spend only O*B* amount. Therefore, total spending would not be sufficient to clear the market at a full-employment level of output. This deficiency in total spending is the deflationary gap. If we are to eliminate this gap, we must increase total spending sufficiently to move the consumption function upward so that it intersects the 45-degree line at point *E'* (a higher level of output and spending).

Chapters 6 and 7 will deal more specifically with methods for shifting the consumption function. However, we might note at this time that what is needed is an increase in one or more of the components of total spending (consumption, investment, and/or government spending). In the case of the deflationary gap, we might (for example) decrease consumer and business taxes. Such a tax decrease would leave a larger amount of income in the hands of consumers and businesses and should, therefore, lead to higher levels of spending by these two sectors. Coupled with this action could be an increase in government spending. However the spending increase is accomplished, it should be of sufficient magnitude to shift the consumption function to the desired higher level. Figure 4-8 shows the higher equilibrium we hope to accomplish.

Figure 4-8

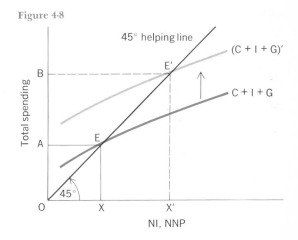

Note that the consumption function (or the level of total spending) has risen from $C + I + G$ to $(C + I + G)'$. A new equilibrium point has been established at E'. Thus net national product now stands at OX', total spending has risen to OB, and the economy is in a *full-employment equilibrium*.

THE INFLATIONARY GAP

An inflationary gap represents the exact opposite of the deflationary gap. The inflationary gap is defined as *the amount by which total spending exceeds what would be necessary to clear the market at a full-employment level of net national product (at current prices)*.

Figure 4-9 depicts such an inflationary gap. Assume now that the economy is producing at OX level of output, with the level of total spending at OA. Once again, we are in an equilibrium situation. But suppose further that a level of production of OF is all that is necessary to provide for full employment of our available resources. We have, then, an inflated net national product.

We cannot, of course, operate at OF level of output since we are in equilibrium at OX level. The 45-degree line indicates that at an output of OF we would require a level of total spending of only OC to

Figure 4-9

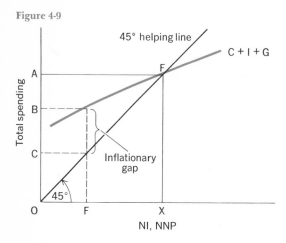

clear the market. However, the consumption function shows that we would, in fact, spend *OB* amount. This would be a disequilibrium situation, in which total spending exceeded total output. This excess of spending over what is necessary to clear the market at a full-employment level is the inflationary gap.

What is called for is a reduction in total spending, so that the consumption function will shift downward, as in Figure 4-10.

If this decrease in spending can be accomplished, the economy would establish a new point of equilibrium at *E'*. Output would then stand at *OF* (a full-employment level), and total spending would be *OB* (an amount just sufficient to clear the market). Once again, we would have established a full-employment level of output.

Closing the inflationary gap requires measures which are the opposite of those called for in eliminating the deflationary gap. Since we desire a spending reduction, personal and corporate taxes could be raised. Such an action would leave less money in the hands of individuals and businesses, causing the desired decline in spending. In addition, government spending could be reduced.

THE MULTIPLIER

We have pointed out that if we desire to close a deflationary gap, we

Figure 4-10

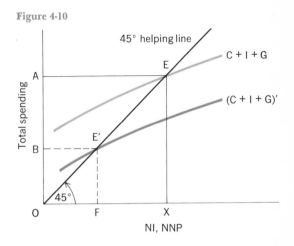

must increase total spending and if we desire to close an inflationary gap, we must decrease spending. However, the increase or decrease in spending which is called for need *not* match the change in national income and output which we desire to attain. That is, it may take only a $10 million change in spending to accomplish a $40 million change in income and output. This effect of spending on income and output is called the *multiplier effect*.

As an example of the multiplier effect, let us suppose that there were, for some reason, an increase in spending of $1,000. Perhaps, say, a business firm has decided to buy a new machine costing this amount. If the businessman bought his machine from you, you would gain $1,000 in income. Then you would turn around and spend a portion of this $1,000 income. (How much you would spend would depend upon your marginal propensity-to-consume.)

If you had an MPC of .75, you would spend $750 of your new-found income to buy something you need or want—say, groceries. But the people who supply your groceries then receive $750 in income, and they will spend a portion of their new income (the amount again being dependent upon their MPC). This process will repeat itself again and again, generating new income and output all along the way. In the data below we will assume an initial change in spending of $1,000 and a marginal propensity-to-consume of .75. The data indicate the amount of new income generated at each step.   Note that the total new income generated by the initial spending change of $1,000 is $4,000.

$1,000.00   (initial new income)
   750.00   (new income, 2d stage)
   562.50   (new income, 3d stage)
   421.88   (new income, 4th stage)
      .
      .
      .
$4,000.00   (total new income)

Fortunately, however, we do not have to add each level of new income to determine the total effect of a change in spending on total income. There is a formula which does this for us: [2]

$$k = \frac{1}{1 - MPC}$$ where: k = the multiplier
MPC = the marginal propensity-to-consume

In our example, the MPC was .75.   Substituting in the above formula,

$$k = \frac{1}{1 - MPC}$$
$$= \frac{1}{1 - .75}$$
$$= \frac{1}{.25} \text{ or } \frac{1}{1/4}$$
$$= 4$$

The multiplier is found to be 4, which means that an initial change in total spending will be multiplied four times before its full impact is felt.   Symbolically, we can say that

$\Delta TS \times k = \Delta NI$ where: Δ = change
TS = total spending
k = the multiplier
NI = national income

Again, in our example $1,000 × 4 = $4,000.

Thus the $1,000 initial change in total spending leads to a $4,000 change in national income.   Graphically, we can show the effect of the multiplier as in Figure 4-11.   In this example, the consumption function has increased from C + I + G to (C + I + G)'.   But note that the

[2] An alternative formula for computing the multiplier is $k = 1/MPS$, where MPS is the marginal propensity-to-save. This is so because $1 - MPC = MPS$.

increase in spending is significantly less than the increase in national income.

The important point about the multiplier effect is that if we know how much we need to change our national income and output in order to provide for full employment and if we can estimate the nation's multiplier, then we will know how much of a change in spending will be necessary to close the deflationary or inflationary gap.

CHAPTER SUMMARY

In this chapter we examined the determinants of the level of employment, income, and output. We found that the equating of total spending with total output will determine these levels. Graphically, we saw that the economy is in equilibrium where the aggregate consumption function crosses the 45-degree helping line. But this point of equilibrium told us nothing about the level of employment.

Specifically, it was pointed out that the economy could be in a slump (with a deflationary gap) or in a boom period (with an inflationary gap). We examined methods of closing these gaps to ensure a full-employment level of output.

Several specific "tools" were developed in this chapter. Among these

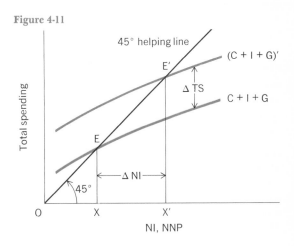

Figure 4-11

were the propensity-to-consume, the propensity-to-save, saving, dissaving, the consumption function, the marginal propensity-to-consume, the marginal propensity-to-save, the marginal efficiency of capital, and the multiplier.   Each of these notions is extremely important to an understanding of methods of closing deflationary and inflationary gaps.

In Chapter 5 we will look at our banking system, which plays a very important role in helping us to adjust to full-employment levels of output.   After gaining an understanding of the banking system, our attention will turn to *monetary policy* (Chapter 6) and *fiscal policy* (Chapter 7)—these are the two major policy techniques at our disposal for ensuring a prosperous, full-employment economy.

STUDY QUESTIONS
1. How does the level of total spending determine the nation's income, output, and employment?
2. How do inflationary and deflationary gaps occur?   What can be done to eliminate them?   How does the concept of the multiplier relate to the closing of these gaps?

IMPORTANT CONCEPTS IN CHAPTER 4

Total spending
Propensity-to-consume
Marginal propensity-to-consume
Propensity-to-save
Marginal propensity-to-save
45-degree helping line
Consumption function
Investment
Marginal efficiency of capital
Cost of capital
Equilibrium level of income and output
Deflationary gap
Under-full-employment equilibrium
Full-employment equilibrium
Inflationary gap
Multiplier

CHAPTER 5

MONEY AND
THE BANKING SYSTEM

In the previous chapter we discussed in some detail the notions of inflationary and deflationary gaps. Our objective in this chapter, and in the two chapters which follow, is to learn how these gaps can be closed. In short, we will examine techniques for restoring the economy to a full-employment level of output and income.

As was previously indicated, monetary policy is one of the important policy areas in this regard. However, before we can decide upon appropriate monetary policy, we must understand the theory upon which such policy is based. It is to this end that the present chapter is directed.

In the pages which follow we will examine the nature of money itself, the history of the development of our current monetary standard, and our banking system.

WHAT IS MONEY?

Most of us feel that we know very well what money is. But we will find that our common conception of money is probably inadequate. Money is really *anything* which fulfills certain functions. A half-dollar is, of course, money. But rare stones may also be money, as can almost any other convenient commodity—so long as it fulfills the *functions of money*.

The Functions of Money

It is commonly accepted that anything can be considered as money if it serves as (1) a medium of exchange, (2) a standard of value, (3) a standard of deferred payments, and (4) a store of value.

Money exists because it is a convenience to us. If it were not for money, it would be necessary for us to barter goods from each other. That is, I might trade a pound of sugar to you for a pound of potatoes. Such a barter system would be extremely clumsy. Fortunately, money enables us to circumvent barter; and when it does, we say that it is performing as a *medium of exchange*. When money acts as a medium of exchange, I can *sell* my sugar and *buy* your potatoes. Obviously, it is more convenient to exchange goods for money and money for goods than to engage in the bartering of goods for goods.

When money acts as a *standard of value,* it provides a common base for estimating the worth of a good or service. We say, for example, that an automobile is *worth* $3,000. This is a much better statement of its value than to say that it is worth 10,000 chickens (or some other commodity). Furthermore, when we state an item's value in terms of money, we can directly compare the worth of one commodity with the worth of another.

Money also acts as a *standard of deferred payments*. Acting in this capacity, money enables us to engage in credit buying. In other words, we can pay some *money* now and additional sums of *money* later.

Finally, money acts as a *store of value*. In order for money to fulfill this function, we must be able to hold it for a period of time without its losing significant value. When we store (save) money, we are actually storing (saving) value.

The Development of Money

The use of money probably first arose in prehistoric societies, where a commodity came to be valued not for its own intrinsic value but because it could be exchanged for commodities having value. The earliest coinage of money began during the seventh century B.C.—over 2,500 years ago.

Over the years, two metals came to be used most often in the making of coins. These metals were gold and silver. The reasons for using these particular metals are that they are relatively durable, they are rare, and they are small in relation to their value. In addition, man has always, it seems, been particularly attracted to gold as a precious metal.

Paper money as a part of the money supply came later.   It is believed that it was invented sometime in the late Middle Ages by bankers in Florence, who had need for a flexible and plentiful money supply for use in trade.

A BRIEF HISTORY OF MONEY IN THE UNITED STATES

Much like the rest of the world, the U.S. government has traditionally relied upon gold and silver in its coins.   Moreover, until the middle 1930s our paper currency also was backed by the precious metals.   We have a long history of backing our currency by gold, by silver, or by both gold and silver (a bimetallic standard).

The Gold Standard Act of 1900 established the U.S. currency as being on a *gold standard*.   (Some persons feel that we are still on such a standard, but this is not the case, as will be indicated later.)   If a nation is to be on a gold standard, three important conditions must be met.   First, the monetary unit (the dollar) must be defined as being equal to a fixed quantity of gold.   A second condition is that the monetary unit must be freely convertible to gold; that is, a citizen holding gold must be able to exchange it for money (or to exchange money for gold).   A last condition of the gold standard is that the government must be willing to buy and sell gold in unlimited amounts. (A fourth condition is sometimes mentioned also—that there be free international movement of gold at the prevailing exchange ratio.)

The United States remained loosely on the gold standard until the period of the Great Depression of the 1930s.   During the Depression there occurred a general loss of confidence in the dollar, and U.S. citizens (and others around the world) began to clamor for gold.   It was felt that gold was much more likely to maintain its value than was the dollar.   As a consequence, the hoarding of gold became commonplace.   The result, of course, was a shortage of gold, so that by 1932 it was becoming clearly evident that the shortage would lead to the eventual abandonment of the gold standard.

This abandonment of the gold standard was actually accomplished by Pres. Franklin Roosevelt in 1934 with the passage of the Gold Reserve

Act. Under the conditions of this act, the monetary unit was still defined as being equal to a fixed quantity of gold. Specifically, gold was officially pegged by the government as being equal to $35 an ounce. (This official ratio still exists.) But the important changes brought about by the Gold Reserve Act were two: the government no longer would issue gold coins, and the private holding of gold (except for special purposes such as dentistry) was made illegal. Since the free exchange of money for gold was terminated, the act effectively took us off the gold standard.

But if gold does not back our currency, what does? The answer to this question is that our *confidence* in the dollar backs the dollar. So long as we believe in the soundness of the dollar, it will remain sound. If we lose confidence in it, then the dollar will lose value. There is still a very loose relationship between gold and the dollar domestically (which is explained below), but not to the extent that we can claim a gold backing for our currency.

It should be pointed out, however, that the United States remains on a gold standard for purposes of international trade. Any nation holding American dollars can trade them to us at will for gold, at the official rate of $35 per ounce.

Paper Currency

As was mentioned earlier, the United States has a long history of experimentation with currency. You may have seen several kinds of paper dollars—including gold certificates, United States notes, silver certificates, and Federal Reserve notes.

Paper dollar bills at one time had the words "Gold Certificate" printed across the top. These gold certificates could be exchanged at will for gold. However, when the United States abandoned the gold standard in 1934, these certificates were called out of general circulation. Now they are of only historical interest to the consumer.

Another type of paper currency once in circulation was the United States note. This type of currency was first issued during the Civil War and was known as the "greenback." It was a *fiat* currency in that it had no metallic backing. While there are a few United States notes still in circulation, these have been largely replaced by Federal Reserve notes.

A third type of currency issued by the government was the silver certificate. This type of paper money was convertible into silver by the holder; that is, it was backed by silver. Silver certificates were in wide circulation until June of 1968, at which time they could no longer be exchanged for silver. The government called this type of currency out of circulation largely because of a domestic shortage of silver, which was causing a steep rise in the price of silver. While silver certificates are still legal currency, they can no longer be exchanged for silver.

The final, and by far the most prevalent, type of currency is the Federal Reserve note. Virtually all our currency is of this type now. Federal Reserve notes are issued by the Federal Reserve banks (to be discussed below). While these notes are *not* exchangeable for gold, they nevertheless had a partial gold backing until 1966. For each dollar issued as a Federal Reserve note, the Reserve banks were required to hold 25 cents in gold (gold certificates). There was, then, a 25 percent gold backing. This 25 percent backing was repealed in 1966, however; consequently, our domestic currency no longer has even partial gold backing.

A NEW DEFINITION OF THE MONEY SUPPLY

In the previous section we talked about the components of the money supply with which we are most familiar—currency and coin. Actually, these two types of money account for only about 20 percent of the total money supply.

Far more important as a part of the money supply are *demand deposits* in our commercial banks. Demand deposits are nothing more than checking accounts, but since we pay by check for about 80 percent of what we buy, demand deposits constitute most (80 percent) of our total money supply.

Can we consider demand deposits to be money? The answer is yes, because checks perform the functions of money just as does currency or coin. Thus the total money supply is made up of three components: currency, coin, and demand deposits. Remember, in the discussion that follows, that when we refer to the supply of money in the economy, we are talking mostly about demand deposits.

Some economists also include *near money* as a part of the money supply. Near money is anything which can be converted very quickly into currency, coin, or demand deposits. Examples of near money are time deposits (savings accounts), very liquid assets, and short-term securities. For our purposes, we will ignore near money as a part of the money supply.

With this understanding of money and the money supply, let us now direct our attention to the banking system. We need to examine the commercial bank and the Federal Reserve bank. Then we can see how the banking system is able to increase and decrease the supply of money in circulation.

THE COMMERCIAL BANKING SYSTEM

A commercial bank can be defined as *a bank for individuals and businesses*. These, then, are the banks with which we are most familiar. It is in these financial institutions that we have our savings accounts and checking accounts.

The primary *economic* function of a commercial bank is to accept checkable demand deposits, that is, to accept our deposits of money and to honor checks drawn upon those deposits. The commercial bank is the *only* financial institution in the United States which can perform this primary function. Of course, commercial banks also perform other important functions, such as accepting time deposits and providing loans.

The commercial bank, like any other private business, is concerned with making profits. There are about 13,500 such banks in the United States at present. Commercial banks obtain about 90 percent of their funds from demand deposits and time deposits of individuals and businesses, and they use their money for cash reserves, loans, and investments.

There is another type of bank in our economy, however—one with which we may not be as familiar. This is the Federal Reserve bank.

THE FEDERAL RESERVE SYSTEM

In the United States, in 1907, we experienced an economic crisis known as the "Panic of 1907." This crisis followed on the heels of many years of uncontrolled banking in the United States, and during that year hundreds of commercial banks failed. The public almost completely lost confidence in the banking system and, as a result, demanded some form of centralized control over the commercial banks. Hence, six years following the Panic of 1907, the Congress of the United States passed the single most important piece of legislation ever passed in the field of banking—the Federal Reserve Act of 1913.

Under the provisions of the Federal Reserve Act, the country was divided into twelve *Federal Reserve districts.* (See Figure 5-1.) A Federal Reserve bank (with branches) was set up in each of the twelve districts.

Now, a Federal Reserve bank is vastly different from a commercial bank. One important difference is that a Federal Reserve bank can-

Figure 5-1 Federal Reserve Districts

Legend —— Boundaries of Federal Reserve Districts
—— Boundaries of Federal Reserve Branch Territories
★ Board of Governors of the Federal Reserve System
○ Federal Reserve Bank Cities
● Federal Reserve Branch Cities

SOURCE: Board of Governors of the Federal Reserve System, *Federal Reserve Bulletin,* Washington, D.C.

not be used by individuals and businesses—*it is a bank for bankers and for the government.*   Perhaps the most important difference between a commercial bank and a Federal Reserve bank, however, is that the Federal Reserve bank does not have profits as its goal, as does the commercial bank.[1]   Rather, the economic function of the Federal Reserve bank is *to control the supply of money in such a way as to help provide for full employment, stable prices, and economic growth.* Exactly how this is accomplished will be shown below and in Chapter 6.

Control of the Federal Reserve System (and, hence, of the Federal Reserve banks) lies with the Board of Governors of the Federal Reserve System.   This Board was also established by the act of 1913 and is composed of seven members, appointed to staggered fourteen-year terms by the President of the United States, with the approval of the Senate.   The terms of the Board members are purposely staggered so that no one President can exert undue political influence over the Board.   It is, then, relatively independent of pressure by a particular President or political party.

Commercial Bank Membership in the Federal Reserve System

Under the provisions of the Federal Reserve Act, all commercial banks holding a national charter *must* join the Federal Reserve System. Commercial banks holding state charters have the option to join if they wish to do so.

There are certain disadvantages to a commercial bank if it joins the Federal Reserve System.   The commercial bank is subject to a certain amount of control and auditing by the Federal Reserve bank to ensure proper banking practices on the part of the commercial bank. Also, some small banks may not be able to qualify for membership because of inadequate capital.   A final requirement (considered to be a disadvantage by some commercial banks) is that each member bank must keep a portion of its deposits on deposit with the Federal Reserve bank.   These so-called *required reserves* earn no interest for the member banks.   Furthermore, these reserves have nothing to do with

---

[1] The Federal Reserve banks have been very profitable, but this is not their goal.   If necessary, these banks would purposely incur a loss in order to provide for the economic stability of the nation.

safety within the banking system.   The sole purpose of required re-serves is to enable the Federal Reserve System to expand or contract the money supply (as we will see in Chapter 6).

For most large banks, the advantages of membership in the Federal Reserve System far outweigh the disadvantages.   One important ad-vantage to membership is that the member bank has access to Federal Reserve credit.   Another advantage is that the Federal Reserve System maintains *clearinghouses* (where checks drawn on the various member banks are exchanged).

Figure 5-2 provides a summary of the relationship between commercial and Federal Reserve banks.   This chart should be read from top to bottom.   It shows, first, that there are about 5,000 banks with a national charter and about 8,500 banks holding a state charter.   (The type of charter is relatively insignificant.   A nationally chartered bank could choose to be chartered by the state instead with very little diffi-culty, though the reverse is not necessarily true.)

Next, Figure 5-2 shows that *all* banks having a national charter *must* be members of the Federal Reserve System.   State banks have an option of joining or not joining, and about one-third exercise their option to join.   Thus about half of the commercial banks in the United States are members of the System.   (Although only 50 percent in number, these are the larger banks and they control about 80 to 90 percent of all deposits.)

Reading downward still further, Figure 5-2 indicates that *all* members of the Federal Reserve System *must* be insured by the Federal Deposit

Figure 5-2

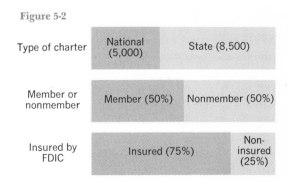

Insurance Corporation (FDIC). Nonmembers may choose to be in-sured by the FDIC, and about half of the nonmembers do so choose. Thus about 75 percent of all commercial banks are insured by the FDIC. The Federal Deposit Insurance Corporation is an insurance organization established by the Banking Act of 1933. Commercial banks which are insured by the FDIC are assessed to ensure the sol-vency of the FDIC. If a commercial bank is insured, individual depositors are insured up to $15,000 of deposits. If, for example, you had a savings account of $15,000 at the XYZ bank and that bank failed, the FDIC would promptly see to it that you received your full $15,000. (If you had $20,000 on deposit, the FDIC would insure only $15,000 of that amount.)

THE FRACTIONAL RESERVE SYSTEM

We mentioned earlier that if a commercial bank is a member of the Federal Reserve System, it must keep on deposit at a Federal Reserve bank a certain portion of its demand and time deposits. While the portion varies, it averages about 20 percent for the commercial bank. Thus, for each dollar you deposit in your bank, 20 cents must be sent by your bank to the Federal Reserve bank in its district or held by the commercial bank in the form of vault cash. Since a *fraction* of all deposits must be kept on reserve, we refer to the banking system as a *fractional reserve system*.

Again, it is important to point out that these reserves are held by the Federal Reserve banks in order that they may expand and contract the nation's money supply. We will see how the Federal Reserve System accomplishes this expansion or contraction in the chapter which fol-lows. But we can have a look now at how the fractional reserve sys-tem *allows* the money supply to grow or to decline.

In order to demonstrate the creation or destruction of the money sup-ply, we will use T-accounts to represent the balance sheets of various commercial banks. Remember, too, that we are really talking about the creation and destruction of bank deposits—which make up 80 percent of the money supply.

THE CREATION OF BANK DEPOSITS

Let us begin with the simple case of a single bank and see what hap-pens when $1,000 is deposited in a checking account. The balance sheet of this bank (bank A) would appear as the T-account below shows:

BALANCE SHEET FOR BANK A

Required reserves (RR)	+$ 200	+$1,000 Demand deposits (DDs)
Loans and		
investments (L & I)	+ 800	
	+$1,000	+$1,000

The right-hand side of the ledger shows that $1,000 has been deposited by someone. The left-hand side shows what the bank does with this deposit. Since we are assuming a 20 percent required reserve ratio, this commercial bank must keep $200 (20 percent of $1,000) on deposit with the Federal Reserve bank. The remaining money ($800) is available for the bank to lend or to invest. And, of course, the T-account balances, with a total of $1,000 on both sides of the ledger.

Now we will introduce several banks in the commercial banking system to see how this fractional reserve requirement leads to a *multiple* expansion in bank deposits. The T-accounts below demonstrate this process.

Let us again assume that a depositor places $1,000 in bank A. With a required reserve ratio of 20 percent, $200 in required reserves are deposited with the Federal Reserve bank, leaving $800 available to the commercial bank for loans or investments. These entries are shown in step 1 in the T-account for bank A. Now let us assume that all the available $800 is loaned to a bank customer. What happens next?

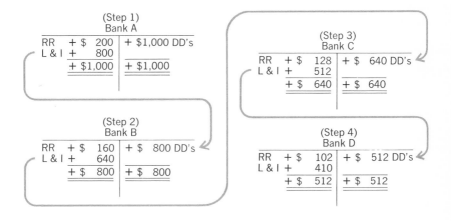

(Step 1)
Bank A

RR	+ $ 200	+ $1,000 DD's
L & I	+ 800	
	+ $1,000	+ $1,000

(Step 3)
Bank C

RR	+ $ 128	+ $ 640 DD's
L & I	+ 512	
	+ $ 640	+ $ 640

(Step 2)
Bank B

RR	+ $ 160	+ $ 800 DD's
L & I	+ 640	
	+ $ 800	+ $ 800

(Step 4)
Bank D

RR	+ $ 102	+ $ 512 DD's
L & I	+ 410	
	+ $ 512	+ $ 512

If a customer borrows $800 from bank A, he will (in all likelihood) not hold the money in the form of cash but will deposit it in his own bank (bank B). In this way, $800 in new deposits is generated in bank B (step 2). Again, 20 percent of the new deposits, or $160 (20 percent of $800), must be kept on reserve at the Federal Reserve bank. But now bank B has new money to lend or invest in the amount of $640 (new deposits less required reserves).

This expansionary process continues in step 3 (bank C). Again we assume that all the money available for loans is borrowed ($640). This amount is borrowed and deposited in bank C. Of this amount, bank C must keep $128 (20 percent of $640) in required reserves at the Federal Reserve bank and can lend out $512.

Step 4 shows that the $512 finds its way to bank D, where $102 (20 percent of $512) is held for required reserves and $410 is loaned out.

Now let us see what has happened through step 4. In bank A, $1,000 was deposited. This is new money (since demand deposits are the major part of the money supply). In bank B, $800 in new deposits is generated; in bank C, $640; and in bank D, $512. Thus we have so far generated an addition to the supply of money of $2,952 ($1,000 + $800 + $640 + $512 = $2,952).

And the process does not end here. New deposits will be generated in the banking system so long as there is money available for loans and investment. How much in total new deposits will be created? Fortunately, we do not have to add all of the new deposits to get the total figure. We have a formula which does this for us. It is as follows:

$$\left(\begin{array}{c}\text{Change in demand}\\\text{deposits}\end{array}\right) \times \left(\begin{array}{c}\text{Reciprocal of the}\\\text{reserve ratio}\end{array}\right) = \left(\begin{array}{c}\text{Change in the}\\\text{money supply}\end{array}\right)$$

In our example, we had an *initial increase* in demand deposits of $1,000. Our assumed required reserve ratio was 20 percent, or $\frac{1}{5}$. The reciprocal of $\frac{1}{5}$ is, of course, 5. (The reciprocal of the required reserve ratio is known as the *deposit multiplier*.) Thus,

($1,000) × (5) = ($5,000)

Our conclusion: $1,000 in new deposits in the commercial banking system will add a total of $5,000 to the money supply! This is made possible by our fractional reserve system.

Of course, this expansionary process assumes that the initial $1,000 deposit was a *net* change in demand deposits.   Had someone simply taken $1,000 from one bank and deposited it in another, there would have been no change in the money supply.   Moreover, had the $1,000 been taken from the cash holdings of the public, that part of the money supply would have been decreased by $1,000, so that the increase in the money supply would have been $4,000, not $5,000.   (Remember that the total money supply is made up of cash as well as demand deposits.)

THE DESTRUCTION OF BANK DEPOSITS

Bank deposits (and hence the supply of money) can be reduced also. The process is just the reverse of what we have been through above. Suppose that for some reason an individual writes a check for $1,000 (reduces demand deposits by $1,000).   The first four stages of this multiple contraction of the money supply would appear as in the T-accounts below.

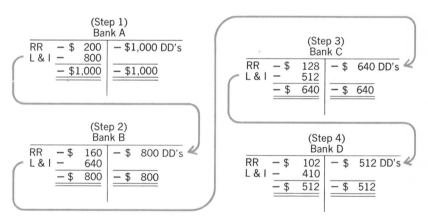

In step 1, demand deposits are reduced by $1,000 because someone wrote a check.   Commercial bank A now no longer needs to maintain a 20 percent reserve at the Federal Reserve bank against this $1,000. Hence, required reserves at the Federal Reserve bank are reduced by $200.   And loans and investments must be called in (in the amount of $800).   By recalling its $200 at the Federal Reserve bank and by calling in loans and investments in the amount of $800, bank A is able to make good the withdrawal of $1,000.

But this process, too, has an impact throughout the banking system. If bank A calls in $800 in loans and investments, it will necessitate the withdrawal of $800 from bank B to pay off these loans. This, in turn, frees $160 in required reserves at the Federal Reserve bank and necessitates the recall of $640 in loans and investments.

The T-accounts, above, carry this process through four stages, showing a total depletion in the money supply of $2,952 (−$1,000 − $800 − $640 − $512 = −$2,952). We have shown the destruction of deposits through only four stages. However, just as before, the process does not end here. It continues until an equilibrium is reached according to our formula:

$$\left(\begin{array}{c}\text{Change in demand}\\\text{deposits}\end{array}\right) \times \left(\begin{array}{c}\text{Reciprocal of the}\\\text{reserve ratio}\end{array}\right) = \left(\begin{array}{c}\text{Change in the}\\\text{money supply}\end{array}\right)$$

In our example,

$$(-\$1,000) \times (5) = (-\$5,000)$$

The withdrawal of $1,000 of demand deposits has reduced the economy's total money supply by $5,000. (Assuming, of course, that the $1,000 is removed from the money supply. If it circulates as currency, the total change in the money supply has been only $4,000.)

LEAKAGE QUALIFICATIONS

While the above explanation of deposit expansion and contraction is a good approximation of the facts, it may not be entirely accurate for several reasons. The change in the supply of money may actually be slightly less than the formula indicates due to several possibilities for *leakage*.

Leakage into Hand-to-hand Circulation

It is possible, for instance, that not all the money borrowed from commercial banks will remain in the form of demand deposits. There may be some leakage into *hand-to-hand circulation*. For example, if you were to borrow $1,000 from the bank, you might choose to keep $100 in cash and leave only $900 in demand deposits.   To the extent that there is leakage into hand-to-hand circulation, there will be a reduction in the amount of new deposits generated.   Money held in the form of cash cannot cause a multiple-deposit expansion.   While this is a qualification to the expansion or contraction of the money supply, it is not a serious qualification.   Why?   Because we know that currency and coin account for only about 20 percent of the money supply.   Hence, at least 80 percent *does* remain in the form of demand deposits.

Leakage into Bank-vault Cash

Another possibility for leakage occurs because commercial banks hold some of their deposits in the form of *bank-vault cash*.   Bank-vault cash is just what it sounds like—money held by the bank in its vaults.   Normally, deposits and withdrawals at a given bank offset each other.   However, for safety purposes, the commercial banks choose to keep about 2 percent of their deposits in the bank vault, just in case withdrawals exceed deposits in a given day.   Thus, again, all the money available for loans and investments is not used for that purpose.   A very small percentage of it is kept in the bank's vault.   This retention of funds, then, minutely reduces the multiple change in the money supply.

Leakage into Excess Reserves

A final possibility for leakage involves the holding of *excess reserves*. We mentioned earlier that a member commercial bank is *required* to hold about 20 percent of its deposits on reserve at the Federal Reserve bank.   There is nothing, however, which prevents the commercial bank from holding *more* than the required amount on reserve.   Any reserves at the Federal Reserve bank in excess of what is required are called *excess reserves*.   And, again, if a commercial bank holds excess reserves, the expansion of the money supply will be lessened.   This type of leakage is not serious either.   Commercial banks do not like to hold large amounts of excess reserves because they receive no interest on this money.   They would much prefer to put their money to work by lending it or investing it.

Considering these various possibilities for leakage, a more accurate ledger of a commercial bank might appear as follows: [2]

Required reserves	+$ 200	+$1,000 Demand deposits
Excess reserves	+ 50	
Bank-vault cash	+ 20	
Loans and investments	+ 730	
	+$1,000	+$1,000

CHAPTER SUMMARY

In this chapter we examined the nature of money, the commercial banking system, and the Federal Reserve System.   And we laid special emphasis on the notion of fractional reserves and how the fractional reserve system allows for the multiple expansion or contraction of the nation's supply of money.

Money, we found, can be anything which fulfills certain functions; whatever serves as money must function as a medium of exchange, a standard of value, a standard of deferred payments, and a store of value.   Currency in the United States is backed largely by our confidence in it, not by gold or some other precious metal, as has been the case in the past.   The Federal Reserve note is the most common form of paper currency.

However, we also saw in this chapter that paper currency is not the major portion of our money supply.   Most of our day-to-day business is carried on by writing checks—hence demand deposits constitute about 80 percent of our money supply.

Next, Chapter 5 differentiated between commercial banks and Federal Reserve banks.   Commercial banks were defined as banks for individuals and businesses, and Federal Reserve banks were defined as banks for commercial banks and for the government.   The structure of the Federal Reserve System was explored, and the relationship between commercial banks and Federal Reserve banks was examined.

Finally, the fractional reserve system was discussed.   Because member

---

[2] Since bank-vault cash can be counted as part of the legally required reserves, leakage into bank-vault cash and into excess reserves could be treated simply as leakage into excess reserves.

commercial banks need keep only a fraction of their deposits on reserve at the Federal Reserve bank, there can occur a multiple expansion or contraction in the money supply.   The size of such an expansion or contraction was seen to depend upon changes in demand deposits and the reserve ratio, in the following relationship: (change in demand deposits) × (reciprocal of the reserve ratio) = (change in the money supply).

In Chapter 6, we will examine monetary policy.   The area of monetary policy deals with techniques available to the Federal Reserve System to *cause* an expansion or contraction in the money supply in such a way as to help ensure full employment, stable prices, and economic growth.

STUDY QUESTIONS

1. What is money, and what function does it serve?   How is it that colorful beads could, under certain circumstances, serve as money?
2. What is the difference between a commercial bank and a Federal Reserve bank?   How do they relate to each other?
3. How does the fractional reserve system aid in the expansion or contraction of the nation's money supply?   What would happen to this expansionary or contractionary process if we insisted that all commercial banks keep 100 percent of their deposits on reserve?

IMPORTANT CONCEPTS IN CHAPTER 5

Medium of exchange
Standard of value
Standard of deferred payments
Store of value
Bimetallic standard
Gold standard
Conditions for a gold standard
Gold Standard Act of 1930
Gold Reserve Act of 1934
Fiat money
Federal Reserve note

Components of the money supply
Near money
Commercial bank
Federal Reserve System
Federal Reserve Act of 1913
Federal Reserve bank
Board of Governors of the Federal Reserve System
Required reserves
Clearinghouse
Federal Deposit Insurance Corporation
Fractional reserve system
Demand deposits
Time deposits
Deposit multiplier
Reserve ratio
Excess reserves

CHAPTER 6

MONETARY POLICY

In the previous chapter we took a rather close look at the "mechanics" of the banking system. We examined the difference between commercial banks and Federal Reserve banks. And, very importantly, we saw how the fractional reserve system allows for a multiple expansion or contraction in the nation's supply of money.

In the present chapter it will be our goal to examine the area of monetary policy. What is monetary policy? It consists of *discretionary decisions on the part of the Federal Reserve System which are designed to control the supply of money in circulation.* While the fractional reserve system *allows* the multiple expansion or contraction of the money supply, it is the Federal Reserve System which makes the decisions actually *causing* such an expansion or contraction.

THE QUANTITY THEORY OF MONEY AND THE EQUATION OF EXCHANGE

In order to fully understand monetary policy, it is first necessary to understand the framework within which the Federal Reserve System operates. Policy, after all, does not just "happen"; it is instituted on some logical grounds.

The logic for monetary policy has been almost four centuries in its development. It began with what is called the *quantity theory of money,* which was first introduced by Jean Bodin, a Frenchman, in the sixteenth century. Bodin observed that as precious metals came into France from her Spanish colonies, prices tended to rise in France.

Hence, he connected the quantity of money to the price level. His conclusion was that there exists a direct relationship between the amount of money in circulation and the level of prices.   If the amount of money doubled, said Bodin, then the price level would double also. This notion of a direct relationship between money and prices was carried through the eighteenth century by David Hume and Adam Smith.   It survived also into the early nineteenth century, when David Ricardo applied the same ideas to paper money.

The reasoning of these early thinkers at first appears sound. If, for example, we were told that, effective now, all $1 bills would be worth $2, what would we expect to happen to the price level?   Obviously, the amount of money in circulation would double.   This, in turn, would double everyone's money income and would double the price on all goods and services.   Everybody's position would remain relatively unchanged.   Thus, *all other things remaining constant,* a doubling of the supply of money would be expected to double prices. The problem is that all other things do *not* remain constant.   Because the early economists oversimplified the relationship between money and prices, we refer to their theory as the *crude* quantity theory of money.

Two very important things do not remain constant—notably, the velocity (or turnover) of money and the level of production in the economy.   Hence, later developments in monetary theory include these two elements (together with the supply of money and the price level).   The resultant refinement of the crude theory is what is called the *equation of exchange.*   The equation of exchange is symbolically stated in the following manner:

$MV = PQ$ where: M = stock of money in circulation
V = the velocity, or turnover, of money
P = a measure of the price level
Q = the physical quantity of goods produced

What the equation of exchange tells us, then, is that the amount of money in circulation, when multiplied by the number of times it is spent during the course of a year, is equal to the price level multiplied by the quantity of goods produced during that year.

But let us take a closer look at the equation of exchange.   On the left side of the equals sign we have MV. These two variables are nothing more than "total spending." If we take the amount of money in circulation and multiply it by its turnover, then, by definition, we have a measure of total spending.

On the right side of the equals sign we have PQ. But this is nothing more than the dollar value of total output—or, roughly, net national product. Hence, the equation of exchange simply tells us that total spending is equal to total output, or that demand is equal to supply—something we already know from past discussions. The advantage of the equation of exchange is that it breaks spending and output into two variables each. This breakdown will serve to help us understand better the rationale of monetary policy, for it is within the framework of the equation of exchange that the Federal Reserve System works.

We said earlier that monetary policy is concerned with increasing or decreasing the supply of money in circulation; hence, the Federal Reserve System is interested in the M in the equation. While the System's *technical* objective is the control of the money supply (M), its *real* objectives are, of course, full employment, stable prices, and economic growth.

Basically, the Federal Reserve System acts as follows: In a *recession,* the price level and the nation's output level are relatively low. (That is, P and Q are depressed.) Hence, the Federal Reserve System will take measures to *increase* the amount of money in circulation (M). If we hold velocity constant and if the System is able to increase the money supply, then something on the right side of the equals sign must rise. The hope is that prices will rise a little but that most of the impact will be felt on output. Thus, in periods of recession, the Federal Reserve System will increase the supply of money, hoping that the resultant increase in total spending will spur additional output.

In periods of *inflation,* the reverse is true. Now the Federal Reserve System will decrease the supply of money in circulation. This time, their hope is that the resultant decline in total spending will decrease the price level. In summary, then, the Federal Reserve System wants to increase the supply of money in recessionary periods and to decrease the supply of money in inflationary periods.

The basic question we face in this chapter is how the Federal Reserve System accomplishes these desired increases or decreases in the money supply.   The answer lies in an understanding of the tools available to the System and of their relation to the fractional reserve system of commercial banks.

For purposes of brevity, we will shorten the term "Federal Reserve System" to, simply, the "Fed," as is commonly done.

FEDERAL RESERVE POLICY CONTROLS

It may be helpful in our discussion of the controls available to the Fed to remember the relationship between the Fed and commercial banks.   Basically, it is as described in the diagram below:

This diagram indicates that the Fed has methods at its disposal to control the reserve position of commercial banks and that the reserve position of commercial banks largely determines the money supply. If the Fed can create excess reserves and if these excess reserves are loaned out or invested, then there will result a multiple expansion of the money supply.   On the other hand, if the Fed can lower the commercial banks' excess reserves, then there will be a multiple contraction of the money supply.

In order to accomplish the desired effect on commercial-bank lending and investing, the Fed has at its disposal two categories of controls: *minor* (or qualitative) controls and *major* (or quantitative) controls. We will examine each of these groups of controls in turn.

Minor (Qualitative) Controls

Four of the controls available to the Fed are known as minor controls. These are (1) control of consumer credit, (2) control of real estate credit, (3) control of stock market credit, and (4) control of interest-rate ceilings.

During World War II, and again in the Korean War, the United States faced periods of rapidly rising prices.   To combat this inflationary trend, the Federal Reserve Board was given the power to regulate *consumer credit*.   Specifically, Regulation W of the Board stipulated their power to regulate minimum down payments on purchases and to regulate maximum maturities. Obviously, if the Fed were to require larger down payments and shorter maturities, they would to some extent curtail total spending. And to the extent that total spending was curtailed, there would be downward pressure on the price level. While Regulation W was fairly effective during the war years, such control was always very unpopular. As a result, this authority over consumer credit expired in 1953 and has not been renewed.

Another wartime policy tool used during the Korean War was provided by Regulation X. This particular regulation gave the Fed the power to control *real estate credit*. The thinking here is much the same as in the control of consumer credit. If the Fed raised the minimum down-payment requirements on residential mortgages, then fewer people could buy homes and total spending would therefore decline. This authority, too, was unpopular and was not renewed when it expired in 1953.

Two of the minor controls are still used by the Fed. One of these is the control of *stock market credit*, the authority for which is contained in Regulations T and U. Under these regulations, the Fed is empowered to set *margin requirements* for the purchase of stocks. If, for example, the margin is set at 50 percent, a potential stock purchaser can borrow 50 percent of the purchase price of the stocks he wishes to buy. If the margin is raised to 70 percent, he can borrow only 30 percent of the purchase price. Hence, by increasing the margin requirement, the Fed can reduce the general public's ability to buy stocks. (The hope here is not so much to control total spending as it is to control wild speculation in periods of rapidly rising stock prices, such as occurred in the late 1920s.)

A final minor-control technique of the Fed is control of *interest-rate ceilings* (Regulation Q). Under this regulation, the Fed has the authority to set the maximum amount of interest which commercial banks may pay on time deposits (savings accounts). In theory, if the interest-rate ceiling is raised, consumers will save more money and hence spend less. If the interest-rate ceiling is lowered, consumers will be encouraged to spend more and save less.

Major (Quantitative) Controls

Far more significant than the minor controls are the so-called major controls available to the Fed. There are three such controls: (1) con-

trol of the discount rate, (2) control of member-bank reserve requirements, and (3) open-market operations. We will examine each of
these in some detail.

We mentioned earlier that one of the advantages to a commercial
bank of belonging to the Federal Reserve System was the availability
of credit from the Fed. When a commercial bank borrows money
from the Fed, the bank must pay a certain rate of interest—and the
rate of interest paid is called the *discount rate*. In effect, the discount
rate, then, is the rate of interest charged by the Fed for money borrowed by commercial banks.

As we have indicated, the Fed has the power to control the discount
rate, and by so doing it can have an impact on the total supply of
money in circulation. How? Suppose that the discount rate is $4\frac{1}{2}$
percent and that the Fed decides to lower it to 4 percent. Since the
cost of borrowing funds has declined, it might be expected that the
commercial banks would be induced to borrow more money at the
lower rate of interest. The money borrowed by the commercial banks
would constitute excess reserves. Remember that excess reserves are
available for loans and investments; if the excess reserves were used
in this way, there would follow a multiple expansion in the money
supply.

For example, suppose that the lower discount rate caused commercial
banks to borrow an additional $1 million from the Fed. This money
would, let us say, all be loaned out. The borrower would deposit it
in his checking account, causing an increase in demand deposits of $1
million. According to our formula, and assuming a 20 percent reserve
ratio,

($1 million) × (5) = ($5 million)

Thus the lowered discount rate has resulted in an expansion of $5 mil-
lion in the money supply. Obviously, the Fed would *lower* the discount rate during *slack* periods in the economy, when additional total
spending was desired.

If the Fed were to raise the discount rate, we could expect a multiple
contraction in the money supply. The higher rate of interest on funds
borrowed by commercial banks would cause those commercial banks
to deplete their excess reserves since the cost of carrying them would
have risen. Consequently, loans and investments would be called in;

the result of this would be a 5-to-1 contraction in the supply of money.

There is an additional effect of raising or lowering the discount rate. Such a change in the discount rate is a cost to commercial banks. Consequently, if the discount rate is increased, the commercial banks will increase the rate of interest they charge for loans. Such an increase will decrease the public's willingness to borrow and to spend. The reverse is true for a decrease in the discount rate.

A change in the discount rate, then, has a twofold effect: it will encourage or discourage borrowing by commercial banks (depending upon whether the discount rate is lowered or raised), and it will encourage or discourage borrowing by the general public. In recession, the discount rate will be lowered to stimulate total spending. In inflationary periods, it will be raised to discourage spending.

The second major policy tool available to the Fed is *control of the reserve requirement*. We have thus far been assuming a required reserve ratio of 20 percent. But the Fed has the authority to raise or lower this ratio as it sees fit.

If the Fed lowers the reserve ratio, then commercial banks need to keep less money on deposit at the Fed. Consequently, more money is available for loans and investment, leading to a multiple expansion of the money supply. The T-accounts below show this process:

20% RESERVE REQUIREMENT		10% RESERVE REQUIREMENT	
RR +$ 200	+$1,000 DDs	RR +$ 100	+$1,000 DDs
L & I + 800		L & I + 800	
ER 0		ER + 100	
+$1,000	+$1,000	+$1,000	+$1,000

With a lower required reserve ratio (10 percent), $100 in excess reserves is created. If this money is loaned out or invested, it will result in a multiple expansion in the supply of money.

Should the reserve ratio be raised, excess reserves would be depleted, with a resultant contraction in the money supply.

As with the discount rate, there is a dual effect when the reserve ratio is changed. A change in the reserve ratio will cause a change in the *deposit multiplier*. Let us assume an increase in demand deposits of $1,000, with a required reserve ratio of 20 percent. Such an increase in demand deposits would cause a $5,000 increase in the money supply:

$$\left(\begin{array}{c}\text{Change in demand} \\ \text{deposits}\end{array}\right) \times \left(\begin{array}{c}\text{Reciprocal of the} \\ \text{reserve ratio}\end{array}\right) = \left(\begin{array}{c}\text{Change in the} \\ \text{money supply}\end{array}\right)$$

$$(\$1,000) \qquad \times \qquad (5) \qquad = \qquad (\$5,000)$$

Now, if the Fed lowers the reserve ratio to 10 percent, the deposit multiplier would change from 5 to 10. The same $1,000 increase in demand deposits would then result in a $10,000 increase in the supply of money:

$$(\$1,000) \times (10) = (\$10,000)$$

Thus, in a *recession,* the Fed would be expected to *lower* the required reserve ratio in order to expand the money supply. In an *inflationary period,* the Fed would most likely *raise* the required reserve ratio to contract the supply of money.

The final and most important policy tool available to the Fed is *open-market operations.* When we speak of open-market operations, we are referring to the Fed's buying or selling of government securities from a dealer in such securities. If the Fed were to decide to buy, say, $1 million worth of government securities, they would do so by writing a cashier's check for $1 million, payable to the securities dealer. The dealer, of course, would receive $1 million. What would he do with it? He would deposit the check in his own checking account, thereby causing an increase in demand deposits and a multiple expansion in the money supply of $5 million.

If the Fed *sold* $1 million worth of securities, it would receive a check for that amount from the broker. But, of course, when the broker writes a check, he depletes demand deposits and causes a 5-to-1 contraction in the supply of money.

Therefore, in a *recession,* the Fed would *buy* government securities in the open market in order to expand the money supply and total spending. In an *inflation,* the Fed would *sell* government securities in order to contract the money supply and total spending.

These, then, are the major (or quantitative) tools at the disposal of the Fed. As a matter of terminology, when the Fed takes action to expand the supply of money, we say that it is following a *loose-money policy.* When it acts to contract the money supply, we call this a *tight-money policy.*

THE ADVANTAGES OF MONETARY POLICY

It should be noted at this time that the wise use of monetary policy can be a very useful tool in slowing down the rate of recession or inflation. One of the advantages of heavy reliance on monetary policy (as opposed to taxing and government spending) is a noneconomic advantage. Reliance on monetary policy is a politically conservative course of action and is, therefore, more readily acceptable to the Congress and to the public at large. Action by the Fed does not *directly* take money away from people, as would a tax increase. Nor is there *direct* intervention in the allocation of resources, as there would be with a change in government spending. As a result, in the early stages of a downturn or inflation, monetary policy is often used first. Then, if the cyclical fluctuation continues to grow in severity, taxing and spending changes will be brought into play.

Another advantage of monetary policy is the speed with which it can be put to work. The Open Market Committee of the Federal Reserve System can buy and sell securities in the open market on a daily basis, as the needs of the economy dictate. Also, congressional approval is not required for the Fed to take action—as it would be, say, in the case of a tax increase or decrease.

Monetary policy is especially effective during periods of inflationary trends, when the Fed is removing money from the economy. No matter how much the public and the business sector may *want* to spend, they cannot if the Fed makes less money available. In a recessionary period, the Fed can make more money available, but they cannot force people to spend if they do not desire to do so.

All in all, monetary policy provides us with a rather effective "buffer" against depression and inflation. In itself, such policy is seldom, if ever, adequate to *cure* either, but it can slow down the rate of decline in business activity or rising prices.

LIMITATIONS OF MONETARY POLICY

While the appropriate use of monetary policy can be of great benefit to the economy, there are certain limitations which reduce its effectiveness. It will be to our benefit to discuss each of these limitations briefly.

Control over Velocity

The Fed is working to expand or contract the supply of money only. Yet the equation of exchange tells us that there are two elements of total spending: the supply of money and the velocity, or turnover, of money.   In fact, the Fed has little, if any, control over velocity.   It is possible that changes in velocity could act to at least partially offset whatever positive action is taken by the Fed.   For example, if the Fed increased the supply of money and if velocity decreased at the same time, the results would be partially offsetting, as demonstrated below by the equation of exchange.   Or if the Fed were to lower the supply of money while velocity was increasing, there would again be offsetting influences on total spending.

$$\overset{\uparrow}{M}\underset{\downarrow}{V} = PT$$

How likely is it that this will happen?   During a recession, the Fed will act to increase the money supply.   But this is the very time when the general public will reduce its spending (velocity), fearing a continued recession.   On the other hand, during inflation, when the Fed is reducing the money supply, velocity is nearly always on the increase.

This is not to say, of course, that monetary policy is ineffective.   All we are saying, really, is that it is not as effective as it would be if we could somehow hold velocity constant.

Control of Interest-rate Ceilings

In late 1967 the Fed raised the interest-rate ceiling which commercial banks could pay on savings accounts (time deposits).   As we discussed earlier, this move was designed to curtail spending by inducing higher levels of saving.   However, such an action by the Fed has another effect with other financial institutions—particularly savings and loan companies.   As the interest-rate ceiling at commercial banks rises, there will be a shift in savings from savings and loan companies (not regulated by the Fed) to commercial banks, so that those savings will earn a more favorable rate of interest.   The effect of this shift is a partial drying up of funds available for residential and business construction activity.   This is true because savings and loan companies loan out the vast majority of their money for purposes of construction.

Therefore, when the Fed raises the interest-rate ceiling on time deposits, this tight-money policy falls particularly hard on one sector of the economy—the construction industry.

Control of the Discount Rate

In order for manipulation of the discount rate to be an effective tool at the disposal of the Fed, we *must assume that the demand for loanable funds by commercial banks is relatively elastic with respect to the discount rate.* Figure 6-1 graphically shows such an elastic-demand curve.

Figure 6-1 shows that if the Fed lowers its discount rate from 4½ to 4 percent, commercial banks will, in turn, increase their borrowing from OX to OX′ (a substantial amount). The assumption is that commercial banks are responsive to changes in the discount rate.

In reality, the demand for loanable funds is quite *inelastic* with respect to the discount rate, as shown by Figure 6-2. What this diagram shows is that commercial banks are not very responsive to changes in the discount rate. If the rate falls from 4½ to 4 percent, say, commercial banks will borrow very little more. Why? Because the Fed itself discourages such borrowing for purposes other than short-run credit to meet the reserve requirement.

To the extent, then, that the demand for loanable funds is inelastic, changes in the discount rate will not be as effective as might be supposed.

Figure 6-1   Demand for Loanable Funds

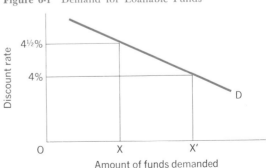

Amount of funds demanded

Figure 6-2 Demand for Loanable Funds

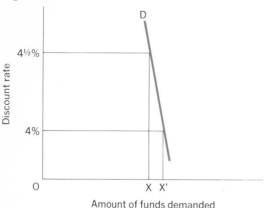

Amount of funds demanded

Other Limitations

There are some other limitations to monetary policy which are a bit less significant. One such limitation is that while the Fed has the authority to change the reserve requirement, it will *not* significantly change this requirement, partly because of tradition.

Another problem is that when the Fed takes a particular action, the business community reacts in an opposite direction. For example, if the Fed followed a loose-money policy in the beginning stages of a recession, the business community might take this action as a sign of impending recession. Consequently, businessmen would curtail their spending and investment activities at the very time the Fed was trying to stimulate spending.

A final limitation of monetary policy revolves around the notion of "internal financing" on the part of business. It is estimated that about 80 percent of all business investment is paid for out of profits retained in the business (internal financing). As a consequence, the business community, at least in the short-run period, is not very responsive to a tight- or loose-money policy. The business community simply does not borrow much from commercial banks. A second result of internal financing is that a tight-money policy hits hardest on the small businessman and consumers, who *do* borrow heavily from commercial banks.

A CONDENSED STATEMENT OF MONETARY POLICY

At this point let us summarize monetary-policy tactics. In times of *recession,* the Fed could be expected to: lower the margin requirement, lower the interest-rate ceiling, lower the discount rate, lower the reserve requirement, and buy securities in the open market. Such action would be a loose-money policy designed to increase the money supply and, therefore, to increase total spending.

In periods of *inflation,* the Fed would: raise the margin requirement, raise the interest-rate ceiling, raise the discount rate, raise the reserve requirements, and sell securities in the open market. Such a tight-money policy would be designed to decrease the money supply and total spending.

A BRIEF HISTORY OF MONETARY POLICY

The first real exercise of monetary policy began in 1914, after the passage of the Federal Reserve Act of 1913. The success of monetary policy has been limited over the years, partly due to overreaction on the part of the Fed and partly due to a failure to act when action was called for.

In 1917 there was a great need to finance the U.S. involvement in World War I and to finance the federal deficit. Hence, during this period there occurred a tremendous credit expansion, made possible both by a reduction of member-bank reserve requirements and by large-scale borrowing by the commercial banks.

As this demand continued, the Fed became very concerned, and in the end it overreacted by instituting a steep increase in discount rates and a generally tight money policy. This overreaction is blamed in large part for the brief recession in 1921.

The 1920s were, for the most part, very prosperous years (though there were two mild recessions during this period). Corporate profits were rising, but not nearly rapidly enough to justify the rapid rise in stock prices. Along with a very "bullish" stock market came a great deal of speculation in the market. Members of the Board of the Federal Reserve System were divided in their opinions. For the most part, they felt that it was not the place of the Fed to be concerned about what happened to stock prices. Yet there was general concern about the growing use of borrowed money to purchase stocks.

The result of this philosophical division within the Fed was that no effective monetary action to control stock buying and spending was taken at all until August of 1929, when the Fed raised the discount rate. The Fed failed to exert any influence upon the stock market's use of credit; and what monetary action the Fed did take was too little and too late to prevent the "crash of 1929," which began the Great Depression of the 1930s.

While the Depression was, of course, a black period in America's economic history, it nevertheless made plain some of our problems and paved the way for passage of legislation clarifying the appropriate role of the Fed. It was during this period (1934) that the Securities and Exchange Act was passed, giving the Fed the authority to set margin requirements (and hence control somewhat the extent of stock buying and speculation).

A year later, the Open Market Committee was established by the Banking Act of 1935. The Open Market Committee is the board whose responsibility it is to buy and sell securities in the open market.

It was also in the Depression years that the Fed developed the philosophy that member-bank borrowings should be short-term in nature (as was explained previously). Such a philosophy was intended to prevent a rapid credit expansion, such as occurred in 1920. It was very successful and continues as policy today.

The Fed was beginning to emerge as an important policy-making group in the 1930s, but mistakes were made, too. Because of its earlier experience with credit expansion, the Fed was reluctant to follow a loose-money policy and actually raised the discount rate in 1931. Belatedly, they did buy heavily in the open market in 1932, but not in time to prevent a serious banking collapse in the following year. After the collapse, the Treasury Department took over monetary policy, but without notable success. It was finally World War II, and not monetary policy, which put the United States on the road to recovery.

Wartime controls over prices and wages were abandoned in 1946, and prices rose to about twice the prewar level (considered a fairly mild inflation under the circumstances). But monetary policy was still largely ineffective because the open-market operations were geared to the maintenance of government-security prices. That is, the Fed was not allowed to buy and sell in the open market as they chose but was expected instead to keep government-security prices stable and interest rates low.   The Treasury did not want interest rates on the public debt to rise.

This conflict between the Treasury and the Fed continued through the period of rising prices during the Korean War.   The Treasury wanted low interest rates to finance the war, whereas the Fed wanted high interest rates to hold down prices.

The controversy was finally settled by the *Treasury Accord of 1951*, which freed the Fed from the necessity of maintaining prices of government securities.   The Fed could now act to control overall prices. Interest rates did rise after the accord but not sufficiently to prevent a 15 percent price rise between 1951 and 1953.

Two important recessions were felt by the U.S. economy in the 1950s: one in 1953–1954 and one in 1957–1958.   During these recessions, monetary policy was largely ineffective and taxing and spending policies came to the forefront.

An additional problem with monetary policy has developed since around 1960 because of the international balance-of-payments deficit experienced in the 1960s by the United States.   We were spending more abroad than foreigners were spending here.   As a result, U.S. money was coming into the possession of foreigners.   The Fed at this time desired to lower interest rates to stimulate spending and investment domestically.   Yet, if interest rates were lowered, foreigners would reduce their investment in the United States.   (A lower interest rate means, of course, a lower return to foreign investors.)   Such was the quandary of the 1960s, and it has not yet been satisfactorily resolved.

CHAPTER SUMMARY

The focus of Chapter 6 was on monetary policy—policy designed to control the amount of money in circulation.   While the fractional reserve system permits the multiple expansion or contraction of the money supply, we saw that it is the Federal Reserve System which actually makes the decisions causing such a change.

The underlying theory upon which monetary policy is based was seen to be the equation of exchange: $MV = PQ$. The Fed is specifically interested in implementing policies to affect the M (stock of money) variable in this relationship.

The controls available to the Fed to manipulate the stock of money include minor (qualitative) controls and major (quantitative) controls. The minor controls are (1) control of consumer credit, (2) control of real estate credit, (3) control of stock market credit, and (4) control of interest-rate ceilings. The major controls are (1) control of the discount rate, (2) control of member-bank reserve requirements, and (3) open-market operations. Of all these controls, open-market operations are the most significant.

In periods of recession, the Fed would be expected to follow a loose-money policy. It would lower the margin requirement, lower the interest-rate ceiling, lower the discount rate, lower the reserve requirement, and buy securities in the open market. A tight-money policy would be followed in an inflationary period; that is, the Fed would raise margin requirements, interest-rate ceilings, the discount rate, and reserve requirements and would sell securities in the open market.

Finally, Chapter 6 presented a brief history of monetary policy and discussed some of the problems of effective implementation of desired policies.

In sum, this chapter examined the mechanics of monetary policy and briefly traced the history of that policy. We indicated earlier that monetary policy is but one of two types of policy available to us. The other is fiscal policy, and it is to this area that we now turn in Chapter 7.

STUDY QUESTIONS
1. What, exactly, is the difference between the equation of exchange and the quantity theory of money?
2. What are the basic tools at the disposal of the Fed in helping to cure a recession or inflation? Can you see evidence of any in use today?
3. Discuss the advantages and limitations of monetary policy.

IMPORTANT CONCEPTS IN CHAPTER 6

Monetary policy
Quantity theory of money
Equation of exchange
Velocity
Minor monetary controls
Major monetary controls
Interest-rate ceiling
Margin requirement
Discount rate
Open-market operations
Loose-money policy
Tight-money policy
Demand for loanable funds
Internal financing
Open Market Committee
Securities and Exchange Act
Treasury Accord of 1951

CHAPTER 7

FISCAL POLICY: PART I

The previous chapter examined the various ways in which the Federal Reserve System attempts to increase or decrease total spending in the economy. As was pointed out, the Fed works by attempting to change the supply of money in circulation.

Another important method of increasing or decreasing total spending is by changing the prevailing tax rates and/or levels of government spending. This area we call *fiscal policy*. Fiscal policy can be defined as effecting *automatic or discretionary changes in the level of government spending or the rate and level of taxation in such a way as to affect the overall level of spending in the economy.*

The objectives of fiscal policy are, of course, the same as those of monetary policy—the achievement of full employment, stable prices, and economic growth. In this chapter we will see how the government attempts to accomplish these objectives. We will also have a look at the effects of fiscal policy on the economy.

Keep in mind the theoretical framework within which we will be operating. This framework was first presented in Chapter 4 and is briefly presented again, below, for purposes of review. Figure 7-1 shows the aggregate consumption function. You may remember that the consumption function relates total spending to total output and that total spending is composed of three elements: consumption spending, business investment, and government spending. Total output is reflected by net national product.

Figure 7-1 shows the economy in equilibrium where the consumption

Figure 7-1   Aggregate Consumption Function

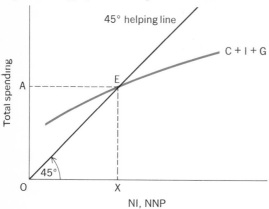

function crosses the 45-degree helping line.   It is at that point that total spending (OA) is equal to total output (OX).

If the economy is at equilibrium at a less than full-employment level of output, it faces a deflationary gap and there is a need for higher levels of total spending.   If, on the other hand, the equilibrium is such that there is excessive spending in relation to the nation's output, the economy is characterized by an inflationary gap and the need is for a reduction in total spending.

Graphically speaking, then, fiscal-policy measures are designed to shift the consumption function upward or downward (as the case may be) to close the deflationary or inflationary gap—that is, to increase or decrease aggregate spending.   Fortunately, the Congress does not have to pass new laws each time a change in spending levels is desired, nor does the President have to make a decision.   The economy has certain "built-in," or "automatic," stabilizers which help to bring about changes in the level of spending without any decision being made.

AUTOMATIC STABILIZERS

If the economy finds itself moving into a recessionary situation, the decline in total spending (which normally accompanies such a recession) is significantly slowed by automatic stabilizers. And when an inflationary situation ensues, the rate of increase in total spending will be slowed by these same automatic stabilizers.

There are many such built-in stabilizers, but we will examine only five of the most important: (1) automatic changes in tax receipts, (2) changes in the level of saving, (3) corporate dividend policy, (4) government subsidies, and (5) unemployment compensation.

Automatic Changes in Tax Receipts

If a recession begins, there is, of course, a need to stimulate total spending. Such a stimulus is partially provided through automatic changes in tax receipts going to the government. A recession means, among other things, falling levels of personal income. But, importantly, as income levels decline, so do tax payments to the government. The less income you earn, the less you are expected to pay in taxes. Moreover, the less you pay in taxes, the greater will be your disposable income. Hence, the declining tax burden will leave the public with a larger amount of disposable income than it would have had in the absence of a progressive tax system. As a result, total spending will decline less rapidly than might otherwise be expected.

Note that we have said nothing about changing tax *rates*—which would require an act of Congress. The decrease in spending we are talking about occurs with an unchanged tax rate.

If an inflation threatens and total spending is rising too rapidly, this built-in stabilizer comes into play in the opposite direction. Money incomes rise during inflationary trends. But rising incomes mean rising taxes. And rising taxes, of course, mean that consumer and business incomes will rise more slowly than would otherwise be the case.

Thus the private sector pays more in taxes during inflationary periods, thereby putting a damper on rising levels of spending. And the private sector pays less in taxes during recessionary periods, so that spending falls less rapidly.

A further effect may also be noted. If we assume a constant level of government spending and if (in a recession) the government receives less revenue from taxes, it may automatically find itself incurring a deficit. And a deficit is exactly what is called for in recessions. Still assuming a constant level of government spending, the government will (in an inflation) receive an increased amount of revenue, so that a budgetary surplus may come about. And, again, a surplus is the proper prescription during inflationary periods.

In summary then, changing tax receipts *automatically* help to reduce total spending in an inflation and help to increase total spending in a recession—all without a discretionary decision on the part of any policy maker.

Changes in the Level of Saving

Empirical evidence suggests that people have a strong desire to maintain their standard of living, even in times of recession. Thus, even though disposable income may be on the decline, families will try to maintain their former spending patterns. How do they do this? By dipping into savings. Thus the attempt to maintain previous living standards causes people to use up their savings during recessions, thereby preventing too rapid a decline in total spending.

In order for this automatic stabilizer to work in reverse, we would have to assume that families would increase their savings more rapidly during inflationary periods. However, the available evidence is not clear on this score. Hence, the primary value of savings patterns as a built-in stabilizer exists on the downward side of the business cycle.

Corporate Dividend Policy

Another of the automatic stabilizers exists because business corporations generally do not change their dividend policies in the short-run period. For example, if a mild downturn is in evidence, corporations will not reduce declared dividends. Nor will they increase dividends during a short inflationary period. This rather rigid dividend policy helps to sustain income levels of recipients in recessions and to restrain income in inflations.

Agricultural Subsidies

Under our current agricultural programs, the federal government has as one of its goals the sustaining of farm income at a reasonably high level. In order to accomplish this goal, the government supports the prices of certain agricultural products at an agreed-upon percentage of parity.   If, for example, $1 per bushel of corn were considered to be a *fair* price (a *parity* price), the government might agree to guarantee 90 percent of that fair price (or 90 cents per bushel).

Now, in the event of falling prices accompanying a recession, the price of corn would also decline.   If the price fell below 90 cents, the government would automatically act to increase subsidies, thereby sustaining farm income.   If, on the other hand, an inflation caused the price of corn to rise above 90 cents, subsidies would automatically cease.   The lower the price of agricultural commodities, the higher will be the level of government subsidies.   And the higher the level of prices, the lower will be subsidy payments.   Hence, farm incomes are bolstered by the government in recession and payments to farmers are lessened in inflation.   In this way, total spending is affected through farm subsidies.

Other sectors of our economy receive subsidies also (for example, the shipbuilding industry), and these subsidies work in much the same manner as those for agriculture.

Unemployment Compensation

Another important automatic stabilizer is found in payments to unemployed workers.   Recessions are, of course, accompanied by rising levels of unemployment.   And as unemployment increases, so do payments to those unemployed (under current federal-state programs).   Such payments prevent income from falling as rapidly as it would in the absence of such programs.

On the other hand, in periods of prosperity, when jobs are plentiful, there is little need for unemployment-compensation payments.

These, then, are the major automatic stabilizers.   Keep in mind two important facts.   One is that this type of stabilizer is built in, requiring no policy (or discretionary) decision.   The other thing to remember is that none of these, alone or together, can act to stop a recession or inflation.   They can serve only to slow down the rate of increase or decrease in total spending.   The actual stopping of a recession or an inflation must be done by the appropriate use of monetary measures and discretionary fiscal policy.   The automatic stabilizers provide only a buffer.   By slowing down cyclical fluctuations, however, they do give policy makers additional *time* in which to make appropriate discretionary decisions.

METHODS OF FINANCING GOVERNMENT EXPENDITURES

As we mentioned earlier in the chapter, discretionary fiscal policy involves taxing and spending by the federal government. We will now take a look at one part of such policy—government spending. Our examination will be concerned with the methods of financing government spending and with the effects of that spending on prices, output, and the level of employment.

When the government decides for any reason to increase its spending, it can finance these expenditures in one of three ways: (1) by printing new money, (2) by taxing the public, or (3) by borrowing money (deficit financing). It will be to our advantage to examine each of these methods, first in a full-employment economy and then in a less than full-employment situation.

In order to understand the impact of the different methods of government financing, we will use two highly simplified diagrams (Figure 7-2).

The block shown in Figure 7-2*a* will be used to represent the total

Figure 7-2

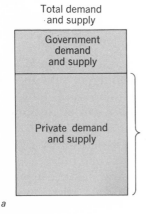

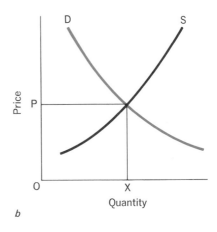

a   *b*

amount of goods and services supplied by the economy. Of this amount, the diagram shows that part is demanded by, and supplied to, the government. The remainder is demanded by, and supplied to, the private sector of the economy. (We are assuming no idle resources.) The supply and demand curves shown in Figure 7-2*b* refer to the *private* sector only. By referring to these basic diagrams, we can better ascertain the effects of different methods of financing on the price level.

Printing Money in a Full-employment Economy

Let us suppose that the government decides to finance its expenditures simply by printing money. What will happen? Figure 7-3 shows the results.

In this case, the government absorbs a larger portion of the nation's output. (This is so because the government has decided to increase its spending.) If all the resources in the economy are fully employed and if the government absorbs some of these resources, then the private supply must decline. This reduced private supply is shown on the right of the block. It is also shown by a shift in the supply curve to the left.

Figure 7-3

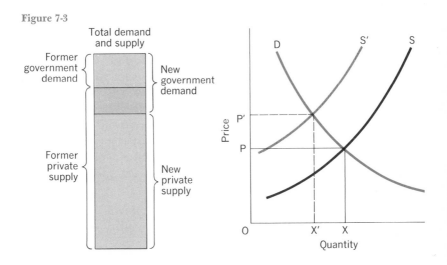

Because the government has taken no money out of the hands of private consumers (remember, new money was printed), there is no reason to assume that private demand will change at all in the short run. Consumers are still willing to buy the amount formerly demanded and still have the money to do so. The only thing missing is the goods and services they wish to buy! Because no purchasing power was removed from the private sector, the demand curve remains unchanged. (It may actually increase as the additional printed money permeates the economy, but we will ignore this aspect for now.)

The result? If demand in the private sector remains constant while supply falls, we can expect prices to rise. In our diagram, the price level would rise from OP to OP' while the amount of goods and services available to the private sector would decline from OX to OX'.

Thus, if the government were to finance new expenditures by printing money, we could expect fewer goods to be available in the private sector—and at highly inflated prices. The rule, then, is that *printing money to finance government spending in a full-employment economy is highly inflationary.*

Deficit Financing in a Full-employment Economy

Figure 7-4 shows the effects of deficit financing in periods of full employment.

As in the former case, if the government buys additional goods and services, supply in the private sector must decline. But what of demand in the private sector? At first glance, it could be argued that if the government borrowed money from the private sector, demand would fall because consumers and businesses would have less money with which to purchase goods and services. But such is not the case. Why? Because consumers and businesses do not curtail their spending in order to be able to buy government securities. Instead, they dip into savings or they sell private securities and replace them with government securities. Hence, private demand for goods and services is not significantly affected.

Thus, again, if supply decreases while demand remains constant, the price level will rise from OP to OP' and the quantity of goods and

Figure 7-4

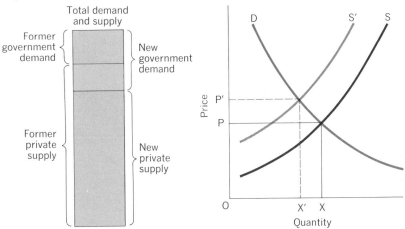

services available to the private sector will fall from OX to OX'. Our conclusion? *Deficit financing in periods of full employment tends to be inflationary.*

Taxation in a Full-employment Economy

Let us assume now that the government will finance its new purchases by taxing the private sector. Figure 7-5 shows the results of this action.

Again we must acknowledge that there will be fewer goods and services available to the private sector because the government is buying more. However, note what happens to private demand in this case. The government now is taking away purchasing power from the private sector through taxation. Hence, consumers have less money and consequently will demand fewer goods and services. The result? Supply in the private sector declines, but so does demand. There will be, of course, fewer goods and services available to consumers and businesses; but to the the extent that the lower private purchases are just offset by higher government purchases, the price level need not be affected. Our conclusion, then, is that *government financing by*

Figure 7-5

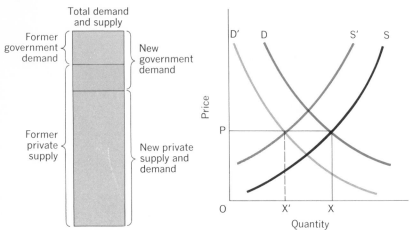

taxation in a full-employment economy does not tend to be inflationary.[1]

Printing Money in a Less Than Full-employment Economy

Figure 7-6 shows the effect on the price level of printing new money to finance government spending in a less than full-employment situation.

We must follow this process a bit more carefully. In a less than full-employment economy, we are faced with *idle* resources. (See Figure 7-6.) In this recessionary period, the government desires to increase its spending to *absorb* these idle resources. Thus the supply of goods and services in the private sector will remain unchanged as a result of the new government purchases. This is so because the government is buying up idle resources instead of buying those goods and services away from the private sector.

---

[1] In reality, there may be some slight inflationary pressure due to what is known as the "balanced-budget multiplier." Because the marginal propensity-to-consume is less than 1, government taxation does not reduce private spending by the full amount of the tax. Consequently, the tax revenue gained is less than the amount spent, leading to a "balanced-budget multiplier" effect.

Figure 7-6

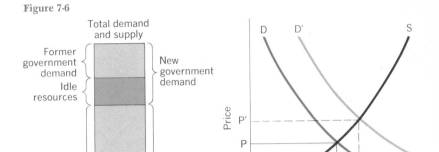

What happens to private demand? As the newly printed money is infused into the economy, private demand will increase because money income has increased. Hence, the demand curve shifts to the right. The result? If demand increases while supply remains constant, the price level will rise. We conclude, then, that *financing government expenditures by printing new money will be inflationary even in periods of less than full employment.*

Deficit Financing in a Less Than Full-employment Economy

Let us suppose now that the government will finance its new expenditures by borrowing the needed funds. Figure 7-7 depicts this situation.

Again, the government desires to absorb the existing idle resources so as to return the economy to a full-employment level. Therefore, the new government spending will have no effect on the supply of goods and services available to the private sector. What will be the effect on private demand? We pointed out earlier that government borrowing does not significantly affect private demand for goods and services because the money to buy government securities comes from saving. Hence, demand remains unchanged. We conclude, then, that

Figure 7-7

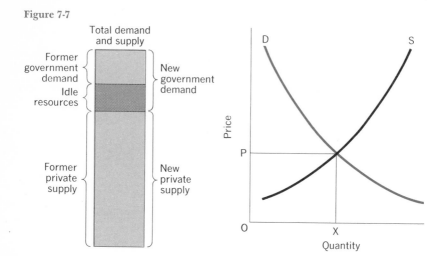

financing government expenditures by borrowing in a less than full-employment economy is not inflationary.

Taxation in a Less Than Full-employment Economy

As a final possibility for consideration, suppose that the government finances its expenditures by taxation in a less than full-employment situation.   Figure 7-8 shows the results.

Once again, private supply is not affected when the government absorbs idle resources, since these are resources not being utilized by the private sector.   But note that private demand falls!   Why?   Because the government has taxed away purchasing power from the private sector.   If supply remains constant and demand falls, the price level must also fall.   Hence, we conclude that *taxing to finance government expenditures in a less than full-employment economy will worsen the recession.*

In conclusion, we should note, then, that if the government decides to increase expenditures in a full-employment economy, such expenditures should be financed by taxation.   Put another way, the budget should be approximately balanced during a full-employment period in order to prevent inflationary pressures.   But if expenditures

Figure 7-8

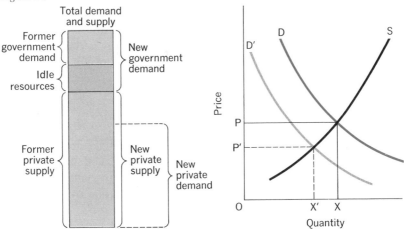

are to be increased in a less than full-employment period, deficit financing should be used.   This would not be inflationary and should help provide for the needed growth in total spending.

In all these cases of changing levels of government spending, it should be kept in mind that any increase or decrease in government spending will have a *multiplied* effect on national income and output due to the notion of the multiplier (discussed in Chapter 4).

THE PUBLIC DEBT

We have just found that under certain conditions (notably, during a recession) it often becomes necessary and desirable for the federal government to engage in deficit financing, that is, to borrow money. Deficit financing, of course, causes increases in the public debt since the government is spending more for goods and services than it is collecting in tax revenues.   This difference between expenditures and receipts is the deficit, which adds to the public debt.

How large is the public debt?   Of what is it composed?   How rapidly is it growing?   What is its effect on the economy?   These, and others, are questions we will examine now.

First of all, we should recognize that our government debt is an *internal debt*—it is owed largely *by* Americans *to* Americans. If the U.S. government were in debt to, say, England, we would consider such a debt an *external* debt. Our debt represents a claim on assets by our own citizens and not by foreign citizens or foreign governments.

Composition of the Debt

If the government raises money by borrowing, it does so by issuing various types of securities. These securities are then purchased by individuals or by financial institutions. Two major categories of such securities exist. One is called *marketable public issues,* and the other is called *nonmarketable public issues.*

Marketable public issues appeal mostly to large financial organizations. They are called "marketable" because they can be bought and sold on the open market. There are four types of marketable securities: (1) Treasury bonds, (2) Treasury notes, (3) Treasury certificates of indebtedness, and (4) Treasury bills.

Treasury bonds have the longest length-to-maturity of all the marketable issues. These bonds mature over periods of from ten to fifty years. Because of their longer length-to-maturity, Treasury bonds pay a higher rate of interest to the holder than do the other securities.

Treasury notes have a shorter length-to-maturity. These securities are issued for periods of two to five years. Treasury notes, together with Treasury bonds, are known as *intermediate* or *long-term issues* (depending upon the specific length-to-maturity).

Treasury certificates of indebtedness pay a lower rate of interest to holders than do either Treasury notes or Treasury bonds. The reason for the lower return is a shorter maturity. These securities mature in one year.

The government issues having the shortest length-to-maturity of all are *Treasury bills* (91 days). And, of course, they pay the smallest return to the holder. Bills and certificates of indebtedness together are known as *short-term issues.* They are purchased mostly by insurance companies, banks, and some large corporations which have funds that are not needed for a short period of time. Rather than let such funds lie idle (earning no interest), the financial organizations will purchase short-term securities.

The second major group of securities comprising the public debt are the nonmarketable issues, which appeal to individuals and non-commercial-bank purchasers. These securities are the "series" bonds with which we are most familiar (Series E, F, G, H, J, and K, depending upon face value, interest, length-to-maturity, etc.). The Series E bond is the so-called "savings" bond, which many of us may have purchased at one time or another. Treasury savings notes are also included in the nonmarketable category. These are notes purchased by businesses in order to pay future federal taxes.

Thus every time a broker or bank buys newly issued securities or every time you buy a savings bond, the national debt increases (providing, of course, that the purchase is not simply an exchange of securities among current holders).

Size of the Public Debt

Since 1945, this country's public debt has grown from about $259 billion to nearly $370 billion. The public debt, then, has shown an increase of about 41 percent between 1945 and 1969.

This increase is, of course, sizable in absolute amounts or in terms of percentage growth. But such a comparison does not give all the facts. The debt must be compared *with something* before we can evaluate its rate of growth. Since our gross national product represents loosely the total productive capacity of the nation at any given time, it is common to compare the debt with GNP.

Immediately following World War II (1946), the public debt stood at 122 percent of the 1946 GNP. It may surprise you to know that since 1946 the debt has *decreased* fairly steadily, so that by 1965 it was only 40 percent of the GNP and by 1969 it was estimated to be only 34 percent of the GNP.[2] Whether or not the debt is considered "too large" is in part a matter of personal philosophy. But there can be no doubt that the debt is steadily declining when compared with our ability to pay it (GNP).

---

[2] President Johnson's message to Congress on the fiscal 1969 budget, delivered Jan. 29, 1968.

Having a good understanding of the methods of financing government expenditures and with a knowledge of the composition of the debt and its relative size, we can now turn to look at government spending and taxation more specifically.

A LOOK AT GOVERNMENT SPENDING

One of the first questions we might ask about government spending is, "For what does the federal government spend its money?" A breakdown of the budget will provide us with the answer to this question. Table 7-1 lists the major categories of federal spending and shows what percentage each is of the total federal expenditures.

It is apparent from the data in Table 7-1 that the U.S. government will spend almost 42 percent of its budget for items directly related to the national defense. Veterans' benefits and services will claim another 4 percent of the budget, and interest on the debt (most of which arose during World War II) will cost over 7 percent of the total budget figure. Thus *at least half* of our total government expenditures is

TABLE 7-1   Proposed Fiscal 1969 Federal Expenditures

ITEM	DOLLAR AMOUNT (MILLIONS)	PERCENT OF TOTAL EXPENDITURES
National defense	$ 79,788	41.75
International affairs and finance	5,153	2.70
Space research and technology	4,573	2.39
Agriculture, agricultural resources	5,609	2.94
Natural resources	2,490	1.30
Commerce and transportation	8,121	4.25
Housing and community development	2,784	1.46
Health, labor, and welfare	51,407	26.90
Education	4,699	2.46
Veterans' benefits and services	7,342	3.84
Interest	14,400	7.54
General government	2,790	1.46
Other	1,950	1.02
Total	$191,106	100.00

SOURCE: *Federal Economic Policy,* 3d ed., Congressional Quarterly Service, Washington, March, 1968, pp. 92–93.

related in some way to national defense.   The figure may actually be closer to 60 to 65 percent when you consider that some of the funds spent for space research and international affairs are certainly related to the nation's defense.

The second major item for which the government spends money is "health, education, and welfare."   This category of spending has grown rapidly since the New Deal era of the 1930s.   It includes payments for health services, public assistance, social insurance, economic-opportunity programs, and other welfare services.

Thus, in answering the question of where the federal tax dollar goes, we can say that most of it goes for the procurement of national defense and the nation's domestic welfare.   It is interesting to note, too, that if we exclude military expenditures, the federal government accounts for only about 15 percent of the total government expenditures for goods and services.   State and local governments account for the remainder of such expenditures.

It is also of some significance to note that federal spending has been declining slightly over the years when compared with the nation's output.   That is to say, the federal government is playing a diminishing role in the economy from the point of view of its relative expenditures.   Excluding Vietnam expenditures, the government's budget outlays as a percentage of GNP were about 18 percent in 1968, compared with 19 percent for the period 1958–1960.

Finally, it should be noted that the U.S. government spends a smaller part of the nation's GNP than do most other governments of industrialized nations around the world.

THE EFFECTS OF GOVERNMENT SPENDING

Federal spending has a great deal of impact on the U.S. economy, in both economic and noneconomic areas.   It would be impossible to examine all these effects exhaustively.   However, it is worthwhile to look at a few areas where government spending is especially important.

Effects of Federal Spending on the Level of Income and Employment

We have already noted that government expenditures for goods and services is one of the major categories of total spending in the economy (the other areas being consumption expenditures and business investment). Such government spending can play a vital role in preventing recessions and providing for high employment levels. And, on the other side of the coin, in inflationary periods a reduction (or a slowdown) in the amount of federal spending can help contain excessive total spending.

Resource Allocation

Another area of influence for government spending is in the allocation of the nation's resources. Because the government makes large expenditures on national defense, for example, resources will flow to those industries providing weapons, airplanes, and so forth. These same resources could have been used to produce consumer goods or business equipment. Thus government expenditures tend to reallocate resources *from* the consumer-goods and capital-goods industries *to* those industries involved in defense production.

Of course, when we talk of resource allocation, we are talking not only of raw materials but of manpower and money as well.

Income Redistribution

Government spending has a further impact upon the way in which the nation's income is distributed. Two major effects on patterns of income distribution may be noted. On the one hand, massive government expenditures for national defense probably tend to take income away from the vast middle-income classes (through taxes) and to distribute that income to large corporations involved in defense production, space exploration, and so forth. In general, this effect of government spending tends to cause an *upward* redistribution of income, from middle-income groups to high-income groups. Payments of interest on the national debt also tend to redistribute income upward, since most of the government securities comprising the national debt are held by upper-income groups and large financial institutions.

But there is also a downward redistribution of income caused by government spending. We pointed out that a large portion of total government spending goes for health, education, and welfare measures (about 27 percent of the budget). Such expenditures are called *transfer payments* because they tend to transfer wealth from the upper-

and middle-income groups down to the lower-income groups, who are the major recipients of these welfare services.

It is impossible to say with assurance to what extent federal spending causes a net upward redistribution or downward redistribution of the nation's wealth. However, with our progressive tax structure, it is most likely that there is a slight downward redistribution.

We will say more about the distribution of the nation's income and wealth in a later chapter. But we should note two aspects of redistribution at this time. An upward redistribution of income tends to provide funds necessary for the investment which is essential for business expansion. This is so because investment funds come from savings and most savings come from high-income persons and businesses. On the other hand, a downward redistribution of income tends to raise the level of total demand—which is also necessary for economic growth. If there is not sufficient purchasing power in the hands of the people, businesses will not invest, no matter how much money is available to them for that purpose.

What is the *appropriate* pattern for the distribution of income? We will ask this question again later. For now, let it be said that no one can answer this question with objective assurance. The answer is dependent upon individual biases and values. The question of the appropriate distribution of income certainly makes politics interesting, however!

Effects of Spending on Economic Growth

A final area where government spending plays a vital role is that of long-term economic growth. We have already mentioned that government spending can affect the level of private investment and private demand; but government spending also affects additional aspects of economic growth.

For example, the government has a direct impact on the rate of technological development by supporting research efforts in corporations and in colleges and universities across the country. Such research is very necessary to economic development.

Also, the government (particularly state and local governments) has a direct impact on the level of education in the United States. The better the schools and the more people who attend them, the more rapid will be our economic growth and social development. In to-day's modern and fast-moving world, one of our most important assets is our "brainpower"!

These are but some of the effects of government spending on the U.S. economy, but they are important areas, to be sure. Now let us turn to the other area of fiscal policy taxation.

A LOOK AT TAXATION

The question is not whether the government should tax or not tax. We can rest assured that the federal, state, and local governments *will* tax. Rather, four other questions should be considered: What is the effect of taxation on business investment? What is the effect of taxation on consumers? What is the burden of taxation? And to what extent do current levels of taxation impair the incentive to work and to invest? It is to these questions that we will now turn.

Taxation and Business Investment

Taxation of businesses can affect investment in two important ways. When the government taxes the business corporation, it is taking away money which otherwise would be profit or would be available for investment in plant and equipment. To the extent that taxes take away needed investment funds, investment will be curtailed. And, of course, investment is vital to growth. There is no evidence to support the idea that the current level of taxation severely limits the availability of investment funds, but such an event is a possibility.

Another way in which taxes may affect investment is through the impact of those taxes on the consumer markets. Individual income taxes do reduce disposable income and, hence, the level of demand for the products produced by the business sector. And if demand is not sufficient, businesses will not invest in new plants and equipment. Again, there is little evidence to support the notion that individual taxes are seriously limiting consumer demand. The United States enjoys the highest level of consumer demand of any country in the world. Therefore, it is not likely that lagging consumer markets will seriously impair the willingness on the part of the businessman to invest over the long-term period.

The Effect of Taxation on Consumers

The most important effect of taxation on consumers is that they have less money to spend! But we must go a bit beyond this contention. Lower levels of disposable income mean that the standard of living of the average consumer will be somewhat lowered. That increase in taxes just may prevent you from buying the color television set you have wanted for so long. Do taxes, in fact, seriously lower standards of living? Certainly not in the United States. We enjoy the highest standard of living in the world—and can still afford to spend vast amounts all over the world for defense, economic development, and so forth. So long as our standard of living is high and continues to grow, this aspect of taxation is largely academic.

The tax system does affect the consumer in another way, however—in its effect on the redistribution of the nation's income. We will examine this effect in more detail immediately below, when we look at the burden of taxation. But we can say at this point that the lower-income people enjoy a somewhat higher standard of living because of our tax structure, while the standard of living of middle- and upper-income groups is probably lowered slightly.

The Burden of Taxation

Without getting into a lot of detail concerning the various types of taxes, we should at least note the two broad types. Taxes may, in their impact, be either *progressive* or *regressive*. A *progressive tax* is defined as *one in which the tax rate rises as the taxable base increases*. The tax base is, of course, income. Thus a progressive tax is structured so that the more income you earn, the more tax you pay as a percentage of that income. The individual income tax is our best example of a progressive tax.

A *regressive tax* is just the opposite in its effect. Such a tax can be defined as one in which the *tax rate falls as the taxable base increases*. In other words, the more money you earn, the less you pay in taxes as a percentage of your income. The state sales taxes are an excellent example of regressive taxes. Why? For the simple reason that persons in the higher-income groups spend a smaller percentage of their income on taxable items than do persons in the lower-income groups. For example, suppose you earn $3,000 per year. The chances are good that you will spend all of it. If the sales tax were 4 percent, your tax bill would be $120 (4 percent of $3,000). You have paid, of course, 4 percent of your income in taxes. But suppose you earn $100,000 per year. With this high level of income, you may spend only $50,000 to live. With the same 4 percent sales tax, your tax bill would be $2,000 (4 percent of $50,000). But now you have paid only 2 percent of your income in taxes ($2,000 is 2 percent of $100,000). Thus the tax burden of a regressive tax is greater on the lower-income families than on the upper-income families.

Exactly what is the burden of taxes in the United States? Such a figure is difficult to ascertain, but Table 7-2 gives a very good estimate for the year 1965.

The data in the table show that federal income taxes are progressive in nature. Families making a yearly income of less than $2,000 pay taxes averaging about 13 percent of their income. This percentage rises to a high of nearly 35 percent for those families earning above $15,000. The percentage of income going to federal taxes remains rather constant for families earning between $3,000 and $10,000 yearly income; that is, there is not much progressivity over this range. All in all, however, federal taxes are progressive and claim between 13 and 35 percent of family income, depending upon income class.

TABLE 7-2   Federal, State, and Local Taxes
as a Percentage of Total Income

FAMILY INCOME	FEDERAL TAXES AS A % OF INCOME	STATE AND LOCAL TAXES AS A % OF INCOME	TOTAL TAXES AS A % OF INCOME
Under $2,000	13.0	15.1	28.1
$2,000–2,999	14.0	12.7	26.7
$3,000–3,999	17.1	12.6	29.7
$4,000–4,999	17.3	11.8	29.1
$5,000–5,999	17.9	11.5	29.4
$6,000–7,499	17.8	10.8	28.5
$7,500–9,999	18.4	10.1	28.5
$10,000–14,999	21.1	9.6	30.6
$15,000 and over	34.9	9.1	44.0

SOURCE: Adapted from *Allocating Tax Burdens and Government Benefits by Income Class*, Tax Foundation, Inc., New York, 1967, p. 7.

However, state and local taxes are regressive in nature. (State and local taxes are largely sales taxes and property taxes, though state income taxes appear to be gaining in importance.) The family earning less than $2,000 pays over 15 percent of its income in taxes on this level, while the percentage declines to just over 9 percent in the "$15,000 and over" group.

In total, the American tax system is progressive but not as progressive as many believe. The last column in Table 7-2 shows the total figures. Total tax payments claim about 28 percent of family income for those families earning $2,000 or less per year. This percentage climbs to only 28.5 for families earning up to $10,000. Thus there is very little progressivity in our tax structure up to the $10,000 level of income. Furthermore, there is not much progressivity when the income level rises to $15,000 (only 2.1 percent more). Finally, there is a significant increase in progressivity when family incomes rise above $15,000; however, this is an open-end class and includes those making extremely high incomes.

So, in answer to the question of who bears the burden of taxation, we can conclude that this burden is fairly well distributed to all income groups up to a yearly income of $15,000. Those earning above $15,000 a year bear more of the burden, though the figure never rises above 44 percent on the average for even the highest-income groups.

Shifting Tax Incidence

There is a further topic we must consider if we are to understand the effects of taxation, and that is the notion of *shifting incidence*. The "incidence" of a tax is nothing more than the burden of the tax, so that the person who is supposed to bear the burden passes it on to someone else. The incidence of a tax may be shifted *forward, backward,* or *absorbed.*

If a tax is levied on a corporation and if that corporation treats the tax as a cost and simply raises prices to cover that cost, the incidence of the tax is said to be shifted *forward* to the consumer. The corporation was meant to pay the tax, but the consumer ultimately paid it through higher prices. The incidence of a tax can generally be shifted forward by a corporation when the demand curve for its products is inelastic (that is, when consumers are not very responsive to price changes).   Forward shifting, then, occurs mostly when the corporation involved produces a product which is a necessity.   Consumers will continue to buy it even if the price rises.

A corporation can sometimes shift the incidence of a tax *backward* by paying less for the factors of production used by the corporation.   For example, an automobile firm could pay less for the steel it uses or pay workers a lower wage.   To the extent that this can be accomplished, backward shifting is said to have occurred.   However, because wages and other costs are relatively "sticky" on the downward side, backward shifting of incidence is much more difficult to accomplish than is forward shifting.

From the viewpoint of the corporation, the best position to be in is one where demand for your product is inelastic and where backward shifting can occur as well.   If the corporation can neither shift the incidence of the tax forward to consumers nor shift it backward to the factors of production, it must *absorb* the incidence, as intended when the tax was levied.   (In the long run, firms seldom absorb the tax incidence.   It can nearly always be shifted.)

Taxes and Incentive

We often hear the statement that high taxes impair incentives.   The assertion here is that people will work less hard if they know that they will pay more taxes on additional earnings or that businessmen will not invest more if they know that their return from that investment will be taxed at a higher rate.

Undoubtedly, some people do lose incentive to work because of the progressive tax structure.   On the other hand, some people work *harder* to raise their standard of living.   There is, then, both an *incentive effect* and a *disincentive effect* to progressive taxation.   Most people, however, cannot choose to work less hard.   They must work their forty-hour week no matter what the level of taxes.   Hence, it is likely that our present tax system has very little effect on the incentive to work.

The same is probably true for the incentive to invest on the part of the businessman.   Most businesses would rather invest at a lower rate of return than to refrain from investing and receive no return at all.

The question of taxes and incentives cannot be definitively answered without a great deal of additional research.   However, at the present time it appears that current levels of taxation have had little, if any, effect on the incentive to work or invest.

CHAPTER SUMMARY

In this chapter we looked briefly at methods of financing government expenditures, the public debt, the effects of federal spending, and the effects of federal taxation.   In the chapter which follows, we will carry our examination of the role of government a bit further.   In Chapter 8 we will discuss some of the limitations of fiscal policy and will trace monetary and fiscal policies since the end of World War II.   We will also present some suggested reforms in fiscal policy.

STUDY QUESTIONS

1. What is the basic difference between automatic and discretionary fiscal policy?   Give some examples of each, and explain how they work.
2. Explain what would happen to the price level (in both a full-employment and a less than full-employment economy) if the government financed new spending by taxing.   By printing new money.   By borrowing.
3. What do we mean when we say that our public debt is an internal one?   Why do we care whether it is internal or external?   What makes up the public debt?
4. For what does the federal government spend its money?   What are the effects of this spending on the level of income and employment, resource allocation, income redistribution, and economic growth?
5. Differentiate among progressive, regressive, and proportional taxes.   How progressive is our tax structure?   Why do we care about the degree of progressivity?
6. What is meant by the "incidence" of a tax?   Under what conditions can this incidence be shifted?   Under what conditions must it be absorbed?   Can you name some taxes where the incidence is borne by you?

IMPORTANT CONCEPTS IN CHAPTER 7

Automatic stabilizers
Financing government expenditures
Public debt
External versus internal debts
Marketable public securities
Nonmarketable public securities
Treasury bonds
Treasury notes
Treasury certificates of indebtedness
Treasury bills
Series bonds
Upward redistribution of income
Downward redistribution of income
Transfer payments
Progressive taxes
Regressive taxes
Shifting tax incidence
Forward shifting of tax incidence
Backward shifting of tax incidence
Absorption of tax incidence
Disincentive effect of taxation
Incentive effect of taxation

CHAPTER 8

FISCAL POLICY: PART II

In Chapter 7 we discussed the various automatic and discretionary fiscal measures which are used to stabilize the economy. At first glance it would seem to be a simple matter to use these policies to prevent both inflation and depression. However, the effective implementation of stabilization policies is more difficult than one might at first imagine, and this is due to three fundamental types of problems: (1) "mechanical" problems, (2) "conceptual" problems, and (3) problems of determining legitimate objectives.

In this chapter we will examine each of these problem areas and will also briefly trace the history of stabilization policy to see how effective it has been. Finally, we will make suggestions for improving our policy tools.

MECHANICAL PROBLEMS

Prognostication

Selection of the most appropriate fiscal measure to implement involves some "crystal-ball gazing." Do we want a tax cut next year? Well, that depends upon what we believe will be the state of the economy next year. How do we know the future state of the economy? We *guess;* and therein lies one of the basic problems of fiscal policy.

There are, of course, some rather sophisticated techniques available which help the economist to guess a little better (such as econometric techniques and regression analysis), but in the final analysis a lot of guesswork is involved.   And, obviously, if we do not know exactly the future state of the economy, then we cannot know exactly the kinds of policies which should be implemented.   If our prognostication (our forecast) is incorrect, then the chances are good that our policy will be incorrect as well.

Time Lags

A second mechanical problem we face is that of time lags.   The democratic process is often a very slow process, particularly in the area of fiscal policy.   Revenue measures (such as tax-rate changes) must originate in the House of Representatives.   Often such measures are tied up in debate in the House for some time.   Then the House-originated bill will be passed to the Senate for its consideration and debate.

If the Senate disagrees with the House, the bill must be passed to still another committee in an attempt to come up with a compromise measure acceptable both to the House and to the Senate.   After agreement is reached and the bill has been passed by both the House and the Senate, it is sent to the President for his final action.   If he approves the bill, it becomes a public law.

But the fiscal measure still is not implemented.   Funds must be appropriated by the Congress, administrative agencies may have to be established and staffed, and so forth.   All in all, the time lag involved between the conception of a fiscal measure and its final implementation can be quite considerable.   As an example, President Kennedy decided that a tax cut was needed in 1961 to stimulate total spending in the economy.   The tax cut was debated and altered for *three years* before it was finally passed as the Revenue Act of 1964.

Rigidities

A third mechanical limitation of fiscal policy can be referred to as *rigidities*.   A simple example will clarify this problem.   Suppose that the economy is faced with high levels of unemployment and widespread recession.   As one of its fiscal policies, the government might decide to build a multimillion dollar dam.   But suppose further that the recession ends after six months and the dam is only half completed. Obviously, the government will not terminate work on the dam but will continue its construction even though the economic situation may call for a cutback in federal spending.

Remember, too, that the majority of all government spending goes for purposes of national defense. Spending such as this does not lend itself to manipulation in order to counter cyclical fluctuations.

Hence, it is possible that these built-in rigidities in government spending can actually induce government-initiated cycles.

CONCEPTUAL PROBLEMS

There is a great deal of honest disagreement among economists as to the exact theoretical relationships confronting us. These disagreements we will call *conceptual problems*.

In past chapters we have suggested that if, say, the economy is in recession, we should increase one of the variables in the $C + I + G$ relationship. That is, we should cut consumer taxes and business taxes and/or increase government spending. The difficulty comes in knowing which variables to change and by how much.

If, for example, we cut business taxes to stimulate investment, that investment still may not occur. Why? Because there is not sufficient consumer demand to buy the hoped-for increased business output.   On the other hand, it will do little good to cut consumer taxes (raising disposable income) if businesses do not have sufficient investment funds to expand output to meet the increased demand.

As a practical matter, both consumer *and* business taxes will probably be reduced in a recession, but economists will always disagree regarding the extent of the cuts that should be made in each; and they will also disagree regarding the extent of the increase in federal spending and *for what* the money should be spent.

Such disagreement among the policy makers is conceptual in nature. We simply do not know enough about the system under which we live. Economic theory has come a long way since the 1930s, but it still does not provide us with all the answers.

DETERMINATION OF OBJECTIVES

A final limitation of fiscal policy is that we cannot really agree upon the appropriate objectives of such policy. Should fiscal-policy tools be used to maintain the status quo, or should they be used to bring about change? We want to stabilize the business cycle, but how stable do we want it? The Soviet Union has a quite stable economy, but certainly we do not want that much stability if it means a dictatorship in the United States.

Should fiscal policy be used to bring about an equitable distribution of the nation's wealth and income? If so, what, exactly, is an *equitable* distribution? Should we attempt to provide for a truly full-employment level of output, or should we simply see to it that unemployment levels do not become too high? And what level is *too high?*

These are all questions of objectives which we have not yet been able to answer with a national consensus. Until there is substantial agreement on such objectives, we will not have a perfect set of policies to forever eliminate inflation and depression.

These, then, are some of the limitations to the effective use of fiscal policy. Now let us turn to a brief historical sketch of some of the major policies implemented since the end of the war in 1945. In this way we can see what the policy makers were trying to accomplish and how successful they were.

A BRIEF HISTORY OF STABILIZATION POLICY (1945–1969)

The Post-World War II Period (1945–1947)

As the war neared its end, economists feared that the nation would be faced with a serious recession as war expenditures were curtailed. This fear (which later proved unfounded), plus the bitter experience of the prewar depression, set the stage for the acceptance by the Congress of the *Employment Act of 1946.* This act has provided the framework for fiscal-policy decisions since that time. The Employment Act opened with this policy statement:

> *The Congress hereby declares that it is the continuing policy and responsibility of the Federal Government to use all practicable means consistent with its needs and obligations and other essential considerations of national policy, with the assistance and cooperation of industry, agriculture, labor, and state and local governments, to coordinate and utilize all its plans, functions and resources*

(1) For the purpose of creating and maintaining, in a manner calculated to foster and promote free competitive enterprise and the general welfare, conditions under which there will be afforded useful employment opportunities, including self-employment, for those able, willing and seeking to work, and

(2)   To promote maximum employment, production and purchasing power.

In short, the Employment Act of 1946 gave the federal government the authority and the responsibility to work with business, labor, and agriculture to maintain full employment and high levels of output and income.

As the fear of recession waned in this period, it was replaced by a fear of inflation.   Consumers began spending for things they could not buy during the war years.   This pent-up demand, together with a tremendous demand for housing and the relaxing of many of the wartime controls, lent credence to these inflation fears.   The Congress reacted by passing Public Law 80-395 (the anti-inflation act).   This act gave the President limited authority to control the prices of scarce commodities through voluntary agreements with producers.

The Period 1948–1949

The fear of inflation carried over into this period.   In mid-1948, President Truman called a recalcitrant Congress back into session for the purpose of passing anti-inflation legislation.   Public Law 80-905 authorized the Federal Reserve bank to reimpose controls on consumer credit and to raise member-bank reserve requirements.   The credit controls required minimum down payments of one-third on automobiles and 20 percent on some major appliances.   Though President Truman vetoed it, tax rates were reduced by the Congress—instead of being increased, as is called for in inflationary periods.

Early in 1949, the President's anti-inflation program was passed, continuing rent, credit, and export controls.   The President asked for, but did not receive, standby authority for selective price and wage controls.

The inflationary trend was brought to an end by a mild inventory recession in 1949, at which time the Federal Reserve officials relaxed the controls over consumer credit, reduced stock market margin requirements, and reduced member-bank reserve requirements.

The Period 1950–1952

The Korean War broke out in June of 1950, creating a general economic boom. But it became clear that the tremendous increase in defense spending would necessitate stringent curbs on private spending in order to avoid inflation.

Consequently, in 1950 the Defense Production Act was passed, authorizing the President to regulate consumer credit and credit on new real estate and to impose price and wage controls if necessary. The Economic Stabilization Agency was established to restrain price and wage increases and did, in fact, order a reduction in automobile prices and call for a wage freeze in that industry. Federal rent control was also extended by the Congress to September of 1952.

As a further aid to controlling the inflationary trend, personal taxes were raised in 1950 to 1945 levels, the maximum corporate tax rate was raised to 47 percent, and an excess-profits tax was reimposed.

Taxes were again raised in 1951. Individual tax rates rose by about 11 percent, the maximum corporate rate climbed to 52 percent, and certain excise taxes were levied.[1]

It was also during this inflationary trend that the dispute between the Treasury and the Federal Reserve System over the policy of pegging government bond prices led to the Treasury Accord of 1951 (as discussed earlier, in Chapter 6). This accord allowed the Fed the independence to buy and sell securities in the open market to stabilize the economy.

The Period 1953–1960

There was a great deal of sentiment in the Eisenhower administration to balance the federal budget. During this seven-year period, monetary policy was relied upon more heavily than was fiscal policy. This was a turbulent period, marked by two rather severe recessions and a third, mild, "inventory" recession.

The nation's economic advance slowed during the spring of 1953 and moved into a recession lasting from mid-1953 until mid-1954. From a

---

[1] These corporate tax rates (47 and 52 percent) are *marginal* rates, not average tax rates. If the tax rate is 52 percent, a corporation will pay that rate on its highest earnings, not on all earnings. Consequently, the average tax rate would be much less.

fiscal-policy point of view, one would have expected a tax-rate decrease to stimulate total spending. Instead, the corporate income and excise tax-rate increases of 1951, which were scheduled to expire in 1954, were continued for one year. There was some reduction in other excise tax rates, and there were other rate reductions for the business community, but these reductions were not particularly significant. The 1951 increase in individual rates was, however, allowed to expire at the end of 1953.

The economy experienced some recovery in the latter half of 1954 and into 1955, though total demand showed some slack in 1956. The only significant tax change during this period was an increase in gasoline and other excise taxes to finance a long-range highway program.

The economy again moved into a recession in 1957, which lasted for about a year. There occurred a significant decline in business investment and in consumer demand as we appeared to reach a saturation point in the buying of consumer durables. The Eisenhower administration responded to this recession by passing three new laws and by giving a small amount of tax relief to business.

An emergency highway bill was passed which increased the authorizations for federal highway grants in 1959, 1960, and 1961. This bill also suspended for two years the pay-as-you-go provisions of the Highway Trust Fund. The hope was to stimulate additional spending on the state level in the area of highway construction.

Public Law 85-386 provided authorization for most of the agencies in the executive branch to spend in the remaining weeks of 1958 up to one-half of their fiscal 1959 estimates for supplies, materials, and equipment. This authorization released about $840 million in procurement funds.

The third significant law passed to counter the 1957–1958 recession was Public Law 85-441. This law authorized the Treasury to advance funds to states agreeing to extend by 50 percent the maximum amount and the duration of unemployment-compensation benefits currently being paid. This law was designed, of course, to help unemployed persons who had exhausted their unemployment benefits before finding work.

The only tax measures during the 1957–1958 recession were the repeal in 1958 of the excise tax on the transportation of freight and $260 million in tax relief for small business.

The economy experienced a slight recovery from the recession in 1959 but then fell into a third recession in that year. This recession, which reached its low point in early 1961, was caused largely by very high inventory levels which could not be sold to the public and by lagging spending in residential construction.

During this period the economy experienced the highest level of sustained unemployment since the Great Depression of the 1930s. Yet the Eisenhower administration again neglected taxes as a fiscal tool. In fact, the gasoline tax was raised from 3 to 4 cents per gallon to meet rising highway construction costs. And taxes on life insurance companies were also increased slightly. Monetary policy was again relied upon, as the Fed lowered the discount rate from 4 to 3 percent in August of 1960.

All in all, the period 1953–1960 was one of serious setbacks. Tax measures were largely ignored in the battle to restore the economy to full-employment levels, and monetary measures had the adverse effect of causing a very tight money market, which greatly curtailed home building.

The Period 1961–1963

This period was a busy one in the area of stabilization policy. President Kennedy's administration was determined to bring unemployment down to an acceptable level.

To help alleviate the problem of unemployment, the Kennedy administration passed its *antirecession program* in 1961. This was a four-point program in the areas of jobless pay, aid to children, social security, and minimum wages.

Because of the prolonged high levels of unemployment in previous years, many unemployed workers had exhausted their benefits under the various state-administered compensation systems (which provided up to 26 weeks of payments). The President was granted authority to extend these benefits for up to 13 additional weeks and to advance about $1 billion to the states over the next year.

A temporary change was made in the federal program of matching state grants for aid to dependent children. (The change was to last until mid-1962.) This move entitled children of unemployed parents to the same aid as that given to children deprived of support because of parental death, desertion, or disability.

As a third part of the antirecession program, the Administration also increased social security retirement and survivor benefits in the amount of about $800 a year.

The final part of the program was an increase in the minimum wage to $1.25 per hour and an expansion of the number of persons eligible for coverage.

Also passed in the period 1961–1963 was the Area Redevelopment Act of 1961. The purpose of this act was to finance industrial and rural redevelopment loans and public-facility loans.[2]

The President, in 1962, asked for, but was not granted, standby tax authority to temporarily reduce individual tax rates to ward off recession. He also requested, but did not receive, similar standby authority to initiate up to $2 billion in public works projects.

There were numerous other monetary and fiscal measures utilized in the period between 1961 and 1963, but we will mention only one other —wage and price guidelines. While the guidelines were not law, considerable pressure was applied on business and labor to adhere to them. The Council of Economic Advisors laid down the following two guidelines:

(1) *The general guide for noninflationary* wage *behavior is that the rate of increase in wage rates (including fringe benefits) in each industry be equal to the trend rate of over-all productivity increase. . . .*

(2) *The general guide for noninflationary* price *behavior calls for price reduction if the industry's rate of productivity increase exceeds the over-all rate—for this would mean declining unit labor costs; it calls for an appropriate increase in price if the opposite relationship prevails; and it calls for stable prices if the two rates of productivity are equal.*

---

2 The law defined redevelopment areas as those *industrial areas* where the past average annual unemployment rate had been 6 percent and (1) at least 50 percent above the national average for three of the preceding four years, or (2) at least 75 percent higher for two of the preceding three years, or (3) at least 100 percent higher for one of the preceding two years. Eligible *rural areas* were to be those "among the highest in numbers and percentages of low-income families, and in which there exists a condition of substantial and persistent unemployment or underemployment."

The Administration urged business and labor to observe these noninflationary guidelines throughout 1962 and 1963.   But all major steel producers nevertheless raised prices on about half of the industry's products, contributing to inflated price rises.

The major items of tax legislation during this period were an investment tax credit and revised depreciation rules in 1962.   The investment tax credit was designed to give tax benefits to businesses actually engaged in investment in new plant and equipment.   The 1962 tax revisions also included the repeal or reduction of most travel excise taxes.

The antirecession program, the Area Redevelopment Act, and other monetary and fiscal measures during the early part of the Kennedy administration put the economy on the road to recovery, although high levels of unemployment persisted between 1960 and 1963.

The Period 1964–1968

The year 1964 was another significant year for fiscal legislation.   President Johnson launched his antipoverty program with $1 billion authorized by the Economic Opportunity Act.

In other important developments, the President appointed a National Commission on Technology, Automation and Economic Progress to study the problems of automation.   Specifically, the fourteen nongovernment members of the Commission were to study the past and current effects of technological change and to recommend steps to promote technological progress while preventing and alleviating any adverse impact on employment.

Perhaps the most significant piece of legislation in 1964 was the Revenue Act of that year.   Unemployment was still a problem, and levels of business investment were lagging.   The intent of the Revenue Act was to stimulate consumer spending and business investment by reducing taxes.   Under the act, individual tax liabilities were reduced $9.1 billion and corporate liabilities were cut $2.4 billion.   And 1.5 million persons were removed from the tax rolls altogether by raising minimum standard deductions.

During 1965, much stress was laid by the Administration on adherence by labor and business to guidelines.   There were two kinds of guidelines or controls.   The first were the wage-price guidelines (previously mentioned), which defined upward limits for price and wage increases by business and labor.   The second type of control was a request that businessmen and bankers reduce overseas investment and lending by U.S. companies and banks, thereby reducing the nation's continuing balance-of-payments deficit.   These controls were purportedly voluntary in nature; however, the Administration was able on several occasions to elicit compliance by using methods other than those of voluntary agreement.

For example, during a twelve-day so-called "aluminum war" in late 1965, the government threatened to sell stockpiles of aluminum on the open market to force down aluminum price increases which the Administration believed exceeded the noninflationary guidelines.   The aluminum producers, led by Alcoa, capitulated and rescinded their price increases.

The same tactic was used later in the year in the copper industry, when the Administration's decision to sell 200,000 tons of copper resulted in a prompt drop in the market price of copper.   Within three days the prices posted by major U.S. copper producers fell accordingly. Taxes were also pared in 1965.   Public Law 89-44 produced graduated excise-tax cuts totaling $4.7 billion.   The cuts provided by PL 89-44 represented the first major revision of excise taxes since World War II. Of particular concern in the fiscal arena was poverty in the Appalachian region of the United States.   Accordingly, in 1965, Public Law 89-4 was passed, authorizing the expenditure of over $1 billion for the development of the eleven-state region [3] (particularly through new highway construction).

The 1961 Area Redevelopment Act and the 1962 Public Works Acceleration Act were broadened in 1965 by Public Law 89-136.   The law provided $3.25 billion over a five-year period in grants and loans for public works and other projects intended to aid economically depressed areas.

By 1966 and 1967, unemployment rates had been brought back to acceptable levels (hovering around 4 percent of the labor force).   The danger now, according to most economists, was inflation.

---

[3] The Appalachian region was defined to include 360 counties, including all of West Virginia and parts of Alabama, Georgia, Kentucky, Maryland, North Carolina, Ohio, Pennsylvania, South Carolina, Tennessee, and Virginia, as well as contiguous counties in New York.

In an attempt to counter this inflationary trend, the Fed engaged in extremely tight policies of credit restraint in 1966.   Interest rates and bond yields rose to the highest levels since the early 1920s.   Other interest rates in the economy rose in relation to bond yields and discount rates, so that, for example, the average interest rate for the purchase of a new home rose from 5.8 percent in November 1965 to 6.4 percent in November 1966.   The construction and home-building industries were hit particularly hard by this tight-money policy.   And, at the same time, the Fed was increasing reserve requirements on time deposits, creating a further shortage of funds in the construction industry.

In a further attempt to discourage price rises, two tax bills were passed by the Eighty-ninth Congress in 1966.   One in March (PL 89-368) increased taxes by providing graduated withholding on individual incomes, accelerating corporate tax payments, and suspending certain 1965 excise-tax cuts.   An October change (PL 89-800) attempted to slow the rate of business investment spending by suspending the 7 percent investment tax credit on the purchase of machinery and equipment.

Although these two laws did not actually levy new taxes, the provisions did have the intended effect of taking money away from businesses and consumers.

Federal minimum-wage protection was also extended in 1966 to cover about 9.1 million new employees, and the minimum wage was raised from $1.25 to $1.60 per hour, in stages.   The added coverage, and other changes, made this the most important revision of the federal minimum-wage concept since its inception as part of the 1938 Fair Labor Standards Act.

The year 1967 began as one in which the economy lagged in the first half of the year but needed restraining in the latter half.   Consequently, the Fed in early 1967 made substantial open-market purchases, reduced required reserves, and lowered the discount rate.   Later in the year, the Fed moved to tighten the money supply.   Tax stimulation was provided when the Administration restored the 7 percent investment tax credit.

As inflation became a threat, President Johnson requested Congress to impose a 6 percent surtax (an additional 6 percent of the tax bill for the individual or corporation).   This request was refused, and pressure was applied on the President to fight inflation by cutting spending rather than by raising taxes.

Major appropriation cuts were made in excess of $5 billion.   On a percentage basis, defense spending was cut by 2 percent, foreign aid by 28 percent, housing and urban development by 24 percent, antipoverty funds by 14 percent, NASA by 11 percent, and transportation expenditures by 8 percent.

The surtax requested by Johnson but refused by Congress in 1967 was finally made effective at a level of 10 percent in 1968.

In summary, there can be little question that the most effective use of stabilization policy in the postwar period was during the Kennedy and Johnson administrations, when the economy experienced one of the longest sustained economic booms in its history.

FISCAL-POLICY REFORM

Numerous reforms have been suggested in the area of fiscal policy; we will make no attempt to examine each of them here.   However, two areas of reform—one accomplished and one suggested—are worthy of consideration.   The accomplished reform is a new budget format, and the suggested reform is standby tax authority.   We will examine each of these in turn.

The Federal Budget

The budget is one of the most important federal documents in that it presents the President's financial plans for the coming year.   The President submits the budget to the Congress each January, six months before the beginning of the fiscal year (July 1 to June 30).   The 1969 budget was submitted by President Johnson in January of 1968, and the figures apply to the period July 1, 1968, to June 30, 1969.   (The 1969 budget is included in this chapter as Appendix 1.)

Prior to the submission of the 1969 budget, three different budgets were prepared, leading to a certain amount of confusion.

One of the old budget forms was known as the *national income accounts budget*.   This budget reported all the income and expenditure transactions of the federal government, including the various trust funds (such as highway programs and social security). However, this budget did not include government loans because they were considered *not* to be an addition to the nation's income since they were repayable.

A second old budget form was the *consolidated cash budget.* This budget included all cash transactions of the federal government, including loans. Also included were the trust funds.

The third old budget form was the *administrative budget,* which excluded all trust funds and hence was less comprehensive than the consolidated cash budget.

Because of the confusion caused by the existence of several budget forms, the President in 1967 appointed a Commission on Budget Concepts to study the feasibility of a single budget. In October of 1967, the Commission reported its findings and called for the creation of a unified budget.

The unified budget includes all federal appropriations, receipts, expenditures, and lending. It also includes the means of financing expenditures and loans, as well as the federal securities and loans outstanding. Thus, while transactions under the federally administered trust funds were excluded in the administrative budget, they are included in the unified budget. And while the national income accounts budget excluded transactions in federal lending programs, these do show up in the unified budget. The Commission also suggested that expenditures and receipts be reported as they become due (on an accrual basis) rather than when payments are actually made (a cash basis, as in the cash budget). This last recommendation was not, however, adopted in the concept of the unified budget.

There is little doubt that the new unified budget will go far toward clearing up the confusion over the budget that has long existed due to the issuance of three different budgets.

Standby Tax Authority

In 1966, the Subcommittee on Fiscal Policy of the Joint Economic Committee requested standby authority for rapid tax increases or decreases. No action has yet been taken on this proposal.

Those who support the proposal maintain that the ability to rapidly change tax receipts would contribute significantly to the stability of employment, output, incomes, and prices. Those who oppose the proposal do so because they feel that the accuracy of economic forecasts is too limited, that tax changes are unsettling for business, and that the federal government is simply not equipped to make rapid changes.

If enacted, the plan would represent a tax surcharge and would work as follows:

If the President felt that a tax increase were needed (perhaps to combat inflation), he would submit a resolution to Congress asking for, say, a 5 percent surcharge. If the Congress agreed, a joint resolution would be issued to that effect. The taxpayer would then compute his tax liability as always, except that now he would add to his tax bill an additional 5 percent of his computed tax. For example, if the taxpayer computed his tax bill to be $1,000, he would add $50 to it (5 percent of $1,000 = $50). His total tax bill would then be $1,050.

CHAPTER SUMMARY

In this chapter we have had a look at some of the problems of implementing effective fiscal-policy measures. We have also traced some of the more important measures since 1945. And, finally, we have taken a very brief look at two reform measures.

Certain mechanical problems were seen to exist in the fiscal arena. These included problems of prognostication, time lags, and rigidities. Also discussed were the conceptual problems which arise because of honest disagreement among economists about the exact theoretical relationships confronting us. The fact that we cannot really agree upon appropriate objectives presents a final limitation of fiscal policy. Should such policy be used to maintain the status quo, or should it be used to bring about change? How stable should our business cycle be? What is an "equitable" distribution of wealth, and should fiscal policy be used to attain this distribution?

Next, Chapter 8 presented a brief history of stabilization policy during the period 1945–1969. This discussion pointed to the successes and failures of fiscal policy over the years.

Finally, we evaluated two reform measures.   One of these measures—the unified budget—has been implemented.   The other—standby tax authority—has been requested by three presidents, but such authority was denied them by a Congress anxious to hold on to its fiscal prerogatives.

In Chapters 3 to 8 we have developed some of the basic fiscal and monetary tools so necessary to the solution of the nation's problems. In Chapters 9 and 10 we will apply some of our newly found knowledge to many of the specific problem areas we face.

STUDY QUESTIONS

1. Discuss the problems of implementing appropriate fiscal policy. Can you think of other problems not mentioned in this chapter?
2. Trace the rising importance placed upon fiscal policy in the period 1945–1969.
3. Discuss some of the reforms suggested in the area of fiscal policy. Can you recommend other reforms?

IMPORTANT CONCEPTS IN CHAPTER 8

Mechanical problems
Conceptual problems
Problems of objectives
Employment Act of 1946
Defense Production Act of 1950
Antirecession program of 1961
Area Redevelopment Act of 1961
Wage and price guidelines
Economic Opportunity Act
Revenue Act of 1964
Surtax of 1968
National income accounts budget
Consolidated cash budget
Administrative budget
Unified budget
Standby tax authority

APPENDIX   FISCAL 1969 BUDGET   (IN MILLIONS OF DOLLARS)

	BUDGET AUTHORITY	EXPENDITURES
National Defense		
Military defense	$ 79,188	$ 76,717
Net lending, military defense	—	−1
Civil defense	77	89
Military assistance	1,860	1,853
Atomic energy	2,755	2,546
Defense-related activities	91	242
Net lending, defense-related activities	—*	−3
Adjustments	−1,654	−1,654
Total	$ 82,317	$ 79,788
International Affairs and Finance		
Conduct of foreign affairs	$ 380	$ 438
Economic and financial assistance	3,393	2,564
Net lending, economic and financial assistance	608	675
Foreign information and exchange	233	255
Food for freedom	918	1,444
Adjustments	−224	−224
Total	$ 5,308	$ 5,153
Space Research and Technology	$ 4,372	$ 4,577
Adjustments	−3	−3
Total	$ 4,369	$ 4,573
Agriculture, Agricultural Resources		
Farm income stabilization	$ 4,178	$ 3,459
Net lending, farm income stabilization	24	24
Financing farming and rural housing	92	32
Net lending, financing farming and rural housing	967	751
Financing rural electrification, etc.	13	13
Net lending, financing rural electrification, etc.	234	360
Agricultural land and water resources	242	350
Net lending, agricultural land and water resources	—	—
Research and other services	648	662
Adjustments	−42	−42
Total	$ 6,356	$ 5,609
Natural Resources		
Land and water resources	$ 2,424	$ 2,536
Net lending, land and water resources	4	6
Forest resources	508	493
Mineral resources	126	131
Fish and wildlife resources	158	158
Net lending, fish and wildlife resources	—	—
Recreational resources	245	309

	BUDGET AUTHORITY	EXPENDI- TURES
General resources surveys and administration	191	239
Net lending, general resources surveys and administration	—	—*
Adjustments	−1,382	−1,382
Total	$ 2,275	$ 2,490
Commerce and Transportation		
Air transportation	$ 1,117	$ 1,282
Water transportation	1,046	1,000
Net lending, water transportation	−6	−7
Ground transportation	4,894	4,420
Postal service	920	767
Advancement of business	400	153
Net lending, advancement of business	150	67
Area and regional development	445	425
Net lending, area and regional development	88	65
Regulation of business	111	107
Net lending, regulation of business	—*	—*
Adjustments	−157	−157
Total	$ 9,008	$ 8,121
Housing and Community Development		
Aid to private housing	$ 23	$ −457
Net lending, aid to private housing	1,914	1,245
Public housing programs	380	350
Net lending, public housing programs	—	−16
Urban renewal and community facilities	2,274	1,432
Net lending, urban renewal and community facilities	80	61
National capital region	140	104
Net lending, national capital region	141	65
Proposed housing and urban development legislation	30	14
Adjustments	−14	−14
Total	$ 4,968	$ 2,784
Health, Labor, and Welfare		
Health services and research	$ 13,609	$ 12,041
Net lending, health services and research	−15	−15
Labor and manpower	1,546	1,492
Public assistance (excluding Medicare)	3,703	3,605
Net lending, public assistance (excluding Medicare)	4	4
Retirement and social insurance	40,472	33,932
Net lending, retirement and social insurance	−530	−530

	BUDGET AUTHORITY	EXPENDITURES
Economic opportunity programs	2,176	1,997
Net lending, economic opportunity programs	4	3
Other welfare services	1,330	1,302
Adjustments	−2,423	−2,423
Total	$ 59,875	$ 51,407
Education		
Elementary and secondary education	$ 2,103	$ 1,931
Net lending, elementary and secondary education	1	1
Higher education	849	1,065
Net lending, higher education	686	334
Science education and basic research	500	480
Other aids to education	1,148	905
Adjustments	−16	−16
Total	$5,272	$ 4,699
Veterans' Benefits and Services		
Proposed legislation	$ 9	$ −18
Compensation and pensions	4,562	4,562
Veterans' readjustment benefits	748	611
Net lending, veterans' readjustment benefits	396	305
Veterans' hospitals and medical care	1,522	1,546
Other veterans' benefits and services	1,167	924
Net lending, other veterans' benefits and services	−94	−94
Adjustments	−494	−494
Total	$ 7,817	$ 7,342
Interest	$ 15,349	$ 15,349
Adjustments	−949	−949
Total	$ 14,400	$ 14,400
General Government	$ 2,901	$ 3,038
Net lending, general government	−36	−37
Adjustments	−211	−211
Total	$ 2,654	$ 2,790
Civilian and Military Pay Increases	$ 1,600	$ 1,600
Contingencies	$ 550	$ 350
Undistributed Intragovernmental Payments	$ −5,049	$ −5,049
Grand Total	$201,723	$186,062

* Less than $500 thousand.

CHAPTER 9

SOLVING DOMESTIC ECONOMIC PROBLEMS: PART I

The economic problems facing this or any other industrial nation are both numerous and highly complex. Suggested remedies for the difficulties, moreover, are never certain to be the appropriate ones. However, it behooves us to diligently try to ferret out the problems and to suggest ways of overcoming them.

The current chapter examines three significant economic problems: city problems, housing problems, and the agricultural problem. While each of these areas contains social and political problems as well, an attempt is made here to deal primarily with the economic dimensions. Too, many of the aspects of the problems discussed here, and in the following chapter, are highly interrelated. However, it generally enhances an understanding of the issues involved if they are each treated as a separate problem. Thus they are treated so here.

THE PROBLEMS OF THE URBAN COMPLEX

The United States has long been characterized by an agricultural tradition. For years the family farm was the cornerstone of the economy, and the majority of our people lived and worked on farms. However, about a hundred years ago, there began a marked migration from the rural areas into the nation's cities. This migration has not been without its problems.

Only 3 out of every 20 persons in the United States lived in urban areas in 1850. Fifty years later, the figure had risen to 4 out of every

10, and by 1920 the figure stood at 1 out of every 2.   This trend toward urbanization has continued, so that today two-thirds of our population live in urban areas.

Slightly over half of those living in urban areas live in the central city
itself, but the other half has settled in the surrounding suburbs.   And
80 percent of the *growth* in the metropolitan areas has been in the
suburbs.   Herein lies a major part of the so-called urban problem.
The shift of population from the central city to the suburbs has caused
our cities to decay faster than they can be rebuilt.

Anyone who makes the daily trip from the suburbs to the city can
attest to the fact that parking is a universal problem and that traffic
is congested both into and out of the city.   But more subtle problems
have also arisen—problems which may not meet the eye of the individual who only travels to and from the city for work.   As industry
moves from the central city, the tax base is eroded, lessening the
sources of revenue for the city government.   A significant part of the
white population is also moving to the suburbs.   These are the middle-
and upper-income white-collar workers, so that the city's tax base is
lessened even more.

But while the tax base in the cities is eroding, the costs of maintaining
the cities rise.   The poor, who cannot afford to move to the outlying
areas, remain in the slums of the city.   The nonwhite population also
remains and is, in fact, bolstered by the migration into the cities from
the southern areas of the nation.   Thus the proportion of poor, nonwhite, and untrained persons in the cities is on the rise—at the very
time when those most able to pay taxes are leaving the central cities
at a rapid pace.

The problems brought about by this shift in composition of the city's
population are serious.   The quality of public education is on the
decline; incidence of juvenile and adult crime is showing an alarming
increase; unemployment rates continue to rise, partly as a result of
more high school "dropouts"; and welfare costs are sharply increasing.
Along with these problems is a political one.   Because of the vested
interests of those in city government, there is little *regional planning*
in the areas of providing appropriate sewerage facilities, securing an
adequate water supply, and meeting the housing and transportation
needs of the area's inhabitants.

The transportation problem is particularly acute.   A particular city may have a daytime population half again as large as its residential population. At the same time, more and more people are avoiding the use of mass transit and public transportation facilities, preferring to drive to and from the cities. "Between 1950 and 1958 transit riding in American cities fell from 17.2 billion to 9.7 billion rides per year, a drop of 43 percent." [1]

Another area of concern for the central city lies in the creation of slums. As the wealthy move to the suburbs and as low-income minorities migrate into the cities, areas of blight develop. Low-income persons owning property find it difficult, if not impossible, to maintain their property; and landlords find it unprofitable. (More will be said below about the housing problem.) The development of slum areas also further increases the need, and the cost, of adequate police and fire protection, as well as public health and welfare facilities.

The property tax is the major source of revenue for the cities. As the value of property declines, so then does tax revenue. Further, when property improvements are made, taxes for the owner rise, providing a disincentive for improvement.

The outlying suburban areas are not without their problems, too. The out-migration from the central cities places increased demands on the outlying regions for schools, roads, police and fire protection, sewage disposal, water, and so forth.

There are some problems common to both the suburban areas and the central cities. The transportation problem, already mentioned, is one of these. Air and water pollution is another. (It is said that simply breathing the air in some of our industrial cities is the equivalent of smoking two packages of cigarettes per day!) Effective land use is another common problem. Ways must be found to allow for industrial development and housing projects and yet ensure the provision of adequate parks—to provide for rapid growth, yet maintain a concern for beauty. The United States is notorious for its ugliness—a reputation we should not enjoy.

The answers to the problems facing the nation's metropolitan areas are not easy ones. Political barriers must be broken down to allow for *regional planning*. Extensive *economic base studies* must be un-

---

[1] *Guiding Metropolitan Growth, A Statement on National Policy*, Research and Policy Committee of the Committee for Economic Development, Washington, August, 1960, p. 19.

dertaken to determine the area's needs and its resources and to enable businessmen and governments to make the proper decisions for urban renewal. Funds must be allocated to enable the cities to *rebuild their slum areas* and to *improve their schools*. Experimentation is needed in building new housing, and existing housing codes must be carefully studied and revised where necessary.

Such programs will necessitate the raising of tremendous sums of money and will be dependent upon cooperation between businessmen and politicians on a level heretofore unthought of. Yet, without this effort, the central city is doomed to decay and the urban areas will be unable to meet the pressing needs of an ever-growing population.

As we have indicated, the housing problem is one of the most severe of the urban problems—both because it is widespread and because it most directly touches the human element of the city. Let us, then, take a closer look at this particular problem.

THE HOUSING PROBLEM

The 1960 census showed that over 9 million housing units in the United States were "seriously deficient." This figure represents 1 out of every 6 houses, and it is likely today that the figure is closer to 1 out of every 5. The "housing problem" is truly one of the most pressing economic problems this nation will face over the next two or three decades.

Obviously, those most affected by deficient housing are the poor. Leon Keyserling points out that:

> *According to the 1960 U.S. Census of Housing, while less than 21 percent of all renter-occupied housing and only about 7½ percent of all owner-occupied housing in metropolitan areas were unsound, about 60 percent of the renter-occupied housing and about 34 percent of the owner-occupied housing were unsound in the case of families with incomes under $3,000. These families lived in more than 46 percent of the unsound owner-occupied housing. And among families and other consumer units with incomes under $2,000, at least 4 out of 5 lived in unsound housing.*[2]

---

[2] Leon H. Keyserling, *Progress or Poverty*, Conference on Economic Progress, Washington, December, 1964, p. 127.

Figure 9-1 shows the extent to which deteriorated housing is occupied by the poor.

The reasons why the poor live in dilapidated dwellings may be several, but the most important is that they simply cannot pay for better housing. Further, most new housing is built for the middle- and upper-income groups—not for the poor. In the first quarter of 1964, for example, only one-half of 1 percent of the new FHA single-family homes were purchased by families with incomes of $4,000 or less. And only 12.5 percent were bought by those with incomes of under $6,000.[3]

Of course, the minority groups are most affected since they are among the poorest in the nation's cities.

Not only are slum areas undesirable from a humanitarian point of view, they are also costly in terms of social services. And, as was indicated, cities derive very little per capita revenue from these areas, while a great deal of municipal expenditure is necessary.

Specific Housing Problems and Proposed Solutions

Much recent study has been made on the housing problem, with the result that specific problems have been isolated and specific proposals made for their solution. Some of the more important of these problems are listed below: [4]

1. HIGH HOUSING COSTS AND SHORT HOUSING SUPPLY   The most obvious solution to this problem, though a costly one, lies in the provision of public housing programs, particularly for the poor. These could take the form of smaller, scattered developments which would neither reinforce the city's ghettos nor create new ones. Government subsidies of several forms will be necessary. Rent and mortgage payment supplements for low-income families would have to be provided. Tax incentives would be necessary for the construction of low-cost housing both in the central city and in the suburbs, and housing producers would in all likelihood have to be subsidized in their pur-

---

[3] *Ibid.*, p. 128.

[4] The majority of the problems presented here, and the proposed solutions, were adapted from *Programs Relevant to Urban Problems, Interim Phase I Report*, Voluntarism and Urban Life Project, Institute of Community Studies, New York, December, 1968, pp. 21–30. This is a preliminary analysis made in the first phase of a three-year ongoing project.

Figure 9-1 Housing Conditions Related to Incomes in Metropolitan Areas, 1960. Unsound housing is a Census clarification based on substantial defects, but the category includes more units than the housing classified by the Census as seriously deficient.

Extent to which Housing Occupied by Selected Income Groups was Unsound [1]

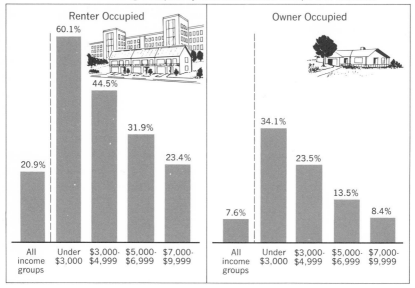

Distribution of Total Unsound [1] Housing among Selected Income Groups
(Note different scale)

Data: U.S. Census of Housing 1960, cited by Keyserling, *Progress or Poverty*, Conference on Economic Progress, Washington, December, 1964, p. 133.

chase of land, in construction, and in their financing costs.   Research would also have to be subsidized to seek breakthroughs in construction efficiency.

2.   SUBSTANDARD HOUSING   Three areas exist for possible improvement of substandard housing.   One suggestion has been for the rigid enforcement of housing codes for landlords.   (The poor living in owner-occupied dwellings would perhaps have to be exempted from such enforcement.)   A second method of improvement would involve the financing of research to develop new and cheaper methods of rehabilitating substandard housing.   And a third possibility would be the provision of tax incentives for home improvement.

3.   SHORTAGE OF LAND FOR DEVELOPMENT   Good land is increasingly becoming in short supply.   Hence, strong zoning laws should be passed to prevent developers from spoiling available areas.   In addition, blighted areas should be reclaimed and redeveloped.   Finally, a rather radical but perhaps necessary policy would involve the use of government funds to provide financial incentives to private firms in the construction of completely new towns.

4.   HARDSHIP TO DISPLACED HOUSEHOLDS   In the process of urban renewal, many families must be displaced.   Generally, of course, these are the poorer families living in slum areas.   All too often in the past, such renewal has occurred with little thought given to those who are to be displaced.   To prevent this inequity, detailed relocation plans should be developed prior to any dislocation.   Moreover, payments should be made to the displaced families so that they can obtain adequate alternative shelter.   Relocation assistance and counseling should be provided as well.

5.   THE PROBLEM OF DISCRIMINATION IN HOUSING   Major steps have already been taken to eliminate racial discrimination in the buying and rental of homes.   To help further in the prevention of discrimination, state and local fair-housing laws could be strengthened and enforced.   Furthermore, new housing could be planned to avoid segregation.

6.   SHORTAGE OF COMMUNITY FACILITIES   It has already been pointed out that rapid urban development has not generated adequate parks

and recreation areas.   This is so particularly in the poorer neighborhoods.   Hence, not only should more areas be planned but priority
should be given to the poorer neighborhoods.

7.   UGLINESS   To prevent what has come to be called "new slums,"
beauty in subdivisions and developments should be encouraged.

Summary of Housing Problems

We have seen that most inadequate housing is occupied by the poor,
who cannot afford decent housing.   We have also noted that the vast
majority of the new housing is being constructed for middle- and
upper-income families.   Slums and ghetto areas are rapidly developing in America's cities.   Such blighted areas are costly in terms of the
social services involved, as well as in humanitarian terms.

Some of the more specific housing problems were seen to be high
housing costs and short housing supply, substandard housing, a
shortage of land for development, hardships imposed on displaced
households, discrimination, a shortage of community facilities, and
ugliness.

A massive effort is needed, involving a great deal of money and extensive cooperation among federal, state, and local governments—in con-
junction with private organizations.   If this effort is not forthcoming,
the United States will face a metropolitan crisis of the first order over
the next decade or two.   A ten-point program for the solution to the
urban crisis was advanced before the second session of the Ninetieth
Congress in June of 1968.   That program is attached as an appendix
to this chapter.

Such is the nature of the urban problem.   We will now move from
the cities to the rural regions to see what misfortunes have befallen
the American farmer—for he, perhaps more than the city dweller, has
undergone an economic crisis of huge proportions in past decades.

THE AGRICULTURAL PROBLEM

Of all the groups in our economy, the American farmer has partici-
pated least in the nation's economic growth.   We will now examine

the extent of the agricultural dilemma, some past attempts to solve the problem, the costs of the farm program, and a suggested program for agriculture.

Farm Income

Between 1947 and 1964, total U.S. personal income rose from $262 to $484 billion, an increase of 84.7 percent. During the same period, nonfarm personal income increased from $235.6 to $464.2 billion, up 97 percent (in constant 1963 dollars). Yet, over the same years, net farm operators' income fell from $19.5 to $12.6 billion, a drop of 35.3 percent.[5] The American farmer has remained poor in the midst of unparalleled prosperity. Figure 9-2 presents relevant data depicting the plight of the agricultural sector of our society.

Why is farm income low? Certainly not because of inefficiency—the American farmer is one of the most productive in the world, both in terms of applying new technology and in yield per acre. As a matter of fact, his very efficiency is one cause of his low income. Rising productivity on the farm, coupled with a relatively slow growth in the demand for farm products, has led the farmer into a general overproduction or underconsumption situation. He is producing more and more, but the demand for his production is largely dependent only upon growth in the nation's population. Hence, this oversupply tends to force down farm prices.

The farmer's increase in productivity occurs because of a *changing labor/capital ratio*. Whereas agricultural production at one time was dependent upon a lot of labor and very little capital equipment, it is now dependent mostly upon the use of machines, with relatively little manpower.

Another explanation for the farmer's low income is the *inelasticity of supply* of farm production. If the demand, say, for wheat were to decline, it would not be possible for the farmer to quickly adjust downward his production level for wheat. Once he has planted his crop, he has little opportunity to alter the output.

One of the most important causes of the farmer's inadequate income

---

[5] Leon H. Keyserling, *Agriculture and the Public Interest*, Conference on Economic Progress, Washington, February, 1965, p. 7.

Figure 9-2 Data on Farm Income, Selected Years

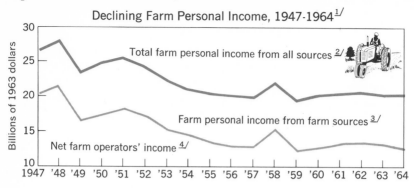

Declining Farm Personal Income, 1947-1964[1]

Billions of 1963 dollars

Total farm personal income from all sources [2]

Farm personal income from farm sources [3]

Net farm operators' income [4]

1947 '48 '49 '50 '51 '52 '53 '54 '55 '56 '57 '58 '59 '60 '61 '62 '63 '64

Disparities in Income Trends, 1947-1964[1]
(Percent changes 1947-1964, in 1963 dollars)

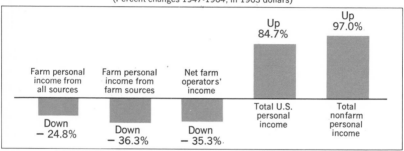

Farm personal income from all sources — Down −24.8%

Farm personal income from farm sources — Down −36.3%

Net farm operators' income — Down −35.3%

Total U.S. personal income — Up 84.7%

Total nonfarm personal income — Up 97.0%

Still More Recent Trends, 1953-1964[1]
(Average annual rates of change in 1963 dollars)

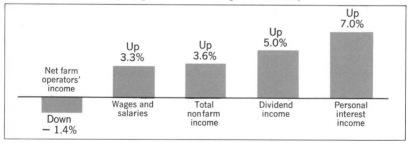

Net farm operators' income — Down −1.4%

Wages and salaries — Up 3.3%

Total nonfarm income — Up 3.6%

Dividend income — Up 5.0%

Personal interest income — Up 7.0%

[1] 1965 estimated on basis of first three quarters.

[2] Total farm personal income is total net income, before taxes, and includes income of farm people from farm and nonfarm sources.

[3] Farm income from farm sources is net farm operators' income of resident farmers, plus wages of farm resident workers and their nonmoney income, less social insurance contributions.

[4] Net farm operators' income is their income from farm marketing, less production expenses, their nonmoney income, government payments, and adjustment for inventory changes.

DATA: Departments of Agriculture and Commerce, cited by Keyserling, *Agriculture and the Public Interest*, Conference on Economic Progress, Washington, February, 1965, p. 11.

is that he is caught in a market "squeeze." The prices he must pay for tractors, cultivators, and other farm equipment are rapidly rising, but the prices paid to the farmer for his output are rising only slowly —and sometimes not at all if the market is glutted. Thus he faces a relative *weakness in the marketplace.*

It is an unfortunate fact that farm income is low also because of past government programs designed to raise it! Though such programs were initiated to sustain farm incomes, they have had the side effect of providing just enough income to keep the "marginal" farmer on the farm. His mobility has declined because he is able (with government help) to eke out a bare living. He is not encouraged by such programs to move into the city, nor can he generally afford to do so. And most of the federal programs have paid no attention to the retraining which would be necessary to encourage the farmer to seek other types of employment. It has been said that the crux of the farm problem is that there are too many farmers. Past legislation has served to aggravate this problem. Below we will look at the major types of government programs aimed at the farmer.

Government Agricultural Programs

Federal farm legislation has taken four forms: (1) programs designed to increase the demand for farm output, (2) attempts to restrict agricultural supply, (3) outright cash subsidies to farmers, and (4) the buying of surplus commodities.

Figure 9-3 shows the intent of programs designed to increase the demand for farm output—say, through expanded school lunch programs. Supply is shown to be inelastic with respect to prices (for reasons mentioned above). If the demand for farm output should increase (from D to D'), the price of such output would rise (from OP to OP') and, of course, farm income would rise from $OPAX$ to $OP'BX$. Such a plan is difficult to implement because the demand for food is also relatively inelastic and is difficult to increase to any substantial degree.

A second plan to aid the farmer takes the form of restricting supply. (The *soil bank* is an example of such a program.) Figure 9-4 shows the intended result of this type of program.

If farmers could be induced to place part of their potentially produc-

Figure 9-3   Increasing Demand for
             Farm Output

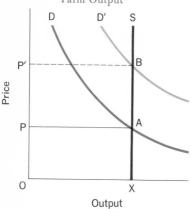

tive land in the soil bank (that is, let it lie idle), the supply of farm
output would decline, as shown by the shift of the supply curve from
S to S'.   Assuming a constant demand, price would be expected to
rise in OP' and farm income would increase from OPAX to OP'BX'.
(Such a change would represent an increase in income because of the

Figure 9-4   Restricting Supply

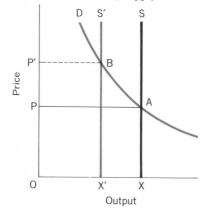

inelasticity of the supply function.   Thus area $OP'BX'$ must be larger than area $OPAX$.)

Attempts to restrict the supply of farm commodities have largely failed.   One reason is that the average farmer will let his least productive land lie idle and will use increased technology on the remaining land.   The result?   Output remains about constant.

A third proposal to bolster farm income is depicted in Figure 9-5. Under a cash-subsidy program of this type, the price of farm commodities would be allowed to seek their normal market level (OP).   No attempt would be made to alter either demand or supply.   Instead, if the government felt that income $OPAX$ was insufficient, a check would simply be sent to the farmer to make up the difference between the income he received and the "fair" income decided upon by governmental authorities.   Such a program has never been implemented, partly because of the difficulty of determining a fair level of income and partly because farmers reject the program as "charity."

A final form of federal aid to the farmer involves the buying of surplus crops in order to guarantee the farmer a fair (or *parity*) price for his output.   A parity price is considered to be a "fair" price for a particular commodity, based upon what the farmer must pay for his tools of production.   Figure 9-6 depicts this type of farm program.   If

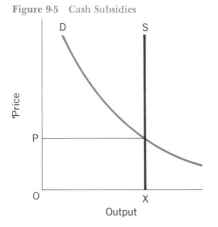

Figure 9-5   Cash Subsidies

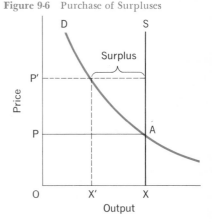

Figure 9-6   Purchase of Surpluses

the market price for, say, wheat were established at OP but if the government felt that OP' was a fairer price, then the parity price for wheat would be set at OP'. But at this higher price consumers are willing to purchase only OX' bushels of wheat (according to the law of demand). Hence, the supply of wheat (OX) exceeds the demand for wheat (OX'). The difference between the supply of wheat and the demand for wheat represents a surplus of wheat production. It is this surplus which the government would buy for storage in order to maintain the higher price, OP'.

Obviously, under a plan such as this there are certain wastes. The consumer pays a higher price for wheat and has less of it available to him. Moreover, the government must pay the cost of storing the surplus wheat. There have even been instances where tremendous amounts of surplus wheat were allowed to rot in storage or were disposed of by dumping!

Costs of the Farm Program

The costs incurred in trying to aid the farmer must be seen in their proper light. If the government pays for highways or dams, such expenditures are *exhaustive* in nature; that is, they cause the using up of manpower and materials. Costs incurred in the farm program are of a very different kind and can be considered as *nonexhaustive* expenditures. Manpower and materials are not consumed; rather, such payments are similar to transfer payments—they channel income form one sector of the economy to another. The money, then, is respent by the farmer. As one economist has put it, the real cost of the farm program is the cost incurred by doing too little. Leon Keyserling states that:

> *instead of unreflective lamentation about "the terrible cost of the farm program," we should ponder the real economic and social costs of doing too little rather than too much under the farm program. . . . During the twelve-year period from the beginning of 1953 to the end of 1964, somewhere in the range of 100–150 billion dollars of the deficiency in total national production, or an annual average somewhere in the range of $8\frac{1}{3}$–$12\frac{1}{2}$ billion, was directly in consequence of inadequate farm income.*[6]

[6] Keyserling, *ibid.*, p. 118.

TABLE 9-1   Farm Outlays in the Federal Budget as a Percentage of Total Budget Outlays and as a Percentage of GNP.

| YEAR | Federal Budget Outlays | |
	AS % OF TOTAL BUDGET OUTLAYS	AS % OF GNP
1961	4.5	0.7
1962	5.0	0.8
1963	5.8	1.0
1964	5.7	0.9
1965	4.6	0.7

SOURCE: Adapted from data contained in Leon H. Keyserling, *Agriculture and the Public Interest*, Conference on Economic Progress, Washington, February 1965, p. 122.

Such a figure is, of course, far in excess of the actual outlay of federal funds over the same period.   Table 9-1 shows the data for federal budget outlays for agriculture, both as a percentage of total budget outlays and as a percentage of gross national product.   The actual adjusted dollar figure for *all* farm programs ranged only between $3.5 and $4.6 billion during the period 1961–1965.

A Suggested Program for Agriculture

We have already mentioned some of the plans which have been used in an attempt to better the lot of the American farmers.   Our conclusion was that these plans were not very effective.   A new approach is vitally needed.   Unfortunately, the farmers in the United States are not represented by a single group—they are highly factionalized. This division has, in part, been the reason why a more effective farm program has not been developed and passed upon by the Congress.

One major program for agriculture has been advanced, and it is worth noting as a possible beginning of a solution for the agricultural dilemma.   It is a plan suggested by the Committee for Economic Development, a private organization composed of 200 leading business-men and educators.[7]   The CED program has two major parts.   One is to attract excess resources from use in farm production.   The second is to cushion the process of adjusting the resources used in farm production.

To entice farmers off the farm, the CED suggests a four-point pro-gram.   First, it is essential to maintain a high level of employment opportunities in nonagricultural industries, so that job opportunities will await those leaving the farms.   Second, the CED notes that fewer farm youths graduate from high school, enter college, and graduate from college.   Hence, it is suggested that both formal and vocational education be stressed for the farm youth.   A third suggestion is to increase the mobility of the farm population through the provision of job information and retraining and by defraying the moving costs of those who leave the farms for industrial employment in the cities.   A gradual removal of government price supports on farm commodi-ties is the final suggestion for getting the farmer off the farm.   As we indicated earlier, the maintaining of price supports often induces the marginal farmer to remain on the farm.

Part two of the CED program—cushioning the process of adjusting the resources used in farm production—involves three steps.   First, the suggestion is made that technical assistance and income be pro-vided for the farmer for purposes of converting cropland to grass.   A temporary income-protection plan comprises the second step.   Pay-ments would continue to be made to farmers, on a declining basis, for a period of five years.   Finally, the CED suggests a temporary soil bank, to last not more than five years.   This soil bank, however, would be on a "whole-farm" basis.   Thus entire farms would be re-tired.

Summary of the Agricultural Problem

We have seen that the American farmer has failed to participate in the high level of prosperity enjoyed by most other economic groups in the United States.   He has remained poor in the midst of prosperity.

---

[7] The plan discussed here is contained in *An Adaptive Program for Agriculture, A Statement on National Policy*, Research and Policy Committee of the Committee for Economic Development, New York, November, 1963. The discussion here is greatly summarized.

One of the causes for low farm income is an underconsumption situation brought about by a changing labor/capital ratio. Another is that the farmer is faced with an inelastic supply function, so that he has little control in the matter of increasing or decreasing supply—at least in the short-run period. A third cause of the farmer's plight is that he is caught in a market squeeze, paying high prices for farm equipment but receiving relatively low prices for his output. A final contributing factor to low farm income was seen to be the very government programs which we designed to aid the farmer. Such programs have encouraged the "marginal" farmer to remain on the farm.

Four approaches to farm aid were examined, all of which were found to be largely inadequate to the task. Some programs are designed to increase the demand for farm products; others attempt to restrict agricultural supply. Outright cash subsidies have been suggested, and the government has engaged in the buying and storing of farm surpluses.

The costs of the farm programs to date have been small when compared with the total outlays of the federal budget and when compared with the GNP. The real cost of such programs has been the loss of total national production caused by an inefficient use of resources and low farm incomes.

Finally, the CED's suggested farm program was discussed. Basically, the program is designed to get excess farmers off the farms and to cushion the hardship of their move to the cities.

CHAPTER SUMMARY

Chapter 9 was concerned with three of the more pressing economic problems facing the United States: the problems of the cities, housing needs, and agricultural problems.

The urban problem has been aggravated by a rapid move of the nation's population from rural to urban areas—compounded by a move from the central city to the suburbs.

Problems have therefore arisen in the quality of public education, in juvenile delinquency and adult crime, in unemployment, and in rising welfare and other municipal costs. Regional planning was called for to improve transportation facilities, to eliminate slums, to handle sewerage problems, to provide adequate police and fire protection, and so forth. Coupled with these more tangible urban problems are the additional ones of air and water pollution and the general ugliness of our American cities.

Because the housing problem was considered to be a vital one, it was also examined in this chapter. Almost one-fifth of the nation's families were seen to live in deteriorating housing units. The major housing problems are high costs and short supply, substandard housing, a shortage of land for development, hardships imposed upon displaced persons, discrimination, a shortage of community facilities, and general ugliness of the communities. Specific remedies were suggested for the various problems.

Finally, the agricultural problem was exposed, with an emphasis on low farm income, the causes of farm poverty, past agricultural programs, and the costs of the farm program. A program for agriculture advanced by the Committee for Economic Development was also summarized.

The problems suggested in this chapter are but three of the serious areas where improvement is needed. Chapter 10 will discuss several others.

STUDY QUESTIONS

1. Urban, housing, and agricultural problems are social problems as well as economic ones. Discuss both the social and the economic ramifications of these problems. Can you list problems such as these which exist in your own city?
2. Discuss the solutions for the housing problem presented in this chapter. How effective do you think these proposed solutions would be? How likely is it that they could be enacted?
3. What, exactly, is the so-called "farm problem"? What are the causes of it? What attempts have we made to solve it? How effective have these attempts been?
4. Evaluate the "suggested program for agriculture" presented in this chapter.

IMPORTANT CONCEPTS IN CHAPTER 9

Migration from rural to urban areas
Migration from the central city to suburban areas
Cities' eroding tax base
Problems of the central city
Problems of the suburban areas
Regional planning
Role of the property tax in the cities
Role of economic base studies
Deficient housing
Specific housing problems and proposed solutions
Level of farm income
Causes of poverty on the farm
Inelasticity of supply of farm products
Labor/capital ratio
"Market squeeze" and the farmer
Soil bank
Government programs for agriculture
Costs of the farm programs
CED program for agriculture

APPENDIX THE URBAN CRISIS: A TEN-POINT PROGRAM *

1. One million public service jobs for persons now unempioyed or seriously under-employed. To provide this necessary means of helping people lift themselves out of poverty and deprivation, Congress must immediately adopt a $4 billion program to fund federal, state and local government agencies and non-profit organizations along the lines of the O'Hara bill. We consider the Clark bill a step in the right direction.

2. Two and a half million new housing units each year, including:

a. Public housing through new and rehabilitated low-rent homes for the 20 percent of city families whose incomes are below requirements for a minimum decent standard of living. New public housing construction, now at a 30,000-to-40,000 annual level, should be immediately increased to 200,000 to 300,000 for each of the next two years and 500,000 a year thereafter. Adequate appropriations for the rent supplement program are a necessity.

b. Housing for lower middle-income families not eligible for public housing and unable to afford decent dwellings in the standard, privately-financed housing market. Federally-subsidized interest rate loans and a federal subsidy for the partial abatement of local taxes on such properties are needed to increase construction of such housing by cooperatives, non-profit and limited dividend corporations. In addition, federal legislation should make it possible for such groups to acquire existing properties, with government insurance of long-term and low-interest loans.

c. Moderate-income housing, already operating with government-insured mortgages, stepped up through measures to increase involvement of pension funds, college endowment funds and private trusts.

d. Open housing, in suburbs as well as in cities, an essential part of a meaningful effort to rebuild our metropolitan areas.

e. Urban renewal no longer confined to commercial and expensive high-rise construction. The focus instead must be on homes in bal-

---

* *Employment and Manpower Problems in the Cities: Implications of the Report of the National Advisory Commission on Civil Disorders, Hearings before the Joint Economic Committee, Congress of the United States,* 90th Congress, 2d Sess., U.S. Government Printing Office, Washington, May–June, 1968, pp. 243–244. The AFL-CIO Executive Council adopted this statement at its quarterly session, Sept. 12, 1967, in New York City.

anced neighborhoods, with families displaced by slum clearance given assistance in finding decent dwellings at rents they can afford.

f. Model cities program, with adequate appropriations.

3. Mass transit, improved and expanded, is an urgent need in all metropolitan areas.

4. Accelerated construction of public facilities, such as water supplies, sewage systems, mass transit, schools, hospitals, day-care centers, playgrounds, libraries, museums, clean air and water, are essential to rebuild America's metropolitan areas. For this, we urge Congress to adopt at least a $2 billion a year grant-in-aid program to state and local governments in addition to categorical grants-in-aid.

5. A substantially expanded Neighborhood Youth Corps program to help youngsters remain in school and to provide work and training for those who have dropped out of school.

6. The opportunity for quality education can be met only by realizing the need to close the educational gap between the privileged and underprivileged schoolchildren of our nation, by special incentives to teachers in slum areas, federal subsidy of the More Effective School type program, full use of school buildings for job-training, adult education and community centers. In addition, vocational training must be realistically geared to the modern job market.

7. Manpower training must be linked with job placement and training allowances must be increased so that trainees can afford to remain in the program.

8. Public welfare assistance must be restructured, with the program based on need alone, a federal minimum standard of payments and adequate federal funds should be provided, state work-incentive programs should enable welfare recipients to retain a substantial amount of the dollars they earn without penalty, and demeaning investigations of applicants should be eliminated on the principle that comprehensive social services are a matter of right to those in need.

9. Relief of rural poverty, concentrated in the southern and southwestern states primarily, by federal legislation to provide farm workers with unemployment compensation and according to them the same right other workers have under the National Labor Relations Act to

organize unions and bargain collectively; by adequate federal funds to assist low and moderate-income rural families to buy or rehabilitate housing; continuation and strengthening of the Vocational Education Act of 1963 and the Education Act of 1965 in rural areas; federal aid in establishment of adequate public facilities, such as highways, hospitals, schools, vocational and technical training institutions; extension of the Agriculture Department recreational and tourist activities in rural areas; and provision of full and fair employment opportunities for Negroes, Mexican-Americans and other minorities to work in the industries of rural areas and in state and local governments.

10.   Economic planning, under federal leadership, and including each state and metropolitan area, should include the development, coordination and maintenance of an inventory of needs for housing, public facilities and services to facilitate application of the nation's resources to meet the needs of a rapidly growing urban population, while also providing a sound foundation for a continually increasing private economy.

America's urban crisis did not come upon this nation without warning. It has been coming for a long time and the government has not been alert to its responsibilities.

The program we have offered will not achieve success overnight.   By its very nature it is a step-by-step proposal for both immediate action and solid achievement.

America cannot wait any longer to get started and the federal government must supply the leadership and resources to the great national effort that is mandatory.

CHAPTER 10

SOLVING DOMESTIC ECONOMIC PROBLEMS: PART II

In Chapter 9, three important economic problems were examined: the urban crisis, housing problems, and the agricultural problem. This chapter will extend our examination of current domestic problems. Specifically, we will look at the problem of poverty and at guaranteed annual incomes as a possible solution. We will also assess the problem of inadequate medical care and its possible alleviation through the Medicare and Medicaid programs. Finally, we will see the extent to which inflation threatens our economy and will suggest measures to curb rising price levels.

POVERTY

Though poverty is all around us, we often fail to see it. The middle-income American does not, of course, spend much time in the midst of slums, and he is unfamiliar with the anguish of being really poor. Moreover, it is a strange characteristic of the middle- and upper-income groups that they are able to deny the existence of widespread poverty even when they are exposed to it. It is only within the past very few years that the American public at large has become aware of the poverty problem. Michael Harrington has referred to poverty as the "invisible land."

> Poverty is often off the beaten track. It always has been. The ordinary tourist never left the main highway, and today he rides interstate turnpikes. He does not go into the valleys of Pennsylvania where the towns look like movie sets of Wales in the Thirties.

He does not see the company houses in rows, the rutted roads (the poor always have bad roads whether they live in the city, in towns, or on farms), and everything is black and dirty. And even if he were to pass through such a place by accident, the tourist would not meet the unemployed men in the bar or the women coming home from a runaway sweatshop.[1]

That the poor exist, there can be no doubt. Questions we must ask are: Who are the poor? Just how poor are they? What are the effects of poverty? Can something be done to alleviate the problem?

It is estimated that the following distribution of income by families existed in 1966: [2]

INCOME CLASS	PERCENT OF FAMILIES IN CLASS	CUMULATIVE PERCENTAGE
Under $3,000	14.3	14.3
$3,000–$5,000	13.9	28.2
$5,000–$7,000	17.8	46.0
$7,000–$10,000	24.4	70.4
$10,000–$15,000	20.4	90.8
Over $15,000	9.2	100.0

Assuming these data to be reasonably accurate, we can see that 14.3 percent of the nation's families (an average family of four) earn less than $3,000 per year. (By way of comparison, the Bureau of Labor Statistics considers the poverty cutoff level to be $3,200 for a family of four.) And many of those earning under $3,000 do, in fact, earn considerably less than that.

The cumulative percentages indicate that almost one-third (28.2 percent) of the nation's families earn less than $5,000 each year. A good estimate is that nearly 1 out of every 5 families in the United States lives in poverty.

If families are divided into fifths, income is distributed among them as follows: [3]

---

[1] Michael Harrington, *The Other America,* Penguin Books, Inc., Baltimore, 1965, p. 11.
[2] Data adapted from Clair Wilcox, *Toward Social Welfare,* Richard D. Irwin, Inc., Homewood, Ill., 1969, p. 8.
[3] *Ibid.,* p. 9.

INCOME CLASS	PERCENT OF INCOME	CUMULATIVE PERCENTAGE
Lowest fifth	5.4	5.4
Second fifth	12.4	17.8
Third fifth	17.7	35.5
Fourth fifth	23.8	59.3
Highest fifth	40.7	100.0

Thus the poorest 20 percent of American families earn only 5.4 percent of the available income.   Moreover, the cumulative column indicates to us that the poorest 40 percent of the families receive under 18 percent of the nation's income.   Such figures give us a notion of the *distribution* of the nation's wealth.   Who reaps the benefits of our society?   Certainly not the bottom 40 percent of its families!   The top fifth of the families receive over 40 percent of the income—more than is received by the lowest 60 percent of the families.

But, we might ask, isn't the distribution of the nation's income becoming more equitable over the years?   Is the spread between the rich and the poor narrowing?   The answer to this question is both yes and no.   The data below show the pattern of income distribution for four periods: [4]

INCOME CLASS	PERCENT OF INCOME			
	1929	1944	1947	1966
Lowest fifth	3.5	4.9	5.0	5.4
Second fifth	9.0	10.9	11.8	12.4
Third fifth	13.8	16.2	17.0	17.7
Fourth fifth	19.3	22.2	23.1	23.8
Highest fifth	54.4	45.8	43.0	40.7

If we compare the distribution of income in 1929 with that existing in 1966, we would conclude that there has indeed been a narrowing of the gap between the rich and the poor.   In 1929, the bottom fifth of our families received only 3.5 percent of the nation's income, while the top fifth received considerably over half (54.4 percent).   By 1966, the lowest fifth was receiving 5.4 percent of the income and the

[4] *Ibid.*, pp. 14–15.

share of the top fifth had declined to 40.7 percent. This relative change in the share of income between 1929 and 1966 has led some economists to conclude that the pattern of income distribution is indeed changing.

However, in the postwar years, little difference in income distribution patterns can be noted. In the nineteen years between 1947 and 1966, the poorest families gained only an additional 0.4 percent of the nation's income (from 5.0 to 5.4). And the wealthiest families lost only 2.3 percent (from 43.0 to 40.7).

The conclusion? While the pattern of income distribution has changed somewhat over the thirty-seven-year span from 1929 to 1966, there has been very little change in the postwar period. The gap between the rich and the poor has remained about the same. Certainly there has been no marked redistribution of income downward. We should hasten to add at this point that the poor in the United States are not nearly as poor as those in many other countries around the world. But they are, nevertheless, poor. When we speak of America's poor, we are describing families living in dilapidated housing. They have virtually no clothing budget. They cannot *afford* a balanced diet. (How they spend what little income they have is another matter entirely.) They can afford no movies, books, or newspapers. And they are faced with inadequate medical and dental care. Thus we are talking not about *relative* poverty, but *absolute* poverty. The poor in the United States do not often lie in the streets in pain from hunger, but they are hungry. And they do starve quietly over a longer period of time.

Who Are the Poor?

The poor in the United States are composed of many divergent groups. *The young* make up part of the group—especially those who have dropped out of high school. Those with a *lower level of education* tend, on the average, to receive less income than those with more education. (It has been estimated that a college diploma adds $100,000 to the graduate's income over his lifetime.)

The *unemployed* also, of course, tend to be poorer since their source of income has terminated. Not only are the unemployed poor, but the *underpaid* are poor as well. Many occupations still are not covered under federal and state minimum-wage laws, and wages paid in some fields remain woefully low.

Minority groups also make up a disproportionate part of America's poor population, particularly the Negroes, Puerto Ricans, and American Indians. This is so even though the majority of the poor are white.

The poor tend to come from the *Southern sections* of the nation, though they are, of course, located to some degree in all parts of the country. And, as we have seen, those in *agriculture* tend to be poorer than their counterparts in the cities. *Female heads of the household* also account for part of our poor population. And, of course, the *ill and elderly* are poorer than the average citizen. A composite picture of the poorest American would be a young, unemployed, female Negro who dropped out of high school. She is the head of her household, is located on a Southern farm, and is in poor health. The society does not hold much promise for her!

Other Dimensions of Poverty

We all know that the major difference between the rich and the poor is that the rich have more money! But there are other aspects of poverty which may have eluded some of us. One such aspect is the *self-reinforcing nature of poverty.* The poor cannot afford the education necessary to lift themselves out of poverty. They cannot educate their children. Often the children of poor families must drop out of school to help support the family. Because of inadequate diet and a lack of proper medical care, the poor may become ill; and if they are sick, they cannot work. And, of course, the unemployed cannot earn the income necessary to lift themselves from poverty.

There are also *political inequities* associated with poverty. The poor are inadequately represented by pressure groups, which have much to do with the passage of legislation. Moreover, those in poverty do not receive equal treatment under the law. They are unable to secure adequate defense attorneys and are less knowledgeable about what is needed in the way of legal defense. (Virtually all of those who have been condemned to death by the courts for murder have been poor.) The list of political and social inequities facing the poor is a long one. We have touched upon only a few.

Other side effects of poverty include the fact that the poor are worse students in school (and often disruptive), they are more often involved in criminal activities, and they have (in many cases) given up any aspirations of ever improving their lot.

A final aspect of poverty which should be noted is that the poor constitute a *subculture* in our nation.   This subculture has recognizable characteristics.[5]   It is, in general, superstitious and poorly informed and feels alienated.   A member of it is willing to believe in the corruptness of leaders; he is self-oriented; and he holds the world (rather than himself) responsible for his plight.   He tends to be more direct in his expressions of aggression and is more content to "get by" rather than "get ahead."   He is conservative in the areas of civil liberties and foreign policy and, in general, is not really very interested in politics at all.   He is very much "anticommunist" but tends to be authoritarian in his own approach to authority.   He is prejudiced, intolerant, pragmatic, and anti-intellectual.

Poverty is one of the most pressing of this nation's problems.   Moreover, most of the governmental programs designed to alleviate the problem either have been largely ineffective or have aggravated the situation.   Federal, state, and local programs have taken three major forms.

There are programs which provide cash assistance to those *outside the labor force*.   These programs include Old Age, Survivors, and Disability Insurance; public assistance programs under the Social Security Act; pensions for needy veterans; and assistance, financed exclusively by states and localities, for needy persons not covered by the Social Security Act.

Other programs are designed to aid those who are *in the work force*. Such programs include training to develop skills for the poor so that their talents are more salable in the labor market, aid to economically depressed areas, unemployment insurance, minimum-wage protection, job creation, and work relief.

The third type of existing program provides goods and services to the poor *regardless of their labor-force status*.   Included in this group of

---

[5] For an excellent discussion of poverty as a subculture, see Frank Riessman, "A Portrait of the Underprivileged," in Robert E. Will and Harold G. Vatter (eds.), *Poverty in Affluence*, Harcourt, Brace & World, Inc., New York, 1965, pp. 74–77.

programs are child care, subsidized housing, medical services and drugs, and several forms of food distribution.

Jacob Hallander has said:

> *Like preventable disease, economic want persists as a social ill only because men do not desire sufficiently that it shall cease. There is still much mumbling of old commonplaces, and it has seemed worth-while to emphasize anew this definite corollary of modern political economy, that the essential causes of poverty are determinable and its considerable presence unnecessary.*[6]

We have made many attempts to help those in need, and new ones are being suggested almost daily. One plan in particular has been receiving a great deal of national attention—a plan to guarantee a minimum level of income for all families. Because the *guaranteed annual income* scheme is being seriously considered, we will turn our attention to the provisions of such a plan.

GUARANTEED ANNUAL INCOMES

The notion of guaranteeing incomes for American families is by no means a new concept or one that is alien to our beliefs and way of life. As we have pointed out, the U.S. government has been attempting to guarantee minimum floors on income at least since the 1930s. Public assistance and social security programs emanating from the New Deal era reflect such an attempt.

However, the public has, in a rather arbitrary sense, defined certain groups as being entitled to public assistance—groups which might be termed the *worthy poor* (the crippled, blind, elderly, etc.). For the able-bodied poor outside these carefully defined categories, only state and locally financed general assistance is available, and grants from this source currently average less than $30 per month per recipient on a scale that starts around $4 per person in Arkansas. Moreover, at least three states have no such program at all.

In addition, our present form of guaranteed income has a fundamental shortcoming in that it is based upon a composite of *wage-*

---

[6] A comment by Jacob Hallander, cited in *Poverty in Affluence, ibid.*, n. p.

related benefits and public assistance programs.   Because such benefits are wage-related, the *employed* poor are excluded, so that about 2 million families, with almost 6 million children, and an additional half-million unrelated individuals are fully employed but are still in poverty.[7]

Public assistance programs now bestow benefits on only about one-fourth of the poor families in this nation.   Further, it is estimated that fully 70 percent of these persons receiving public assistance continue to be poor despite the receipt of such assistance.[8]   It appears that what may be needed is a policy that will provide benefits in the form of income supplements for those who are employed as well as for those whose income-earning potential has been interrupted.

Evolution of the Guaranteed Annual Income Concept

Among many concepts of "justice" in the distribution of a nation's wealth, two stand out.   One, dating to Aristotle, is that the wealth of a nation should be distributed to its members in accordance with the contribution of those members to the generation of that wealth. The other is that the nation's wealth should be distributed according to individual need.   If a nation were to become a truly abundant society—so proficient in the production of goods and services that only a few men are needed to meet the needs of all—a system of justice based upon the first precept would become meaningless.

In the United States, more and more goods are being turned out by machines as business becomes increasingly automated.   Concomitant with this upsurge in productivity is an increase in unemployment, as an expanding number of workers become displaced by the automation-computerization process.   If this displacement continues (and many economists believe that it will), we can expect increasing pressure for the payment of a guaranteed minimum income.

We will need to create about 41 million jobs in the next ten years. Twenty-six million new workers will enter the labor force, and the remaining 15 million jobs will be needed to take care of those workers

---

[7] Martin Rein, "Poverty and Income," *The American Child*, vol. 48, no. 3, The National Committee on Employment of Youth, New York, Summer, 1966, p. 5.
[8] Robert J. Lampman, "Negative Rates Income Taxation," paper prepared for the Office of Economic Opportunity, August, 1965.

displaced by technology. To achieve 41 million jobs means that about 80,000 jobs will have to be created in every week of the next decade.[9] Even if this rapid growth rate in job availability should occur, it would do nothing to wipe out present unemployment or to aid the *employed* poor.

A shortage of jobs means, of course, a shortage of spending power. Thus it is conceivable that even the industrial and financial corporations that own and operate the more efficient equipment for a profit may support the notion of guaranteed annual incomes in order that people may receive (with or without work) sufficient purchasing power to buy the goods and services made possible by the machinery —and at prices sufficiently high to guarantee adequate corporate profits.

In order to deal with this problem of automation, President Lyndon Johnson appointed a National Commission on Technology, Automation and Economic Progress. This committee studied several aspects of the problem but was unanimous in its opinion that technological change was indeed creating surpluses of unskilled labor. The Commission therefore recommended that economic security be guaranteed by a floor under family income. To implement this floor, it suggested a negative income tax.

Whether our abundance, our automated production, and our studies will lead to a national consensus that can be converted into social legislation remains to be seen, but if such legislation in fact appears, it will most likely be in the form of a negative income tax designed to assure every American family a minimum level of living.

The Negative Income Tax

Should a negative income tax be applied universally, it would represent a radical departure from past welfare policies in that it would not distinguish between the able-bodied and the categorical poor. The income level guaranteed by the negative tax would most likely be geared toward the Bureau of Labor Statistics' $3,200 income for a family of four, a level generally considered to provide for minimum

---

[9] Walter P. Reuther, "First Things First," An Occasional Paper on the Free Society, Center for the Study of Democratic Institutions, 1964, p. 4.

health and decency.   Current plans of the Nixon Administration, however, call for a minimum income floor of only $1,600 for a family of
four.

A universal pension to achieve the $3,200 level could be attained by a 15
percent added tax on all personal income above $10,000 or by a 2
percent across-the-board increase on existing individual income taxes.[10]
Such a tax would provide for a total outlay to the economy of about
$30 billion (a figure slightly less than what we are currently spending
for all our public transfer programs).

Most economists concur with the $30 billion figure but indicate that
we could reduce one-half of the poverty gap for $5 billion.   Not only
would this $5 billion cost be small, the tax would have an additional
advantage of reducing the fiscal burden on state and local governments for public assistance programs.   (If such a negative income tax
had been used in 1964, the state-local savings would have totaled almost $1 billion.) [11]

A successful negative income tax would be characterized by three
primary ingredients: (1) it would provide universal coverage, for the
able-bodied as well as for the categorical poor; (2) it would attempt to
provide a break-even family income near the agreed-upon poverty
level (probably $3,200); and (3) it would provide for a reasonably
high incentive structure, in which the individual would always gain
from additional work.

As an example of the third condition, if a family of four earned $2,000
in a given year, the income tax form would be filed and the Internal
Revenue Service would write a check to the family for $1,200.   How-
ever, the family income earner would be allowed to keep, say, 50 percent of all additional income earned up to, perhaps, $6,000.   Under
this method, the wage earner would be encouraged to earn additional
income above the poverty level.

Problems of Implementing the Guaranteed Annual Income

From a purely economic point of view, we have the means now to
eliminate poverty without taking anything very important away from

---

[10] Martin Rein, *op. cit.*, p. 7.
[11] Garth L. Mangum, "Automation and a Guaranteed Income," *The American Child, op. cit.*,
    p. 19.

anybody.   The obstacles are not economic but political, sociological, ideological, etc.   Since it can amply be demonstrated that the cost of the guaranteed annual income program would be relatively small, objection to such a program is generally found in four other areas: (1) the question of incentive, (2) the "Protestant ethic," (3) traditional economics; and (4) the need for social differentiation.

The relationship between guaranteed incomes and economic incentive and motivation has come to be the abiding issue.   There exists a paucity of empirical evidence in this rather nebulous area, so that, in fact, little is known.   If a yearly income were guaranteed, some people would undoubtedly lose the incentive for work.   On the other hand, if the guaranteed level were kept at an amount just sufficient for minimum health and decency, it could be argued that most people would work harder, striving to rise above this minimum level.   There is some reason to believe that when wages fall below around $6,000 annually, people tend to double up on their jobs.   Thus it may be that the incentive question may not be as severe as some would assume.

In addition, it must be remembered that 70 percent of this nation's poor *are* employed but are still poor.   Too, the negative income tax could (as previously suggested) be geared to reward any incentive to raise family income above the $3,200 level.   The problem of a loss of incentive, and its concomitant loss of economic contribution, could largely be solved, it seems, through technical manipulations in the negative tax rates.

Perhaps the most serious stumbling block to the implementation of a plan guaranteeing incomes is the prevalence of the Protestant ethic, which equates the two concepts "work" and "goodness."   The guaranteed income would, of course, be received by those who do not work as well as by those who do work.   Payment for nonwork does not appear to be within the moral-ethical framework of the American mind, which assumes that those who work are good while those who do not work are bad.   Thus it would be necessary for the American public to divorce the notions of contribution and reward.

A further stumbling block is that economic theory as taught in the school systems and as practiced in our acquisitive society is based upon a fundamental notion of "relative scarcity."   It is assumed that man creates desires more rapidly than the system can satiate those desires with its relatively scarce resources.   Put another way, we are constantly striving to distribute our resources in such a way as to meet an ever-expanding demand for goods and services.

But what of the society which has reached abundance?   Clearly, an affluent society is a threat to the notion of relative scarcity.   The basic goal of an economic system has often been described as one of providing the most goods and services for the largest number of people. Yet in the United States there appears to have developed some confusion in this area.   We have become more concerned with acquisition than with distribution.   Our resources have become relatively abundant rather than relatively scarce.

What is indicated is that the establishment of a guaranteed income would be in large part dependent upon a shift in values, so that we become less concerned with production and more concerned with what happens to us *on the way* to achievement.

Lastly, it has been said that we are a nation of scorekeepers, dependent upon systems that render some kind of numerical measure of individual worth.   Perhaps the most significant measuring device we now depend upon is the income differential.   Success is wealth.   The more money an individual possesses, the more successful he is deemed in the eyes of his contemporaries.   It is understandable that such a system has developed since income is easy to measure.   If the guaranteed annual income were to pave the way to a situation in which the income differential were less significant, it would be necessary to establish the *moral equivalent* to the income differential.

If achieved, the guaranteed annual income would not provide us with an economic panacea.   The guarantee of income cannot guarantee anything else the society may desire.   It can guarantee income only. The appropriate use of such income is another matter.   A minimum floor on family income could, however, lead the way to rising aspirations among the poor and could draw attention to an array of contributive possibilities overlooked in our conventional drive to attain material wealth.

MEDICARE

Another of the problems facing the U.S. economy is that of providing adequate medical care for its citizens.   In the past, such care has been largely provided on the basis of ability to pay. Those who could afford the necessary care received adequate treatment. Those who could not afford it received no treatment at all or were poorly treated in overcrowded public clinics.

In recent years, however, we have begun to feel that adequate medical care should be within the reach of all Americans. In virtually every advanced nation except the United States, governments have recognized their responsibilities in this area for years. Lately, two important breakthroughs have come about in this country—the programs known as *Medicare* and *Medicaid*.

The Medicare program, which went into effect in 1965, is designed to provide medical aid for the aged. It was felt that their problems were particularly pressing since they tend to be ill more often than the young and since this illness occurs at a time when their earning capacity is seriously reduced.

Medicare is a compulsory hospital insurance program which covers all persons over sixty-five years of age who are covered by the Old Age, Survivors, and Disability Insurance program under the Social Security Act, plus an additional 2 million persons not covered by OASDI.

The Medicare program pays for the following care: (1) all services rendered during sixty days in a hospital except for the first $40 and all but $10 per day for another thirty days; (2) all services subsequently rendered during twenty days in a nursing home and all but $5 per day for another eighty days; (3) up to 100 health visits by nurses in the year following release from a hospital or nursing home; and (4) four-fifths of the cost of outpatient diagnostic tests.

There is also a voluntary program of medical insurance under Medicare. Should a person elect this coverage, it would pay 80 percent of the charges for the following services after the first $50 in each year: (1) physicians' and surgeons' services; (2) up to 100 home health visits by nurses in a year not following hospitalization; (3) half of the costs of mental illness up to $250 per year; and (4) several other items such as medical appliances and ambulance services. This insurance costs the participant $3 per month, and the government also pays $3. It is estimated that two-fifths of an aged person's medical costs would be covered if he elects both parts of the Medicare program.

The effects of the Medicare program are expected to be several. One, of course, is better medical care for the nation's elderly population. But the program will also affect the nature of hospitals themselves. According to the Brookings Institution,[12] the hospital of the future will become a community health center, with widely expanded services, providing the full spectrum of care from early prevention to rehabilitation and long-term care. The size of the average hospital is expected to grow, though the construction of new ones will slow down. Importantly, with the growing influence of Medicare and Medicaid, it is expected that traditional ward service and free clinical services will virtually disappear.

The Future of Medicare

A great deal of controversy is currently raging over the method of payment to doctors, hospitals, and others under the Medicare program. Fees are virtually guaranteed, so that the question of cost control arises. Physicians' fees are currently unregulated, and as a matter of fact, the income of physicians has risen markedly since the implementation of the Medicare program. Thus it is likely that some form of control over costs will be necessary in the future.

In addition, the Medicare program involves the maximum participation of federal, state, and private organizations under coordinated responsibility. If the program is to prove successful in the long run, the states will have to improve their capacity to carry their share of the financial burden.

Generally, it is expected that the Medicare program will grow significantly, both in scope and in coverage, and that its benefits will be extended to certain groups in the under-sixty-five age bracket.

The Medicaid Program

Prior to the passage of the Medicare program, there was much debate regarding whether medical care should be provided to all potential recipients on the basis of age and need or whether it should be provided on the basis of a "needs" test (for the poor) regardless of age.

Title XIX of Public Law 89-97 incorporates the "needs" test. The

---

[12] "The Future of Medicare and the American Hospital," Brookings Research Report 72, The Brookings Institution, Washington, 1967.

popular name for Title XIX is *Medicaid.* It is expected that all states will have such programs soon and that comprehensive services will be available to all who cannot afford to pay for them. The state average for the maximum allowable income of an average family eligible to receive full medical benefits is $3,514.[13]

If the Medicaid program should prove more beneficial to low-income younger people than does the Medicare program for the older group, interest conceivably could turn away from Medicare to the development of a more extensive Medicaid program.

INFLATION

A final economic problem for discussion in the current chapter is the thorny one of inflation, one of our major unresolved economic problems. Prices in the United States have continuously been rising, largely (but not entirely) because of war and its aftermath.

Economists have been seeking an adequate definition of inflation for several decades, without complete satisfaction. We will use the term here to mean simply a rise of price levels *in general.* We must emphasize the words "in general" because in a free economy such as ours, some prices will rise (and others fall) because of short-run changes in supply and demand.

Since 1939, the prices paid for consumer items have more than doubled, so that the dollar today buys only half as much as it did then. However, we must also be concerned with how many dollars the consumer has. Obviously, if his dollar buys only half as much but if he has four times as many dollars, he is still better off. His *real income* has risen. And, as a matter of fact, real income, *on the average,* has continued to rise significantly in the United States.

The primary reason we worry about inflation is not that rising price levels erode purchasing power in general. That has not happened. The real problem lies in the fact that not *all* real incomes rise along with increases in the price level. Inflation imposes a heavy burden on those having a relatively fixed money income. Moreover, this is

[13] *Ibid.*, p. 9.

no small proportion of the American population. It includes pensioners, holders of life insurance policies, investors in government and other bonds, government employees, school teachers, and others. Thus inflation places a heavy tax on those with fixed incomes, who often are the least able to pay.

The Causes of Inflation

We looked at the theoretical causes of inflation in Chapter 4. But it will be to our advantage to examine these causes a bit more closely at this point. The basic causes of inflation are (1) demand in excess of supply and (2) wage and profit policies. These two causes are sometimes referred to as *demand-pull* inflation and *cost-push* inflation.

There are several aspects of demand-pull inflation that deserve our attention. Demand comes from three basic areas: government, business, and the consumer. In the postwar period between 1947 and 1957, the dollar value of purchases by these three sectors of the economy rose 87 percent, or almost 6½ percent per year on the average. Government purchases of goods and services rose 203 percent, while private expenditures (business and consumers) rose 71 percent. This tremendous increase in demand arose in part due to the requirements for national security during this "cold war" period. Private spending increased rapidly largely due to a backlog of desires which could not be satisfied during the war period ("pent-up demand").

Overall, the increase in demand between 1947 and 1957 outstripped the increase in output—with the result that there was an upward pressure on prices. Total production (supply) rose by about 3.7 percent per year, while spending (demand) increased by about 6.4 percent. Obviously, prices had to rise.

There is also an *accumulative* process associated with increased demand. As spending increases, people earn more in money terms. And as people earn more in money terms, they tend to spend more. Thus a rise in expenditures tends to cause a further rise in expenditures.

Less is known about the cost-push side of inflation—more empirical research is needed to determine the significance of price and wage policies as causal factors in the inflationary process. However, the process can be explained.

If labor unions are able to secure wage increases in excess of increases in productivity, this tends to cause inflation. Or if businesses raise prices in excess of their increase in costs, this tends to cause inflation. Very often these two phenomena tend to work hand in hand. Suppose, for example, that a labor union secures higher wages, costing a company $500,000 in its total wage bill. Next, the company raises prices to the consumer on the basis of increased costs. But, very often, the increase in price is *more* than would be necessary to cover the increased costs. As prices rise, the labor unions again press for increased wages to "meet the higher cost of living." Thus we find ourselves in a *spiraling process* of inflation, where increased costs boost prices, which in turn leads to increased costs. Of course, the spiral process can begin either with an increase in wages (or other costs) or with an increase in prices. The results are the same—higher price levels for the consumer. It is also of importance to note that while wages and prices are flexible on the upward side, the reverse is not true. The failure of prices to fall when demand slackens is due to the fact that wages are "sticky" on the downward side and also to the fact that businessmen are reluctant to reduce prices. This tendency toward wages being "administered" by unions and prices being administered by the business community has accelerated in the postwar years.

Not only does the inflationary process hurt those whose salary rates are adjusted infrequently and those on fixed incomes (pensions, etc.), it also has the effect of reducing the flow of people into many occupations that are vital to society (for example, school teachers).

How to Stop Inflation

In the final analysis, inflation must be curbed through the use of appropriate monetary and fiscal measures. Several specific steps will be suggested here, along with certain policies we should not pursue.[14]

To begin with, monetary policy should not be relied upon too heavily, to the exclusion of fiscal measures. As of early 1969, excessive reliance on monetary measures had boosted interest rates to an all-time high.

---

[14] For more specific proposals to curb inflation, see *Defense against Inflation*, A Statement on National Policy, Research and Policy Committee of the Committee for Economic Development, Washington, May, 1958; and Alvin H. Hansen, *Economic Issues of the 1960's*, McGraw-Hill Book Company, New York, 1960, pp. 31–39.

An appropriate monetary-fiscal policy mix might have avoided these excessively high interest rates.

A second thing we should not do is use the threat of inflation as an excuse for ignoring other necessary domestic and foreign expenditures. Once needed governmental expenditures are decided upon, the tax rate should be altered to provide the necessary revenue on a noninflationary basis.

To the extent that monopolistic power is used to charge excessively high prices or prevent sufficient price competition, effective antitrust action should be taken. At the same time, it would be hoped that both business and labor would exercise voluntary restraints to hold the line on prices.

Alvin Hansen suggests six additional steps to curb inflation: [15]

1. DIRECT CONTROLS The Federal Reserve System is empowered by law to exercise specific and direct controls over real estate purchases and consumer credit arrangements. Such control has been used in the past only in cases of national emergency. However, such control may now be necessary to curb the long-run inflationary trend.

2. AUTOMATIC TAX-RATE ADJUSTMENT Presidents Kennedy and Johnson both asked the Congress to establish an automatic process of tax-rate adjustment, but both were refused. Such an adjustment could be based on agreed-upon indexes of employment, degree of capacity plant utilization, industrial production, and rates of investment. As these measures moved to indicate an impending inflation, taxes would automatically rise. (And, of course, if the indexes indicated recession, taxes would fall.) The advantage of an automatic adjustment in the tax rate is that it would go into effect quickly, to help curb inflation before it became acute.

3. COUNTERCYCLICAL ACCELERATED DEPRECIATION The Internal Revenue Service allows American businesses in some instances to rapidly write off the value of plant and equipment. Such accelerated depreciation is designed to provide a tax advantage for business and thereby stimulate additional investment. But we do not administer this policy

[15] Hansen, *ibid.*

in a countercyclical manner.   Such a program could take the shape of deferred depreciation allowances or, perhaps, the complete denial of such allowances in periods of inflation.

4.   AN ANTI-INFLATIONARY TAX ON INVESTMENT   During periods of rising prices, a tax could be imposed on new investment.   Such a tax would be designed to discourage the unneeded investment (a significant part of the excessive demand).

5.   CONTROL OF ADVERTISING EXPENDITURES   American businesses tend, naturally, to expand their advertising expenditures during boom periods when prices (and profits) are on the upswing and to reduce such expenditures during slack periods.   Yet just the reverse is called for from the point of view of national interest.   If advertising expenditures were to be treated as a countercyclical allowable business expense, they could be encouraged during slack periods and discouraged during boom periods.

6.   THE GOVERNMENT AND COLLECTIVE BARGAINING   In the case of wage-push and administered-price inflation, the public interest might be represented by the government in collective-bargaining procedures. Certainly, the public has a vital interest in such agreements in an economy as interrelated as ours.

The Committee for Economic Development has suggested that:

> *The answer to the problem of long-run inflation calls . . . for but one sacrifice: the sacrifice of the illusion that we can get more out of the economy than we produce.*
>
> *The benefit of winning the fight against inflation is well worth the learning of this simple lesson, for the reward is a society able to spread the products of its economic growth ever more widely in the form of a rising standard of living, for all, in freedom.*[16]

Summary of the Problem of Inflation

Inflation was seen to have two major causes: an excess of demand over supply and wage and price administration.   The U.S. economy has

---

[16] *Defense against Inflation, op. cit.,* p. 64.

been faced with steadily rising prices—partly, but not entirely, due to expanded government expenditures for national defense. Business investment and consumer demand have also contributed to the "demand-pull" side of inflation.

The process of inflation, we saw, hits hardest those on fixed incomes and those whose salaries are adjusted upward too slowly. While *real income* (adjusted for price increases) has risen for the economy as a whole, these particular groups have been unable to participate fully in the rising level of affluence.

Several steps were suggested to curb the inflationary process, including the use of a proper mix between monetary and fiscal measures, the curbing of monopoly power, direct controls over real estate purchases and consumer credit, automatic tax-rate adjustment, countercyclical accelerated depreciation, an anti-inflationary tax on investment, control of advertising expenditures, and the use of government to represent the public in collective-bargaining procedures.

CHAPTER SUMMARY

Chapter 10 was a continuation of the study of some of the economic problems facing this nation. One of the most pressing of these was seen to be poverty. We found that a significant proportion of America's families live in poverty and that the distribution of the nation's income has not changed much since the end of World War II.

While the composition of the poor group in the United States is quite mixed, we did find that the poor tend to be young, less educated, unemployed or underpaid, a member of a minority group, from the South, involved in agricultural production, a female head of the household, or ill and elderly. We found, too, that poverty is self-reinforcing and that it involves political and social inequities as well as economic ones.

The guaranteed annual income (GAI) plan was presented as one partial solution to the poverty problem. The GAI would be set at about $3,200 for a family of four. It would be implemented through a negative income tax and would apply to the employed as well as to the unemployed. Certain problems were seen to exist regarding the implementation of a GAI plan. Among these were the provision of incentive, the Protestant ethic, traditional economic theory, and the need for social differentiation.

Medicare and Medicaid were also examined as techniques for aiding in the field of medical care.   Medicare went into effect in 1965 under the provisions of the Social Security Act.   It provides hospital care for the elderly, and it also provides for voluntary participation in an insurance program to cover physicians' fees and other services.   The future of the Medicare program in part depends upon the control of the costs of administering it and in part upon the close coordination of federal, state, and private organizations.

Medicaid, a program of medical protection based on need, was seen to be growing also; moreover, it was suggested that it is at least conceivable that this program could surpass that of Medicare in the future.

Inflation was the final problem touched upon.   Both "cost-push" and "demand-pull" aspects of inflation were discussed, and several specific controls were suggested.   Inflation hits hardest those living on fixed incomes and must be controlled if economic equity is to exist.

STUDY QUESTIONS
1. How extensive is the poverty problem in the United States?   Why do you suppose this problem exists in a nation as wealthy as ours?
2. Who are the poor in the United States?
3. Evaluate the notion of guaranteed annual incomes as a proposed solution to poverty.   What are some of the problems of implementing such a program?   Do you agree or disagree with such a program?   Why or why not?
4. What has Medicare done to lessen the problems of the sick?   What is the probable future for this program?
5. Inflation is one of the most serious problems facing this nation today.   What, exactly, is inflation?   What are the causes of it?   How can it be cured—or can it?

IMPORTANT CONCEPTS IN CHAPTER 10
Definition of poverty
Distribution of income

Trends in distribution of income
Reasons for poverty
Self-reinforcing nature of poverty
Political and social inequities of poverty
Poverty as a subculture
Guaranteed annual incomes
Automation and poverty
The negative income tax
Problems of implementing the guaranteed annual income: incentive, the Protestant ethic, traditional economics, and the need for social differentiation
Provisions of Medicare
Provisions of Medicaid
Definition of inflation
Causes of inflation
Real versus money income
Demand-pull inflation
Cost-push inflation
Accumulative process of inflation
Wage-profit inflationary spiral
Steps to curb inflation
Automatic tax-rate adjustment
Countercyclical accelerated depreciation
Anti-inflationary tax on investment
Control of advertising expenditures
Government and collective bargaining

PART 3

INTERNATIONAL ECONOMIC PROBLEMS

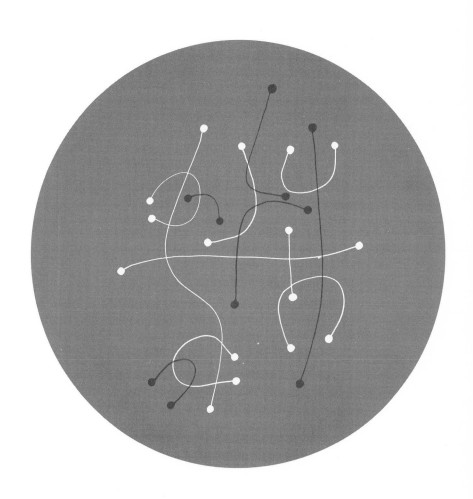

CHAPTER 11

INTERNATIONAL TRADE

With the rapid increase in technological development, the world is becoming a much "smaller" place. The lives of all the world's people are becoming increasingly intermingled. One significant aspect of this increasing reliance on each other is the rapid growth in international trade.

In 1967 alone, the United States exported to other nations about $30.5 billion in merchandise and imported about $27.0 billion. And there has been a more than 100 percent increase in the volume of both exports and imports just since 1951. Figure 11-1 traces the volume of international trade for the United States between 1951 and 1967.

With such a rapid increase in international transactions, and because international trade is such an important part of our economic activity, we would do well to understand at least the rudiments of the theory and practice of international trade. Thus, in this chapter, we will look at several of the more significant aspects of trade, including the idea of "comparative advantage," the accounting technique used in international transactions, economic integration, international trade organizations and agreements, and some recent international developments.

THE NOTION OF COMPARATIVE ADVANTAGE

Prior to the early 1800s, it was felt by most economists, philosophers, and politicians that one nation could gain in international trade only

Figure 11-1   U.S. Balance on Merchandise Trade (Excluding Military Grants)

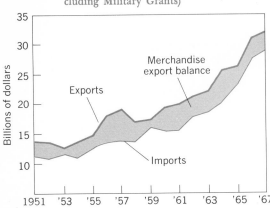

SOURCE: The First National Bank of Chicago, *Gold and the Balance of Payments,* 4th ed., Chicago, July, 1968, p. 5.

at the expense of the other nations with whom they traded.   Thus, if England were to trade with France, for example, one country would gain from the transaction and the other country would lose.

We now realize that all countries can *gain* by trade and that there need be no losers at all!   We owe a debt of gratitude for this knowledge to David Ricardo, who first advanced the notion of the "law of comparative advantage" in 1817.

This law can perhaps be clarified by an example.   Suppose that you are a brain surgeon who is also the best barber in town.   Obviously, you would be much better off to spend your time on surgery and to let someone else do the barbering.   You have a *comparative advantage* in brain surgery, and the barber has a *comparative advantage* in cutting hair—even though you have an absolute advantage in both (you are better at both trades).

These same principles of absolute and comparative advantage apply in international trade.   If the United States can produce both steel and fabrics cheaper than, say, England, it will still be to the advantage of the United States to produce that commodity in which it has a comparative advantage and to let England produce the other commodity. The United States will have a comparative advantage in only one commodity, and England will have a comparative advantage in the other —even though the United States has an absolute advantage in both commodities.

A simple two-commodity–two-country example of absolute and comparative advantage is given in Figure 11-2. It can be seen in this figure that the United States can produce twenty units of product A *or* ten units of product B using one hour of labor. In England, one hour of labor will produce only ten units of product A *or* eight units of product B. Thus the United States has an absolute advantage in the production of both products (twenty units of A to ten for England and ten units of B to eight for England). Yet we will see that the United States has a *comparative* advantage in the production of A and that England has a *comparative* advantage in the production of B.

The United States could get only ten units of B at home for twenty units of A (since they are both equal in terms of labor required for production). But if the United States were to export the twenty units of A, England would provide in exchange sixteen units of B (in a ratio of 10:8). Thus the United States would benefit by exporting product A and importing product B.

England, on the other hand, could get only ten units of A at home in exchange for eight units of B (since they are both equal in terms of labor required for production in England). But if England sends eight units of B to the United States, she will receive sixteen units of A (in a ratio of 20:10). Thus England would be better off to export product B and to import product A.

In this example, the United States has a comparative advantage in

Figure 11-2 Units of Products A and B Produced by the United States and England, Using One Hour's Labor

	U.S.	England
Product A	20	10
Product B	10	8

product A and should, therefore, concentrate her production on that commodity. England has a comparative advantage in product B and should concentrate her productive effort on that commodity.

The notion of comparative advantage depends upon the *ratio* which exists between the two products for each country:

For product A:

The American ratio is: $\dfrac{20 \text{ units of A}}{10 \text{ units of B}}$

The English ratio is: $\dfrac{10 \text{ units of A}}{8 \text{ units of B}}$

Since 20/10 is larger than 10/8, we know that the United States has a comparative advantage in the production of product A.

For product B:

The American ratio is: $\dfrac{10 \text{ units of B}}{20 \text{ units of A}}$

The English ratio is: $\dfrac{8 \text{ units of B}}{10 \text{ units of A}}$

Since 8/10 is larger than 10/20, we know that England has a comparative advantage in the production of product B.

We will shortly see that the problem is not quite this simple (in our discussion of trade barriers, tariffs, etc.); but based upon this simplified analysis, the United States should produce only that commodity in which it has a comparative advantage (product A)—leaving England to produce product B, in which she has a comparative advantage. And both nations benefit. The United States and England each receive *more of both commodities* than they would in the absence of trading. This simplified analysis lays the basis for the mutual desirability of international trade. We can now turn our attention to an examination of the extent and type of trade in the United States and to our method of accounting in trade transactions.

THE U.S. BALANCE OF PAYMENTS

By "balance of international payments" we mean the bookkeeping procedure that records all the international transactions of a nation during the year.   The balance-of-payments statement shows both receipts from abroad and expenditures abroad.   If the outlay of a nation exceeds its receipts, the nation incurs what is called a *balance-of-payments deficit.*   (The United States has had such a deficit every year since 1950, with the exception of 1957.)

Table 11-1 shows the U.S. balance of payments for the year 1967.   The statement is divided into three major categories: the current account, the capital account, and balancing items.   We will discuss each of these in turn.

The Current Account

The current account in the balance-of-payments statement shows the difference between our total dollar exports of goods and services and our total imports of goods and services.   An exportation of goods by the United States leads to money coming into our hands from foreigners.   Hence, exports are shown on the statement as a credit (+), indicating a receipt of money from foreigners.

In 1967, the United States exported $30.5 billion of merchandise.   In that same year, we imported $27.0 billion.   Thus foreigners paid us $30.5 billion for goods we exported, but we paid $27.0 billion for goods we imported.   The balance on merchandise trade is therefore a $3.5 billion credit—that is, we sold $3.5 billion more to foreigners than they sold to us.   (Lines 1, 2, and 3 of Table 11-1 show this information.)

Line 4 shows that we also fared well in the selling of services to foreigners and in the receipt of investment income from abroad.   All told, the United States gained $4.4 billion from these transactions.   Our net military expenditures are shown in line 5 to be $3.1 billion.   This figure is a debit, of course, since it represents money flowing into the hands of foreigners.

If we add lines 3 to 5, we obtain the "balance on goods and services" (line 6).   This figure in 1967 shows that the United States received $4.8 billion more from foreigners than it spent for goods and services.   If we adjust this figure with line 7 (private remittances to foreigners), we end up with the "balance on current account," line 8.   This figure is also known as the "balance of trade."   It shows us that we gained a net of $3.5 billion as a result of our trade of goods and services with all other nations.

TABLE 11-1   U.S. Balance of Payments, 1967 ($ Billions)
Credits (+); Debits (−)

Current Account:	
(1) Merchandise exports	+30.5
(2) Merchandise imports	−27.0
(3) Balance on merchandise trade	+ 3.5
(4) Service and investment income (net)	+ 4.4
(5) Military expenditures (net)	− 3.1
(6) Balance on goods and services	+ 4.8
(7) Pensions and private remittances	− 1.3
(8) Balance on Current Account	+ 3.5
Capital Account:	
Private:	
(9) U.S. long-term investment	− 4.3
(10) U.S. short-term investment	− 1.2
(11) Foreign long-term investment	+ 3.2
Government:	
(12) Grants and capital outflows less repayments on U.S. loans	− 4.2
(13) Balance on Capital Account	− 6.5
(14) Errors and Omissions	− 0.6
(15) Overall Balance of Payments	− 3.6
[Surplus (+) or deficit (−)]	
Balancing Items:	
(16) Gold outflow (+) or inflow (−)	+ 1.2
(17) Convertible foreign-exchange sales (+) or purchases (−)	− 1.0
(18) Foreign liquid dollar holdings increase (+) or decrease (−)	+ 3.4
(19) Total	+ 3.6

SOURCE: The First National Bank of Chicago, *Gold and the Balance of Payments*, 4th ed., Chicago, July, 1968, pp. 2–3.

The Capital Account

While the current account shows the flow of goods and services among nations, the capital account shows the investments and long- and short-term loans of private individuals, businesses, and government to foreign countries and their loans and investments in the United States. The capital account is divided into the private sector and the government sector.

Lines 9 to 11 show that private investment abroad amounted to $5.5

billion (\$4.3 + \$1.2 = \$5.5).   However, foreigners invested \$3.2 billion in the United States.   It is in the government sector (line 12) that we find a large capital outflow from the United States.   Government grants and capital outflows (less foreigners' repayments of loans) amounted in 1967 to \$4.2 billion.

If we sum all items in the capital account (lines 9 to 12), we find that the "balance on capital account" (line 13) shows that private and government investments and grants resulted in a \$6.5 billion outflow from the American economy.

Line 14 represents an attempt to compensate for errors and omissions in the accounting procedure.   Basically, the overall balance of payments for the United States (line 15) is the difference between the balance on current account and the balance on capital account (lines 8 and 13).   With errors and omissions considered, this balance is adjusted to −\$3.6 billion (a deficit).   (+\$3.5 billion − \$6.5 billion − \$0.6 billion = −\$3.6 billion.)

Balancing Items

The \$3.6 billion deficit in the U.S. balance of payments must somehow be financed.   That is, if we run a deficit, the money represented by that deficit must be in the hands of foreigners.   The balancing items (lines 16 to 18) show how we paid for our deficit in 1967.

Part of the deficit was financed by an outflow of gold from the United States.   Line 16 shows that we lost \$1.2 billion in gold to foreign countries.   The remainder of the deficit was financed by our purchase of convertible foreign-exchange sales (line 17) and by an outflow of American dollars (line 18).   The total of the balancing items is shown on line 19 to be \$3.6 billion, which, of course, is exactly equal to the \$3.6 billion deficit in our overall balance of payments (line 15).

In summary, then, the United States in 1967 gained \$3.5 billion by buying and selling merchandise and services to and from foreigners (balance on current account).   But the United States lost \$6.5 billion through private investment and government spending abroad (balance on capital account).   Thus we ended up with a \$3.6 billion deficit in our overall balance of payments.   This deficit was financed largely by an outflow of gold and dollars (balancing items).

ECONOMIC INTEGRATION

In view of our previous discussion on comparative advantage, it would appear that every nation would be in favor of absolutely free trade (that is, no tariffs or other trade barriers), and would concentrate on the production of that commodity in which they had a comparative advantage.   As we mentioned before, however, the case is not this simple. Barriers to trade do exist—and some with good reason.   On the other hand, there are also moves afoot to bring about freer trade.   We will first have a look at the nature of tariffs.   Then we will look at the existing attempts at economic integration.

Tariffs versus Free Trade

A tariff is nothing more than a tax on imported goods.   If you purchase a Volkswagen (produced in Germany), not only will you pay the price of the automobile plus shipping costs, you will also pay a tariff.

Why are tariffs imposed?   Certainly not as a revenue-producing measure, for if the tariff gets high enough, no foreign goods will come into the country and hence no revenue will be generated.

Many advocates of tariffs argue that they must be imposed to *prevent an outflow of money.*   This argument, however, is fallacious.   We have already seen that free trade is advantageous to all nations involved. Moreover, if we refuse to buy foreign goods (e.g., Volkswagens), then foreigners will have neither the money nor the desire to buy our goods (e.g., Chevrolets).

Another partially erroneous argument often advanced in favor of tariffs is that they will *prevent competition from cheap foreign labor.*   It is true, for example, that the Japanese can build ships more cheaply than can the United States (and part of the reason is a lower labor cost in Japan).   Tariff advocates argue, then, that if we do not put a tariff on Japanese ships, our shipbuilding industry will be unable to compete and our shipbuilders will be out of a job.   There is some truth in this argument.

Certainly we would not be able to compete with the Japanese shipbuilding industry.   And workers here would have to leave their jobs and find others (a sometimes painful transition).   On the other hand, the nation as a whole would probably be better off to let the Japanese build ships (since they have a comparative advantage) and to use our workers to produce something in which we have a comparative advantage.   Then both countries would be better off.[1]

A third argument given on behalf of tariffs is called the *infant-industry argument*.   According to this argument, tariffs should be imposed only long enough to allow a newly developing industry to grow and mature to the point where it would be able to compete with similar foreign industries.   Then the tariff would be removed.   (In the age of huge corporations, there are not many examples of infant industries in the United States.)

Perhaps the most valid argument in favor of tariffs is found in the notion of *diversification*.   The United States has such a tremendous comparative advantage in the production of most agricultural products that if total free trade were allowed, we would produce only those products.   Needless to say, we would not want to find ourselves in the position of producing only agricultural goods and buying everything else from foreigners.   (It would be difficult to fight a war with only wheat!)   Thus tariffs are imposed to allow for some desired and necessary diversification in industrial production.

While there are some valid economic arguments for imposing tariffs, it is a fact of life that most of the tariffs in the United States are imposed not for economic reasons but because of *vested interests*.   There is a tariff on steel importation not necessarily because it is the economically sound thing to do but because our domestic steel companies know that they will make more profits if they do not have to compete with foreign steel producers.   Thus the steel industry will lobby for tariffs on steel imports.   The same is true, of course, for the automobile producers, sugar producers, and virtually all other large industries.

The European Economic Community

We mentioned earlier that there have been some recent attempts to bring about freer trade.   The most notable of these attempts is the European Economic Community (the "Common Market").

---

[1] An exception to this argument should be noted.   If the United States feels, for example, that she should maintain her shipbuilding industry for purposes of, say, national defense, then tariffs will help accomplish this purpose.   We will, of course, pay more for ships, but we may be quite willing to pay this additional cost in order to provide for national security.

The Common Market began in 1957. Its membership includes Belgium, France, Italy, Luxembourg, The Netherlands, and West Germany. Recognizing the advantages of freer trade, these nations joined together for the common purposes of trading within the community of nations and of trading as a block with other nations not in the Common Market.

Each nation in the Economic Community has agreed to eliminate tariffs and import quotas on nonfarm goods produced within the area. The nations are also to establish a common tariff against goods coming from outside the Common Market. Finally, these nations have agreed to allow within the areas free trade of both capital and labor. All these goals are to be accomplished by 1970–1973.

The European Common Market has been highly successful and has even led to a substantial group of Europeans who wish to move from this trading arrangement to a "United States of Europe." The Common Market will most likely become the world's second-largest free-trade area (following the United States), and it could perhaps become the world's largest free-trade area if England were allowed to enter. (At this writing, France opposes England's entry because of a fear of domination by England and the United States.)

The European Free Trade Association (EFTA)

Spurred both by the success of the Common Market and by fear of the economic strength of the Common Market, the European Free Trade Association was formed. This group is commonly referred to as the "Outer Seven" and is composed of Austria, Denmark, Norway, Portugal, Sweden, Switzerland, and the United Kingdom.

While the Outer Seven has been a significant development, it is bound together by loose trade agreements, and their success has not been nearly as great as that of the Common Market.

The European Economic Community and the European Free Trade Association have together already had a meaningful political and social impact upon the economy of the United States. It is almost as though another huge industrial trading nation had arisen overnight. One thing is certain: The United States will now have to take a much closer look at its own tariff policies and will have to be willing in the future to compromise a great deal more in the reduction of tariffs and other trade barriers.   Europe is becoming relatively less dependent upon the United States.

INTERNATIONAL TRADE ORGANIZATIONS AND AGREEMENTS

It was pointed out above that the Common Market and the EFTA represent two attempts at economic integration and freer trade.   But there are other very significant trade organizations and trade agreements. Perhaps the four most important of these are the World Bank group, the International Monetary Fund, the Export-Import Bank, and the General Agreement on Tariffs and Trade.   It is to these organizations and agreements that we now turn.

The World Bank Group

The concept of a "world bank" grew out of the Bretton Woods agreements near the close of World War II (1944) in Bretton Woods, New Hampshire.   The World Bank group is composed of three different financial organizations: the International Bank for Reconstruction and Development (the World Bank), the International Finance Corporation (IFC), and the International Development Association (IDA).

While these three organizations are independent ones, there is a great deal of overlap among them in both personnel and resources.   For example, the President of the World Bank is also the President of the International Development Association and is Chairman of the directors of all three organizations.   Most of the World Bank's directors also serve as directors of the other organizations.

The World Bank itself has projects all over the world.   Most of its projects involve the lending of money to the developing nations for electric power and transportation projects.   However, the Bank is now expanding into the fields of education, agriculture, and industry.

The Bank made its first loan in 1947 and has since lent about $11 billion for specific productive purposes in eighty-two countries.   The Bank performs several roles.   If a developing nation applies for a loan for a project, the Bank will examine the project to see that it is financially and technically sound, that it can pay its own way, that it deserves a high place on the list of priorities, and that the country is credit-worthy and pursues reasonable economic policies.

The World Bank also provides technical assistance to the developing nations. The Bank will help draw up national development programs, will advise on economic policies, will assist in the preparation of projects, and will carry out studies of development problems.

The Bank's lending funds come from several sources. There are 106 members in the World Bank. Their usable subscriptions amount to almost $2 billion. In addition, the Bank obtains funds from its own borrowings (about $3.5 billion), from earnings, from sales of portions of its loans, and from repayments. Between 1963 and 1967, the Bank made loans at the rate of nearly $1 billion annually.

The International Finance Corporation (IFC), another part of the World Bank group, was formed in 1956 as an affiliate of the World Bank. The function of the IFC is to assist the *private* economic sector in the less developed member countries.

The IFC, then, provides risk capital for private enterprise, in association with private investors and management. In particular, the IFC supports joint ventures which provide opportunities to combine domestic sponsorship, capital, and knowledge of market and other conditions with capital, technical, and managerial experience available in the more industrialized nations.

The IFC originally financed largely private mining and manufacturing enterprises and supported privately controlled development finance companies. In recent years, however, the IFC has been making larger individual investments and entering new fields such as food processing, distribution services, and tourism.

The IFC has a paid-in capital of about $100 million and can at present borrow up to $400 million from the World Bank. It has eighty-three members and has made 138 commitments, amounting to $221 million, in thirty-six countries.

The International Development Association (IDA) is the third member of the World Bank group. The IDA was established in 1960 to aid the poorest of the less developed nations by providing development capital on favorable financial terms. Loans are made for fifty years and are interest-free (though there is a service charge of $3/4$ of 1 percent). The IDA provides funds for productive purposes of high development priority. It has standards which are similar to those of the World Bank in project appraisal and supervision.

For funds, the IDA relies on subscriptions from its ninety-seven member governments, as well as on contributions from the richer countries of its membership.   As of June 1967, the IDA had had available about $1.78 billion, and it has all been lent.

The International Monetary Fund (IMF)

The World Bank group was the first organization to be discussed.   The International Monetary Fund is the second.   Like the World Bank, the IMF grew out of the Bretton Woods agreements in 1944.

The IMF is concerned with short-term loans and with the cooperative stabilization of foreign-exchange rates.   Short-term loans are made to countries experiencing short-run balance-of-payments deficits.   These loans are made out of currency and gold contributed by participating nations on the basis of national income, population, and volume of trade.   (The United States provides about one-third of the total funds, or about $2.75 billion.)

A nation with a temporary shortage of dollars can borrow dollars from the Fund and supply its own currency as collateral.   However, the dollars acquired in this way are not grants but loans, and they must be repaid with interest within a short period of time.   The maximum amount a nation can borrow in any one year is one-fourth of its own contribution to the Fund.

The IMF also attempts to stabilize exchange rates.   It allows member nations to vary the value of their currency by 10 percent without permission of the Fund's Board of Directors.   Any variation above 10 percent must be approved by the Board.   Such action prevents countries from arbitrarily devaluing their currency to gain a temporary stimulus to their economy.

The Export-Import Bank

The Export-Import Bank is a third organization designed to provide for additional economic integration, economic development, and economic stability.

The Export-Import Bank was formed in 1934.   It is an agency of the United States government and was originally founded for the purpose of financing American exports to lessen the unemployment problems brought about by the Depression of the 1930s.

Over the years since 1934, the objectives of the Export-Import Bank have changed.   The Bank now makes loans to underdeveloped nations (both to governments and to private enterprise).   The Bank currently has close to $4 billion in loans outstanding.

The General Agreement on Tariffs and Trade (GATT)

The major world governments got together in 1947 in an attempt to lessen trade barriers.   The result of these meetings was a compromise agreement known as the General Agreement on Tariffs and Trade (GATT).   This agreement has lasted until today.

GATT conferences are held periodically in Paris.   At these conferences national negotiators meet to swap tariff cuts in which they have a special interest.   When all the separate bargains are agreed upon, they are listed in a single schedule and applied to every member country.   The so-called "Kennedy Round" during the Kennedy administration is an example of a GATT conference.   As a result of the Kennedy Round, substantial tariff reductions were made on selected items among the United States and the other member nations.

GATT outlaws discriminatory tariffs and import quotas (except in the case of a nation experiencing balance-of-payments problems).   It does allow, however, for tariff protection for infant industries.   GATT also has the tools to resolve trade-policy disputes, such as have arisen due to the creation of the Common Market.

These groups and agreements, then, comprise the most significant of the international financial and trade arrangements: the *World Bank group* (including the International Bank for Reconstruction and Development, the International Finance Corporation, and the International Development Association), the *International Monetary Fund,* the *Export-Import Bank,* and the *General Agreement on Tariffs and Trade.*

The final portion of this chapter will examine some of the more important recent developments and problems in the international arena.

RECENT INTERNATIONAL DEVELOPMENTS

The prime internal economic problem facing the United States since 1950 (over two decades) has been one of a balance-of-payments deficit.

The nature of this deficit was explained earlier. It will now be our purpose to look at some of the causes of this deficit and at some of the suggested cures.

Specifically, the balance-of-payments problem originated as a result of our private investment abroad, our military expenditures abroad, and our foreign economic-assistance programs. These expenditures, recent domestic inflation, and the resultant balance-of-payments deficit have all led to what some consider to be a serious outflow of gold from the United States to other countries.

During the years 1941 to 1950, the United States maintained a gold stock amounting to an average of around $22 billion (an abnormally high level due to the inflow of gold during World War II). As a result of the balance-of-payments deficits, the gold stock has declined over the years to the levels indicated in Table 11-2.

From a high figure of about $22 billion, U.S. gold reserves declined to slightly over $10 billion in December of 1968—a reduction of more than one-half of the U.S. gold stock.

The question facing international economists at this point is whether or not the U.S. trend toward balance-of-payments deficits can be reversed. As a matter of fact, the U.S. payments balance improved substantially in 1968.

Inflation of incomes and demand in the United States increased imports sharply and the trade surplus virtually disappeared, while

TABLE 11-2 Gold Stock in the United States, 1960–1968*

YEAR (DEC.)	GOLD STOCK
1960	17,954
1961	16,947
1962	15,978
1963	15,562
1964	15,388
1965	13,799
1966	13,158
1967	12,438
1968	10,367

* In millions of dollars.
SOURCE: *Federal Reserve Bulletin,* vol. 55, no. 4, April, 1969, p. A-4.

stringent controls on U.S. capital flows, restrictive monetary policy,
and other factors resulted in an improvement in the capital accounts
that was considerably greater than the worsening on current account.
. . . it is generally agreed that net capital outflows are likely to in-
crease from their unusually low levels in 1968 and that the current-
account surplus must also increase.[2]

From the above analysis, it appears that the monetary authorities are optimistic concerning the possibility of curbing the U.S. balance-of-payments deficit in future years.

There is a second problem with gold, one which has little to do with balance-of-payments deficits.   Over the years, total world trade has increased tremendously but the world's supply of gold has increased much more slowly.   Because the major currencies of the world are pegged to gold in international transactions, the result has been a chronic shortage of gold in relation to the need for it in international payments.   Consequently, a need has arisen for some form of world reserves other than gold.

To meet this need, negotiations were held in August of 1967 at London.   These negotiations led to an agreement among the Ministers of Finance and the governors of the central banks from a group of ten countries on a plan for establishing a new reserve facility.   It was approved in September by the executive directors of the International Monetary Fund.

This new reserve facility is called *special drawing rights* (SDRs), sometimes referred to as "paper gold."   Basically, the SDRs will provide a great deal more flexibility in the world's reserve capability.   SDRs will be issued according to stringent rules, and the amount of SDRs in existence will be increased every five years.   This new arrangement will be carried out under the auspices of the International Monetary Fund.

Thus, while the United States has been facing a balance-of-payments deficit and an outflow of gold over the past decade, the picture for the future looks brighter.   It is expected that there will be some improvement in the balance of payments, and the new SDRs will make the limited supply of gold less of a problem.

---

[2] *Federal Reserve Bulletin*, vol. 55, no. 4, April, 1969, p. 291.

CHAPTER SUMMARY

We have seen in this chapter that, "all other things being equal," freer international trade can be mutually beneficial to all nations (according to the law of comparative advantage).   However, all things do not always remain equal.   Hence, we saw a need under special circumstances for the implementation of protective tariffs—particularly for purposes of allowing diversification in the nation's industrial structure.

The U.S. balance of payments was another topic for discussion in this chapter.   We found that the United States over the past two decades has typically experienced a balance-of-trade surplus but has been plagued by a balance-of-payments deficit and a loss of important gold stocks.   It is likely that the new special drawing rights and the curbing of inflated demand at home will alleviate these particular problems —and 1968, 1969, and 1970 have already shown that a good deal of improvement may be forthcoming.

In Chapter 12, we will take a look at another economic area having international dimensions—the plight of the underdeveloped nations around the world.

STUDY QUESTIONS

1.   Differentiate between absolute advantage and comparative advantage.
2.   Explain in your own words what is meant by the current account, the capital account, and the balancing items in the U.S. balance of payments.
3.   Give the arguments both for and against the removal of trade barriers.   What is your personal opinion regarding tariffs and more intensive economic integration?

IMPORTANT CONCEPTS IN CHAPTER 11

Law of comparative advantage
Comparative versus absolute advantage
Balance of payments
Current account
Capital account

Balancing items
Arguments for tariffs
European Economic Community (Common Market)
European Free Trade Association (EFTA)
World Bank group
International Bank for Reconstruction and Development (World Bank)
International Finance Corporation (IFC)
International Development Corporation (IDA)
International Monetary Fund (IMF)
Export-Import Bank
General Agreement on Tariffs and Trade (GATT)
Special drawing rights (SDRs)

CHAPTER 12

ECONOMIC DEVELOPMENT

In Chapter 11 we examined one aspect of international economics—that of international trade. And we took a brief look at the various organizations and trade agreements which are designed to foster such trade. In this chapter we will discuss another aspect of international economics—economic development. Specifically, we will attempt to determine the factors which cause a nation to be underdeveloped. We will also make suggestions for spurring a country on to higher developmental levels. Finally, we will see what the United States has done to aid the developing nations and what has yet to be done.

Prior to World War II, interest in the underdeveloped nation was not great. Moreover, the underdeveloped nations themselves were not so vitally concerned with rapid economic growth. Many of the economically deprived areas of the world knew of no other existence. While they were definitely poor, they were not able to see that other nations enjoyed much higher standards of living. However, as American and British soldiers found their way into the underdeveloped nations, comparison became possible.

We do not normally think of an army private's standard of living as luxurious, but compared with the standard of living of those in the economically backward nations, the American soldier was, in fact, quite affluent. Such intermingling of the world's citizens, together with the extremely rapid development of communications in the postwar period, has led to an awareness on the part of the underdeveloped nations. They have become acutely aware of their poverty and are now anxious to participate in economic development.

WHAT IS AN UNDERDEVELOPED NATION?

It is difficult to define an "underdeveloped" country, since such a definition must of necessity be relative. That is, one country is poor compared with other countries. However, certain measures do exist which give a good indication of the degree of economic development.

Most of the underdeveloped nations are concentrated in the eastern and southern continents, including Africa, Asia, and South America. But it is important to remember that there are underdeveloped nations in all parts of the world—even parts of the United States are chronically underdeveloped.

How, then, do we tell if a nation is underdeveloped? We might check the country's availability of national resources and its climate. Often an underdeveloped nation will be short of the natural resources necessary for growth. But more frequently it is not a *lack* of resources which impedes development; rather, it is a failure to effectively utilize the existing resources. By the same token, the climate may be extremely hot and dry (as in some of the African nations). But on the other hand, the nation may be plagued by too much rainfall (as in the case of some of the Latin American countries). The thing which surprises us most is not the *similarity* of climate and resources in the underdeveloped nations, but the disparity. Each underdeveloped nation has its own characteristics and its own specific problems, and they must, therefore, be studied individually.

Nevertheless, there are significant similarities in the emerging nations. For example, the life expectancy of its citizens may be around forty years. A thirty-five-year-old woman in Upper Volta or Burma may be wrinkled, be shaken with palsy, and have all the aging characteristics of a ninety-year-old female in the United States. We might also judge the level of development according to the caloric intake of the country's citizens. In India, for example, the caloric intake is estimated to be between 1700 and 1900 calories per person per day. Yet an individual requires about 2500 calories per day just to replenish the energy consumed by the human body's living cells. And the average American may consume well over 3000 calories per day.

The most commonly accepted measure of economic development is based on money. While such an approach to measuring development is not entirely satisfactory, it is nevertheless the best technique available to us. And per capita gross national product (GNP per person) is the most widely accepted monetary measure.   Per capita GNP varies from a low of $40 (in Malawi) to a world high of $3,270 in Kuwait (a sparsely populated, wealthy nation).   By comparison, the per capita GNP in the United States was $3,240 in 1965.[1]

A few stark statistics will outline the condition of mankind around the world:

Defining countries with a per capita income of under $100 as very poor, those with a per capita income of from $100 to $250 as poor, those with a per capita income between $250 and $750 as being of middle income, and those with a per capita income of more than $750 as the high-income countries, here is how the world's people are distributed:

Very poor	*990 million*
Poor	*1,150 million*
Middle-income	*390 million*
High-income	*810 million* [2]

To show just how poor the two-thirds of the world in the very poor and poor countries are, we might compare their per capita income of less than $250 with the average per capita income of $1,400 in the Common Market countries (population: 175 million) and the per capita income of about $3,000 in the United States (population: 200 million).[3]

Table 12-1 shows the per capita GNP for the world's countries.

Thus far, we know that most underdeveloped nations are concentrated in the eastern and southern continents, that life expectancy in those countries is short, that the caloric intake of the citizens is below the subsistence level, and that per capita income and per capita GNP are quite low.

But these figures do not tell the whole story of economic deprivation in the developing nations.   The average citizen in a poor country will

[1] The per capita GNP figures were taken from the International Bank for Reconstruction and Development, *World Bank Atlas*, Washington, 1967.
[2] George D. Woods, "The Development Decade in the Balance," *Foreign Affairs*, January, 1966, p. 206. The population of mainland China (700 million) is included in the 1,150 million population estimate for the poor countries.
[3] Data from *ibid*.

TABLE 12-1   Gross National Product per Capita (U.S. Dollars)

COUNTRY	GNP PER CAPITA	COUNTRY	GNP PER CAPITA	COUNTRY	GNP PER CAPITA
Kuwait	$3,270	Greece	$600	Malaysia	$260
United States	3,240	Spain	580	El Salvador	250
Switzerland	2,150			Gabon	250
Sweden	2,130	American Samoa	560	St. Kitts-Nevis-	
Canada	2,100	Uruguay	550	Anguilla	250
		South Africa (incl.			
Virgin Islands (U.S.)	2,090	South-West		Trust Territory of the	
Luxembourg	1,820	Africa)	520	Pacific Islands	250
New Zealand	1,790	Hong Kong	500	Swaziland	240
Australia	1,750			Dominica	230
Denmark	1,740	Libya	490	Dominican Republic	230
		Bulgaria*	480		
Iceland	1,630	Chile	480	Ghana	230
France	1,620	Yugoslavia	470	Iran	230
Germany, Fed.		Jamaica	460	Turkey	230
Rep. of	1,620			Brazil	220
Norway	1,620	Panama	460	French Guiana	220
Finland	1,550	Lebanon	450		
		Malta	450	Grenada	220
United Kingdom	1,550	Singapore	450	Iraq	220
Belgium	1,540	Martinique	440	Jordan	220
Netherlands	1,360			Mauritius	220
Germany (East)*	1,260			Rhodesia	220
New Caledonia	1,220	Romania*	440		
		Mexico	430	St. Vincent	220
Israel	1,130	Guadeloupe	420	Algeria	210
Guam	1,120	French Somaliland	410	Ivory Coast	210
Austria	1,080	Ryukyu Islands	410	Saudi Arabia	210
Brunei	1,080			China, Republic of	200
Netherlands Antilles	1,060	Mongolia*	390		
		Costa Rica	380	Honduras	200
U.S.S.R.*	1,000	Barbados	370	Paraguay	200
Puerto Rico	990	Portugal	370	Tunisia	200
Italy	960	Surinam	340	Zambia	200
Czechoslovakia*	900			Korea (North)*	190
French Polynesia	900	British Honduras	330		
		Cuba*	330	Syria	190
Hungary*	870	Nicaragua	320	Ecuador	180
Ireland	830	Guatemala	300	Liberia	180
Venezuela	830	Peru	300	Morocco	180
Poland*	790			St. Lucia	180
Argentina	760	Albania*	290		
		Antigua	280	Senegal	170
Japan	760	Guyana	280	Bolivia	150
Cyprus	640	Colombia	260	Mauritania	150
Trinidad and Tobago	620	Fiji Islands	260	Philippines	150

TABLE 12-1   Continued

COUNTRY	GNP PER CAPITA	COUNTRY	GNP PER CAPITA	COUNTRY	GNP PER CAPITA
United Arab Republic	$150	Vietnam (North)*	$90	Burma	$65
		Yemen	90	Chad	65
Ceylon	140	China (Mainland)*	85	Congo, Dem. Rep. of	65
Sierra Leone	140	Indonesia	85	Laos	65
Papua and		Kenya	85	Mozambique	65
New Guinea	130	Pakistan	85		
Cambodia	120			Nepal	65
Congo (Brazzaville)	120	Malagasy Republic	80	Dahomey	60
		Nigeria	80	Mali	60
Korea, Republic of	120	Central African		Botswana	55
Thailand	120	Republic	75	Ethiopia	55
Cameroon	110	Gambia	75		
Vietnam, Republic of	110	Guinea	75	Lesotho	55
Uganda	100			Somali	55
		Comoro Islands	70	Rwanda	50
Sudan	95	Haiti	70	Upper Volta	50
Angola	90	Niger	70	Burundi	45
India	90	Tanzania	70		
Togo	90	Afghanistan	65	Malawı	40

* The estimates for the U.S.S.R., Eastern Europe, Mainland China, Mongolia, North Korea, North Vietnam, and Cuba may have a wider margin of error because of the difficulties in deriving the GNP at factor cost from net material product and the selection of the most appropriate exchange rates for converting these estimates into U.S. dollars.

source: International Bank for Reconstruction and Development, *World Bank Atlas*, Washington, 1967.

have no furniture in his dwelling (if, indeed, he has a dwelling).   He will own one suit of clothes and will have no household appliances. His food supply consists of some flour, a little sugar, salt, rotten potatoes or rice.   He will consume no meat, fresh vegetables, or canned goods.   His home will have no electricity or plumbing, and several families will be crowded into a single room (250,000 people in Calcutta have no shelter at all and must live in the streets).   There is no television, and there are very few radios and no newspapers or books. (The average citizen cannot read, anyway.)

The poor citizen lives in a community with few government services: there are very few schools, often located at prohibitive distances, little fire and police protection, very few hospitals and doctors.   Automobiles are not owned by the poor in the underdeveloped nations.   The lucky family may have a bicycle, but most walk.   Children may have to ". . . scavenge as do the children in Iran who in times of hunger search for the undigested oats in the droppings of horses." [4]

Almost a billion people live under the conditions described above. And an additional billion and a half live under conditions which are not much better.   Moreover, the description of underdevelopment given so far does not touch on the intangibles of national poverty, such as abject despair, disease, social unrest, open sewers, and so forth.

A bleak situation?   Definitely.   It is virtually impossible for most of us in the United States to envision the squalor which envelops the majority of the world's people.   But, at least on paper, we now know what comprises an underdeveloped nation.   Next let us see why we should be concerned.

WHY DO WE IN THE WEST CARE ABOUT UNDERDEVELOPMENT?

Since the average American is quite secure in his affluence, one might ask why we in the West should concern ourselves with the plight of a nation located halfway around the globe.   The answers to this question are several.

Obviously, one reason we are concerned is because of our *humanitarian ideals*.   It is not within our nature (most of us, at least) to stand by passively while millions of children are afflicted by rickets, while a billion people slowly starve, and while deprivation is a way of life.

But in addition to our humanitarian concerns, there are other, more practical reasons for us to want to help the emerging nations to develop.   We are engaged in an *ideological struggle* for men's minds. In this struggle we hope to convince the unaligned nations that our political and economic system is superior to others.   If we fail to aid the developing nations, we can rest assured that they will become allies with other countries who do offer aid—and, in fact, may become our enemy.   At any rate, if we turn our backs to the problem, it is not likely that we will win many converts to our way of life.

---

[4] Robert L. Heilbroner, *The Great Ascent*, Harper and Row, Publishers, Inc., New York, 1963, p. 26.

A third, and extremely practical, reason we offer aid to the underdeveloped countries is that their development helps us economically.   How? By providing *raw materials* for our production and by providing *markets* for our finished products.   Nigerians cannot buy our goods unless they have money (much of which we must provide).

Finally, we supply economic aid to the developing nations because we know that *people do not starve quietly*.   Many of the world's wars and skirmishes can be traced to this fact.   A poor nation often must starve or fight for additional resources (which may belong to a neighboring country).   While the elimination of the world's poverty would not automatically end hostilities, it would certainly serve to minimize such hostilities.

HOW CAN DEVELOPMENT BEGIN?

We now turn to the all-important question of how economic development can begin.   It is important at this point to reiterate that development problems are vastly different in each emerging nation.   However, certain "average" conditions for development do exist, and it is these that we will explore.   Figure 12-1 will serve as a platform for departure.

The diagram describes the steps to initiating development and the reasons why development has failed to occur.   "Social infrastructure" is used here in its broadest sense to include the basic social institutions (the ways of doing things) of a nation as well as the public goods available, such as transportation, communications, health facilities, and education.

Basically, the diagram suggests that the social infrastructure determines the extent to which a developing nation applies technology in the production of its goods, the use of technology determines the level of productivity (output per man hour), productivity determines the level of the nation's income, the level of income determines the level of consumption and saving, the level of saving determines investment, and the level of investment determines the amount and type of capital accumulation.

For an example, let us assume that in country A the social infrastructure is such that the agricultural workers do not use tractors.   (They

Figure 12-1   The Circle of Poverty

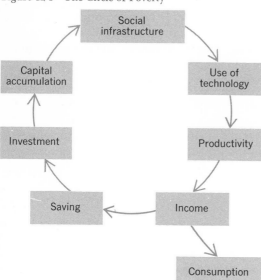

may not be educated in their use, or the use of machinery in farming may even be against their religion.)   The result of A's refusal to use technological developments (the tractor) is that agricultural production is quite low.   Because productivity is low, peasants receive very little in income.   With only a little income, most families spend it all just to survive.   As a result, the level of saving is inadequate to provide for needed investment in plant and equipment.   Capital accumulation does not occur, and country A remains underdeveloped.   Obviously, then, we must at some point reverse the circle of poverty if the problem of underdevelopment is to be overcome.

Shortly after the close of World War II, the United States began an immense foreign-aid program.   A substantial part of this program involved shipping new equipment to the deprived nations.   We were attempting to break into the circle by encouraging the use of new technology.   Unfortunately, the social infrastructure in many cases was such that the recipients of our aid did not know how to use the equipment or did not desire to use it.   Hence, tractors rusted in the fields while farming peasants plowed the ground by hand or with the help of an ox. The provision of aid in the form of technology alone has largely proved to be a failure.

Another approach to stimulating development might be to provide income to the nation through direct grants. The theory would be that with increased incomes, saving and investment would rise. Unfortunately, it would also be a rare case when this approach would succeed. To begin with, it would be financially impossible for the developed nations to provide sufficient funds to lift the emerging nations from poverty. But even if funds were available, growth would probably not occur. Why? Because of the probability of inflation. A rapid infusion of money into the underdeveloped nation would undoubtedly cause a rapid rise in price levels. Thus, even if *money* income were to rise, *real* income probably would not. In addition, people would spend their money as quickly as possible, before the currency lost value due to the inflation. Moreover, most of the population in the developing nations have a high marginal propensity-to-consume, leaving little for saving. Therefore, saving would not appreciably increase, and in fact, the developing nation might be worse off because of our generosity.

What, then, can be done? The solution must lie in the concept of *balanced growth*. By balanced growth we mean that changes in the social infrastructure must accompany changes in technical development. For example, we must teach the peasants how to use a tractor when we provide the tractor. We must provide transportation facilities to move agricultural products as we increase agricultural productivity. And so forth. The key to development lies in changing the social infrastructure along with, of course, the provision of technology and money.

Changes in the Social Infrastructure

In most underdeveloped nations, there are basic parts of the infrastructure which must be changed. The more important aspects are social attitudes, the political structure, education, one-crop economies, and land reform. We will examine each of these in turn.

When we speak of the need to alter *social attitudes* in the developing nations, we are speaking of a very broad spectrum of notions. In some instances, the prevailing attitude may be one which supports a caste system.   Obviously, democratic capitalism cannot thrive under such a system.

Often, too, the governments of the developing nations are very nationalistic.   This rigid spirit of nationalism has grown, in part, as a reaction to past domination by imperialistic powers.   The result of such a nationalistic orientation is that the developing country may be irrational in its demands relating to foreign aid.   For example, a certain nation may want aid from, say, the United States.   But they may be completely unwilling to let the United States have any say whatever regarding the use of that aid.   Consequently, the United States may balk at giving the aid at all.

An additional prevailing social attitude which must be changed if growth is to occur is one of *apathy*.   All too often in the developing nations, it seems that the peasants themselves have little interest in doing what has to be done in order to achieve economic development.   Lest we in the West be too critical, however, we should remember two things: the peasant probably feels that any effort would be futile anyway (as it has been so many times in the past), and a poor peasant in the less developed nations may be afraid to change.   He is, he may feel, at least *existing* presently.   If change were to be for the worst, he might not even be able to do that.

The above are but a few examples of existing social attitudes which must be altered in order to foster economic development.   There are numerous other examples of attitudes which act as a deterrent to growth.   The point is that the aiding nations must discover these social hindrances and attempt to overcome them.

The existing *political structure* may also impede economic development, and two extremes are common in this respect.   Many times the government may be, of necessity, quite dictatorial.   A small group of elite leaders rules with an iron hand.   Since most foreign aid is granted from one government to another, it is little wonder that much of the aid never trickles down to those for whom it is intended.   Instead, that aid may go to purchase a yacht or a mansion for the ruler while the peasants continue to live in poverty.

At the other extreme on the political spectrum, the developing nation may be characterized by a very weak government—so that virtual anarchy prevails.   In cases such as this, the government is too weak to ensure the effective implementation of proper monetary and fiscal measures.   Finally, whether we are talking about anarchy or dictatorship, there is always the possibility that the existing government may be overthrown by revolution.   Yet stable government is essential to the implementation of plans for long-run growth and development.

An important key to development is to be found in *education*.   A university degree in many of the developing nations is equivalent only to a very poor high school diploma in the more advanced nations.   And only a handful of the underdeveloped population get to a university. But more significant than the poor quality of higher education is the lack of good primary and secondary schools and the lack of vocational schools.   Only *5 percent* of the population is literate in countries such as Chad, Dahomey, Ethiopia, Mali, Niger, and the Somali Republic.[5] And the picture is not much different for many others of the developing nations.   Thus the vast majority of persons cannot even read or write.

Together with the need to improve the literacy rate is a need for additional vocational training.   A massive effort is necessary to train persons to operate new machines, to utilize new techniques in farming, and to fill civil servant positions in government.   The tremendous success of the Peace Corps shows that such training can be very effective if carried out on a personal basis at a fairly unsophisticated level. An additional, and crucial, problem with the underdeveloped nations is that their economy is based upon the production and export of only one or a very few commodities.   Such countries are said to have a *one-crop economy*.   This "lopsided" development has resulted, in part, from past imperialism.   To the imperialistic nations, the underdeveloped regions were viewed as a source of raw materials.   Hence the imperialists would develop fully only, say, one resource.   As imperialism has waned, the underdeveloped nations have been left with this one-crop economy as their sole means of economic livelihood.   Diversification and industrialization were simply not encouraged.

Thus today, ". . . Venezuela is dependent for 92 percent of its exports on oil, Colombia for 77 percent of its foreign earnings on coffee, Chile for 66 percent of its exports on copper, Bolivia for 62 percent of its exports on tin, Honduras for over 45 percent of its exports on ba-

---

[5] Data from *How Low Income Countries Can Advance Their Own Growth*, Committee for Economic Development, New York, September, 1966, pp. 62–63.

nanas." [6]   In these cases, a 1 percent fluctuation in the world price of copper or tin may be disastrous to the domestic economy.   Or a bad coffee crop may wipe out millions of dollars of potential national income.

While most of the underdeveloped nations have an agricultural economy (and will continue to have for many years to come), some diversification and industrialization must be encouraged if these nations are to survive.

Finally, land reform is an essential part of the social infrastructure which must be encouraged.   Two problems are evident here.   On the one hand, many countries are characterized by "postage-stamp" cultivation—where many very small plots are farmed by family units.   In such cases, modern methods of cultivation cannot be employed.   On the other hand, there are cases where only a few people own the majority of land and the peasant is propertyless.

In the case of postage-stamp cultivation, what is needed are land-reform measures to combine the small plots into more economical, larger plots of land.   In the case of concentrated ownership, the extremely large areas must be broken up and in some way allocated to the peasants.

But land reform is far from being a simple matter in either case.   You can imagine how difficult it would be to go into an underdeveloped nation and tell the peasants, "We are going to take your land from you so that we can combine it with other plots into a more economic unit."   The peasant's response is likely to be far from friendly.   He takes pride in his land, and he is also afraid of any new technique which, he fears, may eliminate what little food and income he now has.

The aiding nations have also found that it is extremely difficult to instigate land reform in the case of concentrated ownership.   The wealthy leaders in the developing nations are quite reluctant to reallocate their land (and thus their wealth) to the peasant population.   Often such land reform cannot be accomplished short of revolution.

We have said that changes in the social infrastructure are perhaps the most significant changes which must be made so that development can begin.   Specifically, we pointed to a need for change in the areas of social attitudes, the political structure, the educational system, and

[6] Heilbroner, *op. cit.*, p. 66.

one-crop economies and to a need for land reform.   But as the social infrastructure is altered, other problems must also be overcome.

Forced Saving

We saw earlier that saving must begin in the underdeveloped regions, for this is the source of the investment funds essential to capital accumulation.   Thus some technique must be devised to stimulate saving.

In the developed nations of the world, saving is done on a voluntaristic basis or through taxation.   Such savings then find their way into investment channels privately or through the government.   In the underdeveloped nations, the populations are living a hand-to-mouth existence.   Hence, voluntary saving will not occur.   We would be asking the extremely poor to voluntarily become poorer by consuming less and saving more.

Therefore, the governments of the developing nations must turn to a policy of forced saving through taxation.   Some of the meager income of the peasants must be taxed away in order to provide government revenue to be used for the building of highways, hospitals, dams, and so forth.   Increased taxes are a painful, but necessary, policy.   Moreover, a political problem exists here, too.   The rulers of the nation are most often the wealthiest citizens.   What we are asking, then, is that the wealthy policy makers increase taxes on themselves.   Too often, they fail to respond.

The Population Problem

While problems with the social infrastructure and saving are indeed crucial, the most pressing problem facing most of the developing nations is one of overpopulation.   As we will see later, population growth has virtually wiped out the growth of GNP in most of the underdeveloped regions of the world.

Part of the high birth rate can be attributed to ignorance in matters of sex.   Hence, education in such matters could be useful.   But part is also due to a religious orientation which does not allow the use of contraceptive techniques.   Too, a cause of the high birth rate is a need for economic security.   The developing nations do not have elaborate social security and hospitalization programs.   Hence, the elderly must rely upon their children for support when they can no

TABLE 12-2   Average Annual Growth Rates in GNP for Low-income Countries
(1950–1964 and 1957–1964)

| | Percentage Annual Average Increase in GNP (Constant Prices) | | | |
| | TOTAL | | PER CAPITA | |
COUNTRY	1950–1964	1957–1964	1950–1964	1957–1964
Africa				
Algeria	——	——	——	——
Ethiopia	——	4.5	——	3.1
Ghana	——	5.1	——	2.6
Morocco	——	2.0	——	−1.1
Nigeria	——	3.3	——	1.3
Rhodesia (So.)	——	3.6	——	0.3
Sudan	——	4.5	——	1.6
Tunisia	——	4.7	——	2.1
Uganda	——	3.4	——	0.9
Asia				
Ceylon	3.8	3.5	1.2	1.0
India	4.0*	4.4	1.9*	2.1
Iran	——	4.7	——	2.3
Iraq	5.9†	——	3.5†	——
Israel	10.3	10.5	5.7	6.9
Jordan	10.5‡	9.5	7.5‡	6.6
Korea (So.)	——	4.7	——	1.8
Pakistan	3.3†	4.5	1.0§	2.0
Philippines	——	4.9	——	1.7
Taiwan	——	7.1	——	4.0
Thailand	——	7.4	——	4.4
Europe				
Greece	6.5	6.2	5.9	5.7
Portugal	——	5.5	——	4.8
Spain	——	7.2	——	6.3
Turkey	4.9	4.0	1.9	1.1
Latin America				
Argentina	2.1	0.6	0.4	−1.1
Bolivia	1.1	3.5	−1.1	1.2
Brazil	5.3	5.3	2.2	2.2
Chile	3.5	3.3	1.2	1.0
Colombia	4.6	4.6	1.7	1.8
Costa Rica	5.6	4.1	1.6	0.1
Ecuador	4.7	4.3	1.5	1.1
El Salvador	5.4	5.7	2.5	2.8

* Fiscal year beginning April 1.
† 1955–1964.
‡ 1954–1964.
§ Fiscal year beginning July 1.

TABLE 12-2 Continued

	Percentage Annual Average Increase in GNP (Constant Prices)			
	TOTAL		PER CAPITA	
COUNTRY	1950–1964	1957–1964	1950–1964	1957–1964
Guatemala	4.2	4.5	1.2	1.5
Honduras	4.4	3.6	1.2	0.5
Jamaica	——	3.9	——	1.9
Mexico	5.6	5.3	2.6	2.2
Nicaragua	6.1	5.3	3.2	2.4
Panama	4.3	4.9	1.3	1.9
Paraguay	2.8	2.2	0.6	0.0
Peru	5.2	6.4	2.8	4.1
Trinidad and Tobago	——	6.0	——	3.0
Venezuela	6.7	4.5	2.8	0.7

SOURCE: Adapted from *How Low Income Countries Can Advance Their Own Growth*, Committee for Economic Development, New York, September, 1966, pp. 67–69.

longer work. Finally, a large family represents a large agricultural work force to the farmer-peasant and therefore is desirable to him. Until the problem of overpopulation is solved, it is unlikely that meaningful economic development can occur.

THE RECORD OF DEVELOPMENT

In the previous section we examined various problems in breaking into the "circle of poverty" to stimulate economic growth. We should now take a look at the record of development. Have the economies of the underdeveloped countries grown? What has happened to income?

Unfortunately, it is a fact that the richer nations of the world are getting richer in relation to the underdeveloped nations. There is an increasing gap between the rich and the poor. The affluent world *adds* each year to its existing wealth more than the *total* income available to the poor countries.

This is not to say, however, that the poorer countries are not growing. In fact, the *rate* of growth of GNP in the developing regions is in most cases higher than that of the United States. Table 12-2 shows the percentage growth rates in GNP for selected poorer nations. These figures can be compared with an annual growth rate in the United States of approximately 3 percent.

It can be noted in Table 12-2 that the growth rate for GNP in the vast majority of the low-income countries outstripped that of the United States. In only three countries (Morocco, Argentina, and Paraguay) did the rate of increase in GNP fall below 3 percent between 1957 and 1964. Most of the developing regions recorded highly satisfactory rates of growth in total GNP.

The discouraging part of the development picture is shown in the per capita GNP figures. While total GNP increased rapidly, the GNP per person did not. Thirty of the forty nations for which data were available showed per capita GNP growth rates of under 3 percent between 1957 and 1964, and two nations (Morocco and Argentina) actually showed a decline in per capita GNP! It appears, then, that population increases are virtually negating any increases in GNP and hence are preventing satisfactory development. Thus the growth record on a per capita basis has, on the average, been quite poor. Moreover, the record is very likely to continue to be unsatisfactory so long as population growth goes unchecked.

The picture we have presented is, indeed, bleak. But it is not insurmountable. What can we in the United States do to foster development? We can do at least two things: we can attempt to change our attitudes about granting aid, and we can increase the aid we give.

Currently, the United States devotes only about $\frac{1}{10}$ of 1 percent of our GNP to nonmilitary foreign aid—hardly a burden to the average taxpayer. Yet we are surprised when economic assistance of, say, $2 a head—the aid given to India—does not bring decisive results within a decade. We have the financial resources to increase this amount significantly without unduly taxing ourselves.

We must keep in mind, however, that a sudden increase in aid (however well intentioned) could have a disastrous effect on the developing nations. As was indicated earlier, a massive infusion of money into a country could well set off a hyperinflationary process, which of course would impede development.

The future for the developing nations is not bright. At best we can probably expect, on the average, not more than, say, a 2 to 3 percent growth rate in per capita GNP over the next decade. But this low rate of development is certainly better than no growth at all (which would be the case if aid ceased). And the GNP figures do not give the whole picture. The *structure* of the developing economies is undergoing change, with the result that better transportation and communication systems are emerging and the level of literacy is on the rise.

CHAPTER SUMMARY

In this chapter we examined some of the more salient aspects of economic development. We found that the desire for rapid development gained impetus partly as a result of World War II, at which time many of the peoples of the underdeveloped regions became aware of the great divergency in standards of living. Thus, since the mid-1940s, the world has become increasingly committed to the economic development of the poorer regions.

We also found that approximately 1 billion people live under extremely poor conditions, with more than twice that many classified as either "poor" or "very poor" (a per capita income of $250 per year or less).

The Western nations must be concerned about the underdeveloped world for several reasons, including our humanitarian ideals, the existing ideological struggle, the fact that the underdeveloped nations are a source of raw materials and markets, and the knowledge that the poor do not starve quietly.

We posed the question, "How can development begin?" The answer to this question we found in an examination of the "circle of poverty." The social infrastructure determines the use of technology, which, in turn, determines the level of productivity. Productivity sets the level of income, from which savings are derived. These savings, of course, are necessary for investment and capital accumulation. Thus we concluded that we must somehow break into this circle of poverty.

One significant area for an attempted breakthrough is the social infrastructure—which necessitates changing social attitudes, altering political systems, diversifying the industrial structure, and engaging in sweeping land-reform programs. Each of these areas presents tremendous problems, both to the developing nations and to those attempting to aid in their development.

It was pointed out that in addition to changing the social infrastructure, a program of forced saving through taxation would be necessary. Voluntary saving is a virtual impossibility in a nation plagued by poverty.

A final problem was examined—that of overpopulation. This problem is generated by ignorance, religious taboos, a desire for economic security, and the need for a "family work force."

Next, the record of development was briefly discussed. This examination bore out the fact that the gap between the rich and the poor nations is growing yearly. However, the rate of increase in the total GNP of most of the emerging nations is quite satisfactory—and, in fact, exceeds the growth rate of the United States (with few exceptions). On the other hand, population increases have caused the *per capita* GNP to grow at a very slow rate and in some cases to actually decline. About three-fourths of the underdeveloped nations showed per capita GNP growth rates of under 3 percent.

Finally, it was indicated that the United States (as well as other affluent nations) is committing only a very small percentage of its GNP to non-military economic aid. While this amount could easily be increased without burdening the American people, such an increase in aid might have the result of severely inflating the economies of the developing nations.

As to the future, it was suggested that the process of economic development will continue to creep at a snail's pace but that slow development is certainly preferable to no development at all.

One advantage held by the developing nations is that they may *choose* from existing economic systems the system which best suits their needs —whether it be capitalism, socialism, communism, or some other. Chapter 13 looks at these various economic systems and assesses their advantages and disadvantages.

STUDY QUESTIONS
1. Define, to the best of your ability, an underdeveloped nation.
2. Why do we care about the underdeveloped nations, anyway? Why not let them fend for themselves?

3. Describe the so-called "circle of poverty."   How might we break into this circle and begin the process of development?
4. How successful has the record of development been?

IMPORTANT CONCEPTS IN CHAPTER 12

Underdeveloped nation
Role of resources and climate in development
Very poor nation
Poor nation
GNP as a measure of growth
Reasons for caring about economic development
Circle of poverty
Social infrastructure
Role of technology in development
Role of productivity in development
Role of income and saving in development
Role of investment in development
Balanced growth
Problem of social attitudes
Problem of the political structure
Problem of education
One-crop economy
Land reform
Postage-stamp cultivation
Forced saving
Population problem
GNP versus per capita GNP in the developing nations

CHAPTER 13

COMPARATIVE
ECONOMIC SYSTEMS

In an era characterized by an intense struggle for the minds of men
and beseiged by the aura of a "cold war," it is imperative that we know
what the struggle is about. The major powers of the world are attempting to convince the lesser powers to align themselves with a
particular form of government and a particular economic system. We
in the United States are trying to sell capitalism as a way of life. The
Russians and the Chinese are pushing communism. And Britain and
the Scandinavian countries espouse socialism. The purpose of this
chapter is to reach an understanding of these various economic systems.
Then, and only then, will we be able to "judge" which system is best
and under what circumstances.

Unfortunately, the man on the street fully believes himself to be an
expert on such matters. Ask him what communism is, or socialism,
or capitalism for that matter, and he will have a ready answer. But
the layman who thinks he understands these very complex economic
systems is operating under a delusion. A complete understanding of
any of the "isms" requires years of difficult study.

An understanding of the material in this chapter will in no sense make
the student an expert on comparative economic doctrines. The best
that can be hoped for is that the reader will gain some insight into
some of the more important elements of the various systems.

This chapter places the greatest emphasis on the study of communism
and socialism, since these two systems are the least understood by the
average student. However, attention is also given to capitalism and to
two other "isms" (fascism and anarchy).

It should be remembered that no economic system is perfect in the sense that it maximizes the wellbeing of each and every individual living under it.   There are good and bad aspects to *every* system, including our own.   Hence, after each discussion of a particular system, you will find a summary statement attesting to both the achievements and the shortcomings of that system.

COMMUNISM

The system of communism is probably the least understood of all the systems under which man may live.   Moreover, it is probably obscured more to Americans than to those of other nations.   There are at least three reasons why we do not really understand this particular economic system.

The first, and foremost, reason is that the definitive work on communism—Karl Marx's *Capital* [1]—is an extremely difficult work and is quite tedious to read.   Moreover, it was Lenin, not Marx, who gave us the most lucid account of the economic organization of a communist society.   Hence, very few people have tried to glean the tenets of communism from the original source.

A second source of confusion regarding the nature of communism revolves around the fact that there exist two broad types of communism: theoretical communism (as advanced by Marx) and communism as practiced in the world today.   Not only are there vast differences between theoretical and practiced communism, there are also significant differences in communism as practiced by the Soviet Union and China, and also by Yugoslavia.   Some of these differences will be discussed below.

A third source of our lack of understanding of communism is our "anticommunist" bias in the Western world.   Not too many years ago (in the mid-1950s), copies of *Capital* were actually burned in some states!   In other states all copies of the book were removed from the shelves of the public libraries.   Even today it is common to hear someone brand a particular policy as "communistic" or a long-haired male as a "communist"—as though that should be reason enough to dismiss

---

[1] For a popular version of this book, see Karl Marx, *Capital*, Modern Library, Inc., New York.

the policy or person.   Certainly the road to knowledge and understanding is not paved with ignorance and bias.   An *understanding* of the communist system does not imply an *acceptance* of it.

Above all else, when we study Marx's brand of communism, we should bear in mind that he was a true intellectual and that many valuable insights can be derived from a careful study of his works.   The fact that Marx spent many years closeted in the library, that he neglected his family, or that he was plagued with open sores on his face should not negate the fact that he was indeed brilliant.   Obviously, however, the fact that he was brilliant should not lead us to accept his conclusions or prophecies.

With this background in mind, let us now turn to an examination of Marxian (or theoretical) communism, followed by a discussion of communism as practiced in the world today.

Marxian Communism

Over the years, scholars have given a great deal of attention to the interpretation of historical change; they have sought to find the *cause* of social change.   Early in our historical development, a commonly accepted notion of change was *divine providence.*   Those who accepted this motivating force to societal change simply assumed that change was part of God's great design.   Neither man nor conditions of society caused changes to occur—only God could cause change.

Another interpretation of historical change is called the *political,* or "hero," interpretation of history.   Those adhering to this notion believed that great statesmen, kings, and military figures created the growth (or decline) of a society or economic system.

More important to the Marxian theory, however, was the interpretation of change advanced by the philosopher Hegel, from whom Marx was to borrow heavily.   According to Hegel, the all-important maker of change was the *impact of ideas.*   Ideas themselves created the given condition of society, and the clash of ideas introduced a dynamic element causing societies to change.

Put simply, Hegel maintained that any original idea (which he called a *thesis*) would be opposed by another idea (referred to as an *antithesis*).   The result of this clash between ideas would be an entirely new idea (a *synthesis*).   In this fashion, then, societies changed.   An example may help.   Suppose that you are adamantly opposed to a new tax (a thesis); suppose further that your adversary is as strongly in favor of it (an antithesis).   Now, should the two of you clash, you may find that both of you end up supporting a reduction in government spending (a synthesis) instead of doing anything with the tax structure.

It was this idea of thesis-antithesis-synthesis that Marx borrowed from Hegel.   However, Marx narrowed the concept greatly.   He held the thesis to be the values agreed upon by a nation's property owners (*the bourgeoisie*).   The antithesis, according to Marx, was the set of values held by the working class (*the proletariat*).   These two sets of values were bound to clash in a capitalistic society in the form of a class conflict, said Marx.   The result?   The formation of a new economic system—communism.   (Of course, the process was not as simple as this, as we shall see later.)   Thus Marx attributed all changes in society to the economic values held by opposing classes.   Because he emphasized the economic aspects of change, Marx's interpretation of historical change has come to be called *economic determinism* or *materialistic determinism*.

It is significant to note at this point that Marx was not writing his works as an *attack* on capitalist systems as such.   He held no malice toward the capitalists' way of doing things.   Rather, he held that the demise of capitalism would come about due to inherent shortcomings of the system and as a natural phenomenon.   In other words, capitalism held the seeds of its own destruction.   (This notion is sometimes referred to as the *gravedigger theory*.   Capitalism would "dig its own grave.")   Exactly how capitalism was to destroy itself, we will see below.

The Dynamic Aspects of Marxian Communism

We have already indicated that there would be, according to Marx, a class struggle in the industrialized nations between the bourgeoisie and the proletariat.   The basic reason for this conflict would be the notion of *surplus value*.

Marx maintained that the proletariat (workers) in a capitalistic society would be paid wages only high enough for subsistence (that is, just high enough to feed, clothe, and house themselves).   Yet they would earn for their employers an amount greater than this.   The difference between what the workers were paid and what they earned for their employers Marx called *surplus value.*

(Value of production) − (Wages) = (Surplus value)

Because the bourgeoisie owned the means of production, all surplus value would accrue to them. As this surplus value came to be concentrated in the hands of the bourgeoisie, it would be used to build new plants and equipment—that is, it would become capital accumulation. Moreover, the capital equipment would become more and more efficient, so that fewer workers would be needed.

The unemployment resulting from technological displacement would constitute a *"reserve army of the unemployed,"* with the misery of the proletariat increasing at every step.

Increased unemployment, however, means a decline in aggregate purchasing power (falling demand for goods and services). With the bourgeoisie producing more and more with increasingly sophisticated machines but with the proletariat buying less and less, an overproduction situation would develop, said Marx, culminating in a severe depression.

As the capitalist society fell into a depression situation, business profits would decline. In an attempt to prevent falling profits and to avoid the intense competition for the consumer dollar, the industrial firms would join together, causing increased industrial concentration (monopolies). The depression, lagging demand, and overproduction at home would eventually lead the industrial giants to search for foreign markets for their surpluses—that is, to engage in capitalist imperialism.

During this dynamic process, the proletariat would have grown increasingly miserable. Their lot would continue to worsen until a breaking point was reached. At that point, the proletariat would revolt and overthrow the bourgeoisie.[2]

All is not a bed of roses after the revolution, however. Marx maintained that the revolution would only serve to reverse the power structure. Thus there would be established a *dictatorship of the proletariat.* The workers would simply have changed places with the property own-

---

[2] Marx specifically suggested that a revolution may not be necessary to achieve this transfer of power in the United States, Britain, and certain other capitalist nations. For the most part, however, his was a revolutionary doctrine.

ers. Marx considered all governments to be oppressive, and the dictatorship of the proletariat was no exception. It, too, must go in the final analysis.

Here we reach what many consider to be the weakest point in Marxian theory. Marx did not clearly explain how the industrial nation was to move from the dictatorship of the proletariat into the next prescribed stage—that of socialism. It seems that Marx simply assumed that the proletariat, in search of the good society, would relinquish part of their power and set up a socialistic economic system. Finally, as all members of the society began to work for the common good, communism could be ushered in. Figure 13-1 diagrams these dynamic steps in the move from capitalism to communism, as we have described them.

As to the actual form to be taken by the communist system, Marx gave us little to go on. Presumably, the communist nation would have a highly democratic government, greatly decentralized. The government would have little authority, with policy being created and carried out collectively by all citizens. It was to be a largely stateless society based on cooperation and conformity.

Not only did Marx fail to describe the communist state adequately, he also was remiss in explaining exactly how the revolution was to occur. Presumably, it was to come naturally and spontaneously. At least one communist theoretician, V. I. Lenin, was not satisfied with Marx's explanation of the revolutionary process and set out to outline it in more detail.

Lenin's Contribution to Marxian Communism

Lenin was a leading theoretician of the communist doctrine. His notions on revolution were most clearly laid out in his pamphlet "What Is to Be Done," published in 1902. It was here that Lenin developed his concept of the *professional revolutionary*.

Lenin was not content to rely upon the unorganized proletariat to lead a spontaneous revolution. Instead, he suggested that a body of well-trained, highly disciplined revolutionaries be developed. This group was to be similar in structure to a police force or a small army and was to be highly secret.

The proletariat in the industrialized nation, according to Lenin, were

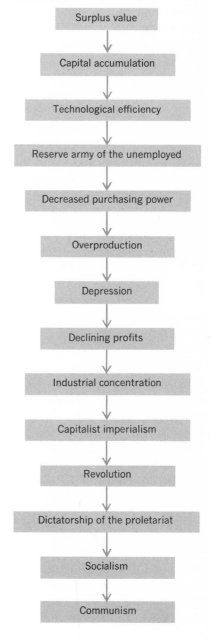

Figure 13-1 The Move from Capitalism to Communism

to form perfectly legitimate and lawful organizations such as labor unions and church groups.   But each of these groups was to be infiltrated by professional revolutionaries.   These professionals were to infiltrate virtually all organized groups in the nation (schools, political parties, churches, etc.).   They were to train spies, saboteurs, and so forth, so that when the time for revolution was ripe (perhaps in times of depression or serious civil strife), a well-trained professional army could lead the proletariat to victory over the bourgeoisie.

Lenin also recognized the importance of trying to win the developing nations over to communism.   Marx had felt that communism would come naturally to the highly industrialized nations.   But Lenin saw no reason to wait for industrialization.   Instead, he suggested moving into the backward regions of the world at once.

These few short paragraphs cannot do justice to Marxian communism. Perhaps, however, they will give the reader some basic insight into the nature of theoretical communism.   Needless to say, Marxian communism is practiced nowhere in the world today and probably never has been—with the possible exception of the American Indian tribes. For this reason, we will now turn to an examination of communism as it is practiced currently.

Communism as Practiced

The communist system, as practiced in the Soviet Union, Red China, and elsewhere, is vastly different from the economic system described by Marx.   The Soviet system probably aligns more closely with the socialist tenets (described later) than with those of communism, and in fact, the Soviets call themselves the Union of Soviet *Socialist* Republics (U.S.S.R.).

A harsh, inequitable Tsarist regime was overthrown by a bloodless revolution in Russia in October of 1917.   At that time, the Bolsheviks seized power.   (They were not called communists until 1919.)   This revolution represented the beginning of the communist society in the Soviet Union.   Since that time the Soviet government has sought to bring about a highly collectivized economic system, characterized by rigid economic plans for agricultural and industrial output.   The expected output of each factory and farm is dictated to those who run them (after consideration by the Planning Committee), and it is ex-

many agricultural specialists. The United States, however, led in
e humanities and the social sciences. The ratio of physicians in the
viet Union is 19 per 10,000 persons. In the United States, this ratio
13 per 10,000 persons. As a result, thousands of doctors must be
ported into this country (about 1 in 4 are foreign-trained). The
tional income of the Soviet Union is only 40 percent of that of the
nited States. Yet they spend proportionately twice as much of their
ational income on education as does the United States. Moreover,
percent of the students in Russia receive a stipend approaching the
verage pay of a factory worker.[4] Certainly, we must admit that the
viet Union has made great strides in the field of education.

nother area where the Soviet Union has excelled is that of military
ower. Although total output in the Soviet Union is less than half
f that of the United States, they spend about the same amount of
oney on national defense as we do.

Weaknesses and Failures of Communism

While the above discussion stresses the achievements of the Soviet government, the total picture is not so rosy. The Soviet system has several important shortcomings.

One of the most important of these shortcomings is the stress placed
on conformity. In various stages of Soviet development, conformity
has been demanded in social thought, in political thought, in the
sciences, and in the arts. As an example, scientific questions were
often decided by the political Central Committee of the Communist
Party rather than by the scientific experts. Such conformity does not
encourage the experimentation so necessary to progress.

Another shortcoming in the Soviet Union is the failure of reality to
match their stated ideals. For example, the Soviet Constitution makes
the following guarantees:

Article 10—*The right of citizens to own, as their personal property,
income and savings derived from work, to own a dwelling house and
a supplementary husbandry, articles of household and articles of*

---

[4] Ebenstein, *ibid.*, pp. 65–68.

pected that the agreed-upon quotas will be met. Ince
surpassing their quotas are significant. Failure to mee
result in a demotion.

Advantages and Achievements of Communism

While the average American abhors the collectivism and
the communist way of life, the system is not devoid of acl

The Soviet system is much more egalitarian than was (
under the Tsars. Power and riches in Russia once accru
small, elite ruling class. Now, however, race, sex, and
tions have been largely eliminated—providing a great deal
and economic mobility for the average Soviet citizen.

Another distinct achievement of the Soviet Union has l
tremely rapid industrialization. Prior to World War I, t
of Russia was based almost totally on agricultural prod
the end of World War II, the Soviet Union was second (
United States in industrial production—a truly remarkab
such a short period of time. Unfortunately, growth in the
of consumers' goods has not kept pace with the growth in
production. Nevertheless, particularly in those industries (
war and national defense, Russian growth has been phenc
steel, iron, coal, petroleum, electricity, and cement, for exam

Soviet strides in the field of education are also noteworthy.
the launching of the first Sputnik in October 1957, the nonce
world had paid little attention to Soviet achievements in e
Since that time, they have been taken more seriously—and
might be! Between 1926 and 1952, the Soviet Union incr
professional manpower at a fantastic rate. The number of (
rose ten times; there were five times as many teachers and fo
as many physicians as at the beginning of the period.[3]

By way of comparison with the United States, the following fig
revealing. During the period 1928–1959 (for the Soviet Uni
1926–1958 (for the United States), the Soviet Union trained 1.8 ;
engineers as the United States, 2.4 as many medical doctors, ;

---

[3] William Ebenstein, *Today's Isms*, 4th ed., Prentice-Hall, Inc., Englewood Cliffs, N.J., 19(
citing Nicholas DeWitt, *Soviet Professional Manpower*, National Science Foundation, 195!

personal use and convenience, is protected by law, as is also the right of citizens to inherit personal property.

Article 118—*Citizens of the U.S.S.R. have the right to work, that is, the right to guaranteed employment and payment for their work in accordance with its quantity and quality.*

The right to work is ensured by the socialist organization of the national economy, the steady growth of the productive forces of Soviet society, the elimination of the possibility of economic crises, and the abolition of unemployment.

Article 119—*Citizens of the U.S.S.R. have the right to rest and leisure. . . . ensured by the establishment of a seven-hour day for industrial, office, and professional workers, the reduction of the working day to six hours for arduous trades and to four hours in shops where conditions of work are particularly arduous . . . annual vacations with full pay. . . .*

Article 120—*. . . the right to maintenance in old age and also in case of sickness or disability . . . free medical service . . . and the provision of . . . health resorts for the use of the working people.*

Article 124—*. . . freedom of religious worship and freedom of anti-religious propaganda is recognized for all citizens.*

Article 125—*. . . freedom of speech, freedom of the press, freedom of assembly, freedom of street processions and demonstrations. These civil rights are ensured by placing at the disposal of the working people and their organizations printing presses, stocks of paper, public buildings, the streets, communications facilities and other material requisites for the exercise of these rights.*[5]

Obviously, many of the above guarantees of the Soviet Constitution are honored in the breach, and these lofty ideals are not always conformed to.

Another shortcoming in the Soviet system can be cited. While much of the class system has been eliminated, there still exists an elite group. The political commissars hold a very powerful position (often having

[5] *Constitution of the Union of Soviet Socialist Republics,* Foreign Languages Publishing House, Moscow, 1962.

the power of life and death over dissenters).   By the same token, the Soviet Union espouses international equality as well as domestic equality.   Yet Soviet foreign policy has been imperialistic and domineering.

Summary Remarks on Communism

We have seen that two brands of communism exist—that advanced by Karl Marx and that as practiced in the world today.   According to Marx, capitalist nations hold the seeds of their own destruction, so that, ultimately, communism must prevail.   It will be brought about by a class struggle between the bourgeoisie and the proletariat, culminating in revolution.   His doctrine of historical change is known as economic or materialistic determinism.   We saw also that communism as practiced in the Soviet Union more closely approximates a highly regulated socialist system.

While the level of achievement in the Soviet Union has been unusually high (particularly in the scientific and professional fields), serious shortcomings were also noted.

The Sino-Soviet struggle can be taken as further evidence of differing brands of communism even within the communist-bloc countries. China endeavors to follow a "hard" line based strictly on Marxian theory, while the Russians have tended toward a "softer" line.   This dogmatic dispute, coupled with border clashes, has generated very strained diplomatic relations between these two communist nations.

Next, we will analyze a socialist economic system and compare this system with the communist one just discussed.   Again, the advantages and disadvantages of such a system will be brought to light.

SOCIALISM

Socialism is another term which is widely misunderstood by the general public.   The word itself is often applied to any program of social welfare, such as social security, unemployment compensation, and Medicare.   But welfare measures do not, in themselves, constitute socialism.   Socialism is defined as an economic system in which the major means of large-scale production are owned by the government. Short of nuclear power and the Tennessee Valley Authority (TVA), the United States government owns very little in the way of factories and other means of production. In order for this country to be classified as socialist, our government would have to own the utilities, General Motors, U.S. Steel, and the other large organizations. Such, obviously, is not the case. (The system we do have might be termed "regulated capitalism" or "modified capitalism," but more will be said of this later.)

It is generally accepted that the formal economic system of socialism had its early beginnings under Robert Owen (1771–1858). Owen was a man we would think least likely to found a socialist system. He was a wealthy industrialist. Nevertheless, he was the founder of socialism in Britain and was the first to coin the word "socialism."

Owen's brand of socialism was, however, different from most socialist systems today. As we have defined socialism, it involves government ownership of the major means of production. But Owen looked to society, not to the state, to bring about desired social change. He stressed *self*-help rather than help by the government.

With Owen, as with the majority of socialists, gradualism was stressed instead of revolution. His belief was that men were rational beings and that they could cooperatively work together to create a new and better environment. Owen specifically opposed the practice of working young children for twelve hours or more a day in the factories (which, incidentally, was a revolutionary notion at the time). Owen's major stress was on education; he felt that virtually all of society's problems could be solved if the members of that society were well educated.

Robert Owen experimented with his notions of socialism by founding a cooperative movement in Indiana, called New Harmony (certainly an optimistic name!). The co-op ultimately failed, but Owen's ideas were to remain and were to serve as the basis for the establishment of other socialist systems such as those in Great Britain and in the Scandinavian countries.

It is very important to stress that when we speak of socialism, we are speaking of an *economic,* not a political, system. Socialism is a particular way of producing and distributing goods and services. This economic system is quite compatible with democracy and with most other political systems. For example, in Great Britain the voters determine the degree of socialism. It is the ballot box, not revolution or totalitarianism, which is the determinant factor.   Hence, we can refer to *democratic socialism,* indicating a socialist economic system and a democratic political system.

The Procedure for Nationalization

As with communism, there are as many different kinds of socialism as there are socialist countries.   A common thread running through all of them, however, is some degree of nationalization of the productive factors (that is, converting them to state ownership).

This transition from private to state ownership of the major means of production can occur suddenly or gradually.   It can be revolutionary in nature or quite peaceful.   While there is no hard-and-fast rule, most transitions are gradual and peaceful.   There still remain a few revolutionary socialists, but their impact is negligible.

Most likely, if the voters under a democratic system wanted socialism, a gradual nationalization of industry would ensue.   Moreover, the government would make every attempt to compensate the private owners for their property at a "fair" market value.   Needless to say, the determination of a fair value for property would be a most difficult task; undoubtedly some inequities would occur as the government took over the property.

In compensating the owners for their property, the government very likely would pay them with income-yielding securities (bonds).   Thus the property owner would continue to receive compensation for the remainder of his life.   These securities probably would be non-transferable.   (That is, they could not be bought and sold in the marketplace.)   To complete the nationalization process, these securities could not pass to the heirs of the property owner but instead would revert to the government upon the owner's death.   Thus, over a gradual period, private property would be shifted to government ownership.

There is no certain order for the nationalization of industry.   However, it is likely that the government would first nationalize the *banking* industry in order to gain control over the money supply.   Since the banking system is only a quasi-private industry, the transfer of ownership could be accomplished more easily than in other industries.   The next industry to be nationalized would very likely be the *public utilities* (including fuel and power, communications, and transportation).

Following the nationalization of the banking and public-utilities industries, the government would move to transfer ownership of heavy industry. In some countries, this step might not occur at all, or only one or two key industries might be nationalized (say, steel and automobiles). In other countries, all heavy industry might be nationalized. In most socialist countries, small businesses and agriculture would be left in private hands. If, however, they were to be nationalized, they would be taken as a last step.

Socialism versus Communism

As we pointed out earlier, the Soviet Union really is more of a socialist system than a communist one. Hence, the difference between socialism and Soviet communism is slight. *Politically,* the differences may be great. For example, the Soviet Union represents a totalitarian form of socialism, while Britain and the Scandinavian countries represent democratic socialism.

Socialists generally desire to vest the ownership of producers' goods used in large-scale production in the government. This is also done under communism. But under Marxian communism, there is also social ownership of consumers' goods.

An additional difference between socialism and communism is that under socialism the economic motivation of the individual would not be significantly altered. The same people would manage and work in the factories as managed and worked there before nationalization. And they would be paid much as before. Those who made more money would continue to have command over more consumers' goods. Under Marxian communism, however, the distribution of consumers' goods and services would be on the basis of *need,* not income. The slogan "from each according to his ability, to each according to his need" applies to communism, whereas under socialism the slogan might be "from each according to his ability, to each according to his ability."

Finally, a major difference between communism and socialism is that socialism holds more promise for a peaceful and gradual transition, while communism is more prone to a sudden and revolutionary transition.   As we have already pointed out, however, this need not be the case.   Socialism can be brought about by revolution, and Marx himself suggested that revolution was not always necessary.

Advantages and Achievements of Socialism

It is difficult to talk of the advantages of socialism for the simple reason that what are advantages to some are disadvantages to others. For example, free medical care for the poor would certainly be an advantage to the sick poor.   But such a program would involve a sacrifice on the part of the middle- and upper-income groups, who would pay for it through increased taxes.   In spite of this difficulty in isolating advantages, most people agree that the British and Scandinavian experience with socialism has had its achievements.

The British National Health Service is one of the best examples in the world of socialized health services.   Under this program medical and hospitalization care is provided for all, free of any direct charge.   At its inception there was a great deal of opposition to the National Health Service.   However, over the years, it has been widely accepted and is deemed a success even by most British medical doctors, who opposed its beginning most vehemently.

The British also have instituted what has come to be called a "cradle-to-grave" social security program.   The reason for its name becomes obvious when we look at what it does.   The program has maternity grants for prospective mothers; it provides family allowances after the child is born (based upon the number of children in the family); it protects against sickness and unemployment; it provides old-age pensions; and, finally, it provides burial allowances.

An additional advantage of socialism *may* be the elimination of excess business profits due to the existence of monopoly power in the heavy industries.

The socialist governments have traditionally increased the educational opportunities for all.   In the United States, many young people cannot go on to college because of financial pressures.   In the socialist countries, higher education is provided free of charge, and often stipends are given to the student.

Finally, while the high degree of planning in the socialist nations has its drawbacks, such planning has effectively eliminated the problems of severe unemployment and depression.

Weaknesses and Failures of Socialism

While the socialist systems have been largely effective in the health, welfare, and educational areas, they are not without their weaknesses. Nationalization of industry can best be done only with industries which are highly developed, well established, and standardized.   Even so, it is *possible* that nationalization may have a stifling effect on the risk taking and entrepreneurship so necessary to economic growth.   (We do not have the evidence to say with assurance that such is the case, but the possibility does exist.)

It is difficult to determine whether public ownership is more or less efficient than private ownership.   There are at least two reasons, however, why we might suspect some loss of efficiency.   First, there are management problems associated with any large bureaucracy—and government bureaucracy is no exception.   Second, profits are normally assumed to provide a motivating force for efficiency.   If a private firm can reduce its costs by utilizing its resources more efficiently, it will make more profit.   However, under government ownership, the profit motive is not operative.   Thus there might be some waste of resources and a lessened desire to improve technology.

Summary Remarks on Socialism

We have seen that socialism involves government ownership of the major means of large-scale production.   It is an economic, not political, system, and may be quite compatible with either democracy or totalitarianism.

The process of nationalization would involve the compensation of the private owners at the fair value of their property.   Payment would probably be made in the form of nontransferable, income-yielding securities.   And the probable order of nationalization would be the banking system, public utilities, heavy industry, small businesses, and agriculture (though the last two might be left in private hands).

The major differences between socialism and communism were seen to be several.   Under Marxian communism there would be social ownership of consumers' goods; under socialism, only producers' goods. Under socialism the economic motivation of the individual would not be significantly altered.   Distribution of goods would be made on the basis of individual contribution for the most part.   Under communism, the distribution of the nation's output would be on the basis of need, regardless of the individual's contribution.   A final difference between socialism and communism was seen to be that socialism holds more promise for gradual and peaceful change, while communism would most likely call for sudden and revolutionary change.

A socialist system was seen to offer certain advantages, particularly in the areas of health, welfare, and education and in the area of economic stability and full employment.   The drawbacks to socialist systems included a possible stifling effect on risk taking and entrepreneurship and a possible waste of resources due to the lack of a profit motive.

The next system we will study is our own—capitalism. It, too, as we will see, has its advantages and disadvantages.

CAPITALISM

To begin, it should be pointed out that capitalism does not exist in the United States in its pure (or classical) form.   Our system is a modified one but can be referred to as capitalistic since it is primarily that.

Fundamental to a capitalistic economy is a philosophical notion referred to as the "Protestant ethic."   Space will not permit a detailed examination of the history of the development of the so-called Protestant ethic, but we should know basically what it is all about. The notion began in our churches and later spread into virtually all our social and business institutions.   The Protestant ethic originally stated that God would reward those who suffered most in their service to Him.   As the notion has come into modern usage, however, it has come to mean that those who *work* will be rewarded and those who do not work will not be rewarded.

The Protestant ethic is germane to capitalism because it lays the justification for profit taking and free enterprise—both of which are designed to reward *individual,* not collective, effort. Thus, under capitalism, men *compete* for society's rewards.

Classical Capitalism

There are several important characteristics of capitalism in its pure form. One of the most significant of these is *private ownership of the means of production.* Whereas under socialism and communism ownership of the means of production is vested in society as a whole, under capitalism ownership remains in the hands of individuals.

A second major characteristic of capitalism is that it is a *market economy.* Goods are bought and sold in the marketplace, and the level of production and prices are determined by the forces of supply and demand. We saw in Chapter 2 how the market mechanism works to set prices and output.

Closely akin to the idea of a market economy are two other characteristics of capitalism: the *profit motive* and *consumer sovereignty.* Under capitalism the desire for profits motivates men and businesses to produce goods and services and to take the risks necessary in their production. At the same time, the consumer is the final judge of what should be produced. He is sovereign. His dollar votes tell the business community what he wants. If he is willing to pay for hula hoops, then hula hoops will be produced. If he votes against hula hoops (by not buying any), then they will not be produced.

Thus the cornerstones of a capitalist society are seen to be private ownership of the means of production, a market economy, the profit motive, and consumer sovereignty. All this implies that the role of the central government should be minimized—and, in fact, relegated to the performance of only those necessary duties as would not be done by the private sector of the economy. Free and unregulated enterprise should prevail.

Alterations of Classical Capitalism

A pure form of capitalism can operate effectively only when the members of society are all intelligent, rational, and well; and only so long as the system itself does not find itself in the throes of depression or inflation. A further requisite for the effective operation of capitalism is that the business sector be composed of a very large number of small businesses—each too small to control price or output (that is, the absence of monopoly power).

For many years (in fact, until the 1930s), this nation operated as though classical capitalism did exist. The government took a "hands-off" position in regard to the regulation of business enterprise. The results of this "hands-off" policy are now widely known. In the 1800s, we experienced an era characterized by "robber barons." Business, in its unchecked quest to maximize profits, was defrauding the public, working children long hours at arduous tasks, and making billions of dollars of profit through stock swindles and other techniques. The working man had no rights and, in fact, could be jailed for conspiracy if he tried to form a union with his fellow workers. Only a handful of very wealthy people owned the vast portion of American business, and they exploited the rest of the population.

The absence of government regulation also meant that the American economy underwent violent swings in economic activity. We had periods of hyperinflation and dark depression. Millions often would become unemployed as the result of a depression over which they had no control.

The beginnings of the end of our belief in classical capitalism came in the 1930s. With the stock market crash of 1929, the U.S. economy (along with the rest of the world) was plummeted into its most chronic depression. Millions of people walked the streets homeless and without jobs. Breadlines sprang up all across the nation. The worst of the Depression lasted from 1930 until about 1939, but damaging effects lasted until well into World War II, in the early 1940s. This was a black period, indeed, in America's economic history. There was widespread talk of revolution, communism, and socialism, and our government perhaps came its closest to being overthrown at that time.

Recognizing the dangers to democracy and capitalism, the administration of Franklin Roosevelt ushered in a series of economic programs called the *New Deal*. More important than the actual programs of the New Deal was the fact that a new philosophy came to pass. We realized that members of the society often suffered, not out of laziness, but because of the nature of the system itself. We saw that the old and sick were often left at the impersonal mercy of the market-place.   If they could not work (because of depression, illness, or age) and if they had no family to care for them, they starved.

For these reasons, the Roosevelt administration implemented the social security system.   Under the system, each working member of society contributed so that the elderly and the unemployed could be cared for.   This philosophy was, of course, recently expanded to provide hospital and medical care for the elderly.

Together with the New Deal came more government intervention into the regulation of business and labor.   The Sherman Antitrust Act, which was passed in the late 1800s, began to be enforced.   Huge monopolies were either broken up or regulated to prevent the recurrence of earlier abuses.

The government also began to take a hand in the prevention of economic crises, such as depression and inflation.   This role for the government was greatly strengthened by the unanimous passage of the Employment Act of 1946.   Under this act, the government (together with business and agriculture) assumed the responsibility for maintaining stable price levels, full employment, and economic growth. From that time until the present, the government has attempted to achieve these goals through the appropriate use of monetary and fiscal policies.   While we have not always been successful, we have at least been able to lessen the violence of the upswings and down-swings.

This, then, is what we mean by modified or regulated capitalism. While the role of the government is still minimized and while rigid economic planning is avoided, the government nevertheless does regulate business, labor, and agriculture to prevent abuses and to protect against the economic defects of the system itself.

Capitalism Compared with Socialism and Communism

The most vital differences between capitalism and the other systems are those already mentioned.   Capitalism stresses private ownership of the means of production; both socialism and communism advocate collective ownership.   A capitalist economy is a market economy, with supply and demand determining the level and output of goods and services.   Both of the other systems have *planned economies,* with the government determining what should be produced, how much should be produced, and at what prices it will sell.

Production for profit is a basic part of capitalism. Under socialism and communism, the profit motive is not operative for those industries owned by the state. Finally, the consumer plays a much more important role, with his dollar votes, under capitalism than under the other two systems.

Advantages and Achievements of American Capitalism

One of the most remarkable advantages of the American capitalist system is its economic freedom. Aside from the necessary regulation discussed above, businessmen, workers, and farmers are free to pursue their own economic interests so long as they do not unfairly impinge upon the economic freedom of others. That such a free system would work at all is surprising; that it would work so well is truly astounding! Another achievement of the capitalist system is found in the profit motive. While there are drawbacks to our profit orientation (discussed below under weaknesses of capitalism), it has served to a large degree as a motivating force for all sectors of the economy. The expectation of profits induces businessmen to invest and take the risks associated with new and improved products. The promise of financial advancement gives incentive to workers and farmers as well.

The capitalist system also provides many more opportunities for varied employment. One may choose to be a butcher, a baker, a candlestick maker, or virtually any other profession he likes. No one dictates to us the line of work we must follow.

The most remarkable achievement of capitalism, however, is the tremendous material output that has been possible under it. We have no way of knowing exactly how much of our material wealth is due to capitalism as such or how much is due to the availability of resources or to the type of person in the United States, but we do know that we have become far and away the wealthiest and most productive nation in the world. And we have done this under a capitalist system.

Weaknesses and Failures of American Capitalism

We would be remiss if we did not also take stock of our weaknesses and failures. No economic system is perfect, including ours. Moreover, if we are to improve our system, we must recognize its short-comings.   Chapters 9 and 10 examined specific problems which must be overcome here at home.   Hence, this discussion will deal only with weaknesses inherent in the capitalist system itself.

One such weakness is found in the market system.   While a market system does a superb job of determining levels of output and prices, it pays virtually no attention to distributive justice.   We get what we pay for, and those who provide us with what we want reap the economic rewards.   Since the sick and the elderly cannot provide us with useful goods and services, they tend to be poor.   Because we demand the services of a particular singing group, for example, they can earn more money in a two-hour performance than the President of the United States earns in a year!   Thus the market system fails us when it comes to distributive justice.   Some of the measures mentioned earlier lessen the inequities, but the problem still remains.

A second weakness of capitalism is its inherent bias toward violent swings in the business cycle.   Left to its own devices, our system would fall into serious inflationary periods and chronic depressions, with the concomitant unemployment, misery, and slow growth.   Again, the government has taken measures to alleviate these fluctuations; yet inflation and recession still remain problems of serious proportions.

The profit motive, too, has its bad side.   Because of the business interest in maximizing profits, the tendency exists to defraud the buyer.   While this tendency to defraud has been largely checked by regulation, it still exists.   Products very often do not match up to the claims of the manufacturer.   Often, too, quality is sacrificed in order to keep costs as low as possible and thereby maximize the returns to business.   Additionally, the profit motive leads the businessman to conclude that whatever sells is "good."   Hence, the market abounds with pornographic literature and movies, cereals that "snap, crackle, and pop," and numerous other goods having very little real economic value.   If the public will buy it, it will be sold (with the exception, of course, of drugs and other potentially harmful goods).

The capitalist system also causes to be created powerful vested-interest groups.   These are formed and financed by business, labor, agriculture, professional groups, and virtually every other large group in the country.   Their purpose?   To influence federal legislation to the benefit of the organizations which they represent.   What is good for one segment of the economy *may* be good for the others as well, but very often it is not.

Another area for concern under capitalism lies in the provision of "public goods." The emphasis in the United States is to produce more and more industrial and consumer goods, with inadequate attention being paid to the creation of public goods (goods which are used by all collectively). Thus larger and more powerful automobiles are built, but there is a shortage of good highways over which to drive them. Ugly slums blot our cities, and air and water pollution are a very real threat to health in some areas of the country.

Finally, the "competitive spirit" itself may be at the root of many of our social problems. Our economic system is one of exclusion. One man competes with all others for the available resources and income. If he gets more income, someone else must get less. Some writers maintain that we are paying too much in terms of personal and social stress for our material wellbeing. We cannot, of course, conclude that capitalism alone is the culprit, but the United States does have the world's highest rates of mental illness, divorce, and ulcers.

Summary Comments on Capitalism

We have seen that the capitalist economic system is based on the idea that those who produce will be rewarded accordingly. This notion has its roots in the "Protestant ethic." This philosophical base led to a system which is characterized by private ownership of the means of production, a market economy, the profit motive, and consumer sovereignty.

Because of abuse by certain sectors of our economy and because of the system's inherent tendency toward violent economic fluctuations, the classical notion of a free capitalist society had to be altered. The beginnings of this alteration occurred in the 1930s, and it is continuing at present. The federal government now accepts limited responsibility for the growth of the economy and for the elimination of violent cyclical fluctuations.

The lack of centralized planning was found to be the major difference between capitalism and socialism and communism. The market, not the government, determines what will be produced, how much of it will be produced, and at what price it will sell.

Some of the advantages of capitalism, we noted, were its freedom from regulation, its ability to provide incentives to invest and work, and its provision of many varied employment opportunities. And, of course, the most remarkable achievement of the system is its material wealth. But, as we also noted, the system has its disadvantages. The market system pays virtually no attention to distributive justice. The economy also has an inherent tendency toward inflation, depression, unemployment, and slow growth. These tendencies have been checked somewhat, but they are still major problems. The profit motive was seen to have its negative aspects also. It causes a tendency on the part of the seller to defraud the buyer, it often affects quality, and it may result in the production of goods with limited usefulness. The formation of vested-interest groups and a slighting of public goods were mentioned as two final weaknesses of capitalism.

We will now turn our attention to the other "isms," fascism and anarchy.

OTHER "ISMS"

Fascism

Fascism is really more of a political arrangement than an economic system. But because it is always intricately involved with economics and because fascist systems have had such an impact on the world, we will treat it as though it were an economic system.

More than any of the other systems, fascism differs drastically from nation to nation. Nazi Germany was vastly different from fascist Italy. And both of those nations were unlike the current fascist regime in Spain. Nevertheless, there are certain characteristics which run as a common thread through virtually all fascist systems. Among these common characteristics are the following: [6]

1. Distrust of reason
2. Denial of basic human equality
3. Code of behavior based on lies and violence
4. Government by elite

---

[6] Items 1 to 7 are suggested by Ebenstein, *op. cit.*, p. 110.

5. Totalitarianism
6. Racialism and imperialism
7. Opposition to international law and order
8. A high degree of nationalism
9. A union of business, government, and the military

This list certainly does not paint a very pretty picture. But fascism is not a very desirable system of government. Fascist regimes have led us into two world wars and into numerous other skirmishes.

Fascist movements generally have their beginnings in periods of great civil strife, when the population is clamoring for someone to create order out of chaos. (Hitler's rise to power began during a German recession.) When we say that fascism distrusts reason, we are implying that the movement is one of "faith," not intellectualism. It is often made possible by a charismatic leader who promises to lead his people to better times. There will usually be no organized plan for growth; rather, there will be an appeal to emotion. Hitler, for example, was considered to be one of the world's best public speakers and was able to sway millions of people with his dramatic appeals.

If Nazi Germany is taken as an example of fascism, we can see that the elements listed previously certainly apply. The Aryan "race" was considered to be the "master" race, and all other religious groups and nationalities were denied their basic human rights and were treated as inferior beings. Hitler's was a totalitarian regime of the first order; his word was law. He, and a very elite group of others, ruled Germany with an iron hand. This was the period also of the "big lie." Hitler is purported to have said that small lies may not be believed by the public but that if the lie is large enough to be preposterous, the public will believe it. Hence, he was able to convince millions of his followers that the Jews were responsible for the economic and social ills that had befallen Germany.

That the German government was imperialistic and opposed to international law and order there can be little doubt. While the world was attempting to negotiate and while Hitler himself was talking peace, the German army began its scourge of Europe. Racialism and violence, too, were apparent—attested to by the murder of 6 million Jews.

As to the form of government under fascism, most fascist governments take the form of a strong dictatorship, with a collusion between the

government, the military, and the business sector.   These sectors benefit at the expense of the country as a whole.

Unfortunately, there is a tendency on the part of capitalist nations
(such as ours) to support fascist regimes, at least in the early stages of
development.   This is so, in part at least, because of their political
stability and because of the high level of economic output made possible by rigid planning.   Thus we found ourselves allied with fascist
Germany, Japan, and Italy in the early stages of these governments,
prior to World War II.   We also had close ties with Cuba when it was
under the rule of the dictator Batista.   And, even today, we maintain
strong military ties with Franco's fascist Spain.

Anarchy

At the other end of the "ism" spectrum, we find anarchy—which is
really not an economic or political system at all; rather, it is the
absence of one.

Anarchy is characterized by a lack of centralized government and a
breakdown of law and order.   It usually follows or occurs simul-
taneously with periods of civil disorder and strife, riots, revolutions,
and so forth.   Put simply, anarchy is the absence of a system of government.

Because a nation cannot survive without stability in government and
in the economic system, anarchy is a short-run phenomenon.   The
vacuum of anarchy will be filled by some economic and political system similar to one of those we have discussed.   Unfortunately, fascism
usually follows a period of anarchy since there exists an urgent need
for order.   Populations at that time are most willing to give up their
freedoms in exchange for stability.

MILITARY COMPETITION AMONG THE ISMS

The differences among nations today are not only ideological—that is,
based upon notions of what constitutes the "good society."   Nor are
these differences based strictly upon economics, that is, concerned
with the best economic methods of achieving increased material output.   The various systems of the world today are also involved in a
tremendous struggle for superior military power.   This struggle is

worth our notice because of its impact upon our standards of living and our way of life.

At this writing, young people throughout the United States are gathering together in large numbers to protest our involvement in the war in Vietnam. Moratorium demonstrations in October and November of 1969 were the largest demonstrations for military withdrawal in the nation's history. And more will be forthcoming. What are the economic issues being discussed? Aside from the "moral" question of large budgets for war and defense, two fundamental economic questions arise: (1) Is our military budget so large that we are ignoring important domestic economic and social problems? (2) Is there developing (in this country and others) a "military-industrial complex" which threatens our democratic way of life and our economic system?

Table 13-1 shows the percentage of the national budgets of some of the world's major powers which is committed to national defense. A cursory glance at the figures in this table can leave little doubt that spending for war and defense does, in fact, drain badly needed resources away from the domestic economies. Of course, it can be argued that without such defense spending the will of foreign powers might prevail, so that the domestic standard of living might decline even further. Nevertheless, if the world could disarm and nations live without threatening each other, it is quite clear that the world's people could live a much better material life.

The question of a "military-industrial complex" is perhaps more germane to the U.S. economy than to other, more collectivized economies around the world. With tremendous military budgets, the importance of defense contracts to our nation's industrial firms is ever increasing. Some will argue that this wedding of the military and industrial sectors of our economy creates a power bloc which is antithetical to the American way of life. Can the military-industrial bloc unduly influence federal legislation to the detriment of the average citizen? Can the lobbyists for this group divert the nation's resources from the domestic economy against the will of the people? Does this powerful "organization" lessen the impact of the vote in a free society?

These and other questions are the ones raised by those who fear the "military-industrial complex." We cannot, of course, answer these

TABLE 13-1   National Defense Expenditures, 1966 *

| | Expenditures | | DEFENSE EXPENDITURE |
COUNTRY	TOTAL (MILLIONS OF U.S. DOLLARS)	PER CAPITA PER YEAR (DOLLARS)	AS PERCENTAGE OF GNP (MARKET PRICES)
United States	67,950	346	9.2
Australia	1,120	96	4.7
Canada	1,461	73	2.8
China (Mainland)	6,500	8	10.0
China (Taiwan)	270	21	8.9
Czechoslovakia	1,270	89	5.7
France	4,465	91	4.4
Germany, East	975	57	3.3
Germany, Federal Republic of	4,335	76	3.6
India	1,259	25	3.3
Italy	1,982	38	3.3
Japan	958	10	1.1
Poland	1,589	50	5.3
South Vietnam	150	10	10.5
United Kingdom	6,081	120	6.4
U.S.S.R.	29,800	129	8.9

* Gross national product figures upon which percentages are based for East European countries and China have been estimated in terms of Western purchasing-power equivalents.

SOURCE: *The Military Balance, 1967–1968*, The Institute for Strategic Studies, Ltd., London.

questions here.   It is enough that we be aware that they are being asked.

CHAPTER SUMMARY

In this chapter we have examined the various major economic systems under which the peoples of the world live.   Basically, any economic system is designed to answer the fundamental questions of what to produce, how much to produce and at what price, and how to distribute the society's wealth.   The ends, then, of all the systems are essentially the same (with the exception, of course, of fascism and anarchy). What differs is the means to achieve the desired ends.

Some nations have chosen a modified form of communism, with its attendant economic planning both in the area of production and in the area of consumption and with its necessary collectivization. Other nations have chosen socialism, in which ownership of the banking system, the utilities, and at least the major productive enterprises is vested with the state. Other nations, the United States included, have chosen the path of capitalism.

It was indicated that no economic system has achieved a level of perfection. There are both weaknesses and strengths inherent in all economies. With a knowledge of these shortcomings and achievements, man may better continue his search for the most equitable and productive system possible.

STUDY QUESTIONS

1. Review the basic tenets of Marxian communism. How closely does Marxian communism relate to communism as practiced in the Soviet Union?

2. What did Lenin contribute to Marxian communism?

3. Define socialism and describe the likely procedure for nationalization if a nation decided to adopt this particular economic system.

4. Define capitalism. What is the difference between "classical" capitalism and capitalism as we know it?

5. Discuss the advantages and shortcomings of each of the economic systems discussed in Chapter 13. This list is by no means complete. Can you add others?

IMPORTANT CONCEPTS IN CHAPTER 13

Communism
Marxian versus practiced communism
"Divine providence" interpretations of history
Political, or "hero," interpretations of history
Hegelian interpretation of history
Thesis, antithesis, synthesis
Economic or materialistic determinism
Bourgeoisie

Proletariat
"Gravedigger" theory
Surplus value
"Reserve army of the unemployed"
Dynamic demise of capitalism according to Marx
Class struggle
Dictatorship of the proletariat
Lenin's contributions to communism
"Professional revolutionary"
Bolshevik
Socialism
Robert Owen
New Harmony
Democratic socialism
Nationalization
Compensation for nationalized industry
Order of nationalization under socialism
"Cradle-to-grave" social security system
Capitalism
Protestant ethic
Classical capitalism
Market economy
Role of the profit motive under capitalism
Consumer sovereignty
Robber barons
New Deal
Sherman Antitrust Act
Employment Act of 1946
Modified or regulated capitalism
Planned economies
Public goods
Fascism
Elements of fascism
Anarchy

INDEX